THE
DEATH VIEW REVOLUTION

Best wishes,
Madelaine Lawrence

THE
DEATH VIEW
REVOLUTION

A guide to transpersonal
experiences surrounding
death

by

MADELAINE LAWRENCE

www.whitecrowbooks.com

ABOUT THE AUTHOR

———⫸⏺⫷———

D
r. Lawrence is a researcher, author, educator, professional life coach as well as a certified hypnotist and instructor of hypnosis. She has taught research to graduate and undergraduate students for over 20 years and has been a Director of Nursing Education and Research for a large urban hospital in Connecticut. Her research and writings include an investigation of the experiences of unconscious patients, a prospective study of near-death experiences, and a study of the incidence of deathbed communications. She has been interviewed for several lay publications and appeared on a number of television shows including ABC's *Turning Point* with Diane Sawyer. The author of a book entitled, *In a World of Their Own: Experiencing Unconsciousness*, she is currently researching the fear of death of hospice patients who have had a near-death experience at a previous time.

CONTENTS

ACKNOWLEDGEMENTS

No writing concerning transpersonal experiences could be possible without the contributions of those who have had these experiences. They have shared their descriptions, reactions and aftereffects which has enormously assisted other experiencers, families, healthcare professionals, educators, and researchers.

Many individuals and organizations through their continuous efforts create building blocks for others to add to the knowledge of transpersonal experiences associated with near death and dying. The works of Carlos Alvarado, William Barrett, Nancy Evans Bush, Maggie Callahan, Mark Chorvinsky, Peter and Elizabeth Fenwick, Bruce Greyson, Bill and Judy Guggenheim, Patricia Kelly, Raymond Moody, Melodie Olson, Joseph B. Rhine, Kenneth Ring, Scott Rogo, Michael Sabom, Penny Satori, Kimberly Clark Sharp, Jenny Streit-Horn, Charles Tart, and Pim van Lommel have been particularly helpful in the writing of this book.

I offer heartfelt acknowledgement to those who have taken their time to review chapters providing valuable insights, comments, encouragement, and support: Fred M. Karas, Sandra McCourt, Joannie McMahon, and Kathy Ryan. Particular thanks goes to Karen Newman for her careful editing and formatting.

It is with warm appreciation to my friends and family who have provided emotional support and loving and fun distractions when needed. Thank you Barbara, Becky, Bernie, Betsy, Deborah, Debra, Donna, Joanna, Jennifer, Paul, Rebecca, Suzanne C, Suzanne H and Suzanne P.

Much recognition needs to be offered to Jon Beecher, publisher of White Crow Books. He is responsible for the publication of this book and so many others on significant transpersonal experiences. A huge gap in the publication of information on this topic would exist without his considerable efforts.

INTRODUCTION

As a doctoral student at the University of Connecticut, I was encouraged by my major advisor, Dr. Arthur Roberts, to sign up for a course on death and dying taught by Dr. Kenneth Ring. He had heard excellent feedback about the course. I was reluctant but since have been eternally grateful.

One day, Ken played a tape recording of a man who he interviewed about the 1,000 out-of-body experiences (OBEs) he'd had. This was incomprehensible to me who knew nothing about transpersonal experiences. Then Ken brought four near-death experiencers to class and asked them to describe their near-death experiences (NDEs). It was a discordant event. How could these events happen? I entered the course thinking as a health professional I knew a lot about death and dying but realized I was still a novice.

One experiencer while unconscious could hear what the doctors, nurses, and family members were saying. That prompted a detailed interview with this experiencer and a 50 page paper on unconsciousness and NDEs. Poor Ken! I went from the reluctant student to enthusiastic researcher, presenter, consultant, and writer of transpersonal experiences.

In the 1990s, in my role as Director of Nursing Education and Research in a large urban hospital and later as a hospice coordinator, I heard many individuals describe the transpersonal experiences they had just encountered. Many of them were reluctant to talk about them for fear of being called 'crazy'. If the experience was hellish, they were afraid others would not only think they were mentally ill, they feared they would be thought of as immoral. Many were told not to talk about these experiences by doctors, nurses, clergy and even relatives.

However, these individuals wanted to talk about what had occurred. They wanted to know what these events meant. They wanted assistance processing these occurrences. They wanted to know what resources were available to them. When I asked if I could tape the interviews for my research, they frequently would double check to make sure the tape recorder was working properly. They wanted to be heard.

Nurses on the hospital units would frequently call me to talk with patients or relatives when one of these events occurred. They were unsure about what to say and wanted to be helpful. One woman patient was being told by her deceased mother to come with her but the patient did not want to die yet. The nurses wanted to know what to do. Should they call a psychiatric consultant? Was this woman's experience normal after nearly dying?

This book is designed to assist professionals and friends and family members who counsel and care for individuals experiencing transpersonal events surrounding near-death and death. It includes a comprehensive description of all known transpersonal phenomena occurring to survivors of near death, dying patients and family members. Knowledge of transpersonal experiences should be an integral part of the education of all individuals who assist those who come close to death or are dying. Most of us are schooled in the biological paradigm that governs our thinking about these transpersonal experiences. A new paradigm that includes the addition of these transpersonal experiences is necessary to give complete care and assistance to the millions of individuals who experience the phenomena.

In all, there are nine distinct transpersonal events discussed in this book, most of which have aftereffects requiring both instruction and intervention. Some background in transpersonal experiences and frameworks for assisting experiencers are discussed. Two chapters are devoted to the current levels of evidence achieved through the research on the phenomena, an ever growing body of information. Here is a brief description of each chapter:

Chapter 1. The structure of revolutions

History describes many scientific revolutions. As Kuhn states, anomalies that are unexplained by the presiding paradigm push the boundaries of knowledge eventually creating a new way of thinking. Kuhn's understanding of how revolutions in science take place provides a framework for understanding how a revolution in our view of death and dying has been developing during the last 50 years. This chapter also includes a brief description of the development of parapsychology as a scientific field of study, the definitions and descriptions of terms, and research methodology.

Chapter 2. Frameworks for assisting experiencers

Descriptions of frameworks for communicating with individuals who have transpersonal experiences such as transpersonal psychology, client-centered care, neurolinguistic are presented in this chapter.

Chapter 3. Near-death visits

Near-death visits are a lesser known and lesser described phenomena. Different from near-death experiences and deathbed communications, the individual does not leave his or her body and experience events while out of body. This individual sees, hears, or feels someone in their presence, often occurring in a hospital room after a close encounter with death.

Chapter 4. Out-of-Body experiences

This chapter includes information about circumstances under which individuals close to death have out-of –body experiences as singular events and as part of an NDE.

Chapter 5. Near-death experiences

Of all transpersonal experiences associated with dying the near-death experience (NDE) is the best researched phenomena. In this chapter there are descriptions of the various components of the NDE and research on incidence and triggering factors.

Chapter 6. NDE aftereffects, explanations, and supportive measures

The most common after-effects of NDEs include interference with electronic devices, increased psychic abilities, increased spiritualism, decreased materialism, and the loss of fear of dying. These are described in this chapter along with responses to these phenomena by the experiencers.

Chapter 7. Angels, grim reapers, and shadow figures

These are the only transpersonal experiences during which a symbolic apparition is seen as opposed to someone or something normally visible. These are visions commonly occurring but rarely discussed.

Chapter 8. Deathbed communications

Deathbed communications were previously called deathbed visions. Some deathbed communication involves hearing and feeling the presence, or being touched by someone within hours or a few weeks of death.

Chapter 9. Choosing the time of death

We health professionals historically have believed physiological interventions are what controls the time of death. This chapter includes descriptions of how near-death experiencers often chose to 'come back' from death and how hospice patients wait to die until loved ones arrive or leave their room. Some of the individuals described in this chapter have been pronounced dead but return.

Chapter 10. Miscellaneous occurrences at the time of death

Family members, friends as well as doctors and nurses frequently report a mist or smoky substance leaving the body, usually the chest or head, at the time of death. Reports of this phenomena, evidence for the presence of ultraviolet light in the room at the time of death, glowing faces and hands reaching down at the time of death are included in this chapter.

Chapter 11. After-death communication with family and friends

There are many anecdotal reports of family and friends reporting communications with deceased loved ones after death. This chapter also includes highlights from the considerable research on this phenomena.

Chapter 12. Evidence for near-death visits, out-of-body experiences, and near-death experiences.

Chapter 13. Evidence for the aftereffects of near-death experiences, deathbed communication, and after-death communication

These two chapters include analysis of what constitutes evidence or proof, about the existence and veracity of the transpersonal experiences described in this book. In everyday life we determine evidence or proof from the following ways: what we experience through our senses, what makes logical sense to us, what we have been told to be true by authority figures, and what is traditionally established as truth. In science, there are levels of evidence. The content in these chapters describes those levels achieved by research in this field of study

Chapter 14. Viewing the transpersonal experiences in totality

All these experiences describe events that occur before, during, and after death. Each experience is in some way like the proverbial elephant being viewed from different perspectives by the blind men. It is not until we view these phenomena in total that we have a truer and more holistic description of the nature of this phenomenon.

One hospice patient I interviewed three weeks before his death provided the exemplar description for the need of a new paradigm for viewing death. Eight years before he developed cancer, he had a near-death experience from a bleeding episode. He described the experience as full of love and beauty. I asked him how he felt now being close to death on the hospice program. He said, while not wanting to leave his family, he could not wait to die. He knew he would feel the exquisite feeling of love again. At the time of his death, his wife said he raised his hands up toward the hands he saw coming down toward him. A peaceful glow covered his face.

PREFACE

The 21st century is an exciting time in medical science. Medicine is becoming increasingly specialized; targeted therapies and laser precision are now the norm. These advances make death seem like just another medical condition waiting to be "cured." But, alas, death remains an inevitability.

Death also continues to be a mystery. No one knows what happens when we die. In fact, determining an exact time of death continues to evade us. There are obviously legal and medical definitions available. Death is a process; clinical death is followed by biological death. But what happens to the essence of the person—that part that makes us who we are (call it identity, personality, or soul). This question generates numerous possibilities for what happens to the essence of the person as the physical process unfolds. In the absence of facts, the answers are determined by religious and cultural beliefs.

As a parapsychologist, the experiences centered on death are of particular interest. The roots of parapsychology are found in formal investigations of the Spiritualist Movement and the belief of being able to communicate with the dead. The first major study was a survey conducted by the Society for Psychical Research in 1890. The Census of Hallucinations was based on answers to the question, "Have you ever, when believing yourself to be completely awake, had a vivid impression of seeing or being touched by a living being or inanimate object, or hearing a voice; which impression, so far as you could discover, was not due to any physical cause?" Approximately 10% of the 17,000 respondents reported having one or more experiences. The data were analyzed to determine if a pattern existed. It was concluded that most cases were reported at the time of the death of the agent (or sender) and, as time passed after the death, the number of reported cases declined.

Many decades later, and after considerable research, additional patterns have emerged indicating that paranormal events occur at times and in places when a person is in transition. For example, many people report apparitions in hallways and on staircases. The dying report seeing deceased loved ones and being seen by family and friends.

The patterns indicate that when the boundaries between life and death become blurred, our identity seems to expand beyond the personal, which by definition is transpersonal. Though the patterns have been identified, conclusions about the exact cause and nature of these experiences cannot be drawn. Unfortunately, our desire for specialization and targeted precision cannot be applied to transpersonal experiences. Tempting as it is to draw conclusions and deem all experiences centered on a dying person to be the product of oxygen deprivation, endorphin release, the grief process, or proof of an afterlife, such simplification does not do any of the experiences the justice they deserve. Instead, there is a need to adopt a collaborative care model and view them from a multidisciplinary perspective. In the same way that disease management and care coordination programs are designed to improve outcomes, examining death experiences holistically provides a richer, more complete framework.

Dr. Lawrence has reviewed the entire panorama of transpersonal experiences that center on the dying. Her exploration into the complexity of these experiences highlights their life-changing impact. The current volume goes to great lengths to shed light on a subject that is fraught with the prejudice, scientific supremacy, and the fervor of personal beliefs and desires. To date, no study has so effectively and objectively examined transpersonal experiences at the time of death.

Joanne DS McMahon, PhD
Parapsychologist

CHAPTER 1

THE STRUCTURE OF REVOLUTIONS

Keywords: Clairaudience, clairvoyance, paradigm, parapsychology, psychokinesis, revolutions, seventh sense, sixth sense, telepathy

No phenomenon is without history. Our understanding of transpersonal experiences surrounding near death and dying is no exception. Edmund Burke (1729-1797) once said, "Those who don't know history are destined to repeat it (Bartlett, 2012, p. 323)." Scientists look to those who came before them to attempt to avoid the misadventures of previous researchers. Scientists also build on the successes and insights of preceding researchers to extend knowledge. This chapter includes a brief description of the development of parapsychology as a scientific field of study, the definitions and descriptions of terms, and research methodology. It also includes a discussion of Kuhn's (1962) description of *the structure of scientific revolutions* with examples in the biological and medical sciences. Kuhn's understanding of how revolutions in science take place provides a framework for understanding how a revolution in our view of death and dying has been developing during the last 50 years.

In 1962, Thomas Kuhn wrote an extraordinary book entitled, The Structure of Scientific Revolutions. Kuhn believed scientific communities operate under paradigms which include basic, and assumed to be, uncontroversial assumptions about the nature of a discipline. The paradigm includes theories derived from facts and research shown to successfully explain common occurrences within the discipline.

According to Kuhn (1962), science progresses by what he called normal science. That is the type of scientific study that enables researchers to add more and more information about what is believed to be true in a discipline. The largest progressions in science, however, occur through revolutions which are often fraught with difficulties. The revolution begins with anomalies. These anomalies are occurrences that cannot be explained by the prevailing paradigm. Once these anomalies occur, scientists will try to use the known paradigm to try to explain their existence with great tenacity. The current paradigm filters the interpretation of events. Even when the current paradigm is unsuccessful in explaining the anomaly, individuals cling to the old paradigm. Often even factual data does not help produce a change in the way of thinking about a new phenomenon. The history of the development of germ theory provides a good example.

After Antonie van Leeuwenhoek (1632-1723) built his microscope, he noticed small living things he called "animalcules" moving in teeth scrapings he placed under the microscope. The idea of microscopic creatures was unheard of during this time. He sent his findings to the Royal Society of London whose members were full of misgivings about his reports. No one had heard of microscopic organisms before this time. In 1676, Leeuwenhoek reported to the Royal Society signs of microscopic life on pond scum. Fortunately, he could convince the members of the truth of these findings when they could see the one-cell organisms themselves under the microscope (de Kruif, 2002).

As early as the 1840s, a Hungarian doctor, Ignaz Seemelweiss, argued for aseptic techniques during surgery and when doctors examined patients. Doctors who worked for him washed their hands in calcium chloride between patients. Deaths on Semmelweiss' patient wards decreased from 12% to 1%. However, his findings were ignored by the conservative doctors in Hungary. The paradigm those doctors believed in was that diseases were spread in the form of "bad air," also known as miasmas. Also, it was believed diseases were the result of an imbalance of the "four humours," the treatment for which was bloodletting. Semmelweis's ideas contradicted all established medical science of the time. The doctors also believed because they were gentlemen of high social status, they could not possibly have dirty hands. Semmelweis argued for the validity of the use of antiseptic techniques until his death in 1865 at the age of 47. His legacy lives on today, being recognized as a pioneer of antiseptic techniques. Semmelweis University in Budapest is named after him. There is also a Semmelweis Medical History Museum and a hospital for women in Vienna that carries his name (Carter & Carter, 2005).

Louis Pasteur (1822-1895) followed the development of this revolution when he proposed his germ theory. It was also difficult for Pasteur to convince others of the validity of this theory. One of his major efforts was to convince surgeons that germs existed and carried diseases. He argued intensely about the need for surgeons to clean instruments and wash their hands between patients. During the American Civil War (1861-1865), surgeons did not wash their hands and clean instruments between patients. More soldiers died from infections than bullet wounds during that time. Many of these infections could have been prevented if the new aseptic techniques proposed during that time had been used (de Kruif, 2002).

As the above example shows, current paradigms filter perceptions. Those who advocate for a new paradigm are often ignored for centuries until the evidence is too overwhelming. Those advocates can be rejected by society and even persecuted. When there is a change in the paradigm, it is referred to as a paradigm shift.

Paranormal events and parapsychology

In the biological sciences it has been determined we have five senses: sight, touch, smell, taste, and hearing. Reality in our current biological paradigm is determined by what we experience through those senses. We have recognized these five senses for centuries. Early Buddhist literature (sixth century BC) described the five material faculties. Shakespeare (1564-1616) discussed the five wits or senses in his writings. Depictions of these five senses were a popular subject for artists as early as the seventeenth century. In 1630, Pietro Paolini, an Italian artist, executed a painting entitled *Allegory of the Five Senses*. In this painting at the Walters Art Museum in Baltimore, MD, the artist depicts the functions of these senses through the actions of the figures. A woman with a lute represents sound. Taste is represented by a man drinking from a flask of wine. Another young man smells a melon next to a man holding a pair of spectacles. Touch is represented by two people fighting (Walters Art Museum).

Thus, for centuries, we have held to be true that there are five senses. Normal science, in accordance with Kuhn's thinking, has led us to develop

3

explanations of how these senses work and operate within the physiology of our bodies. We know our senses have ranges leading to some individuals being better than others in certain activities. An acute sense of taste allows some individuals to distinguish fine wines from mediocre ones, where others could not taste the difference between even a merlot and a cabernet. Normal science has helped us understand much about our five senses. There are those who argue we have evidence of a sixth sense and even a seventh sense. Normal science still says we have only five senses.

The sixth sense

Extrasensory perception (ESP) is often referred to as *the sixth sense.* This sixth sense idea was made popular in modern culture in the movie, The Sixth Sense. Anyone who saw this movie will forever remember Cole Sear (Haley Joel Osment), the six-year-old boy, telling Malcolm Crowe (Bruce Willis), a child psychologist, that he "sees dead people."

ESP is defined as the reception of information gained through the mind and not the physical senses. It also can involve knowledge of the future and not just knowledge of the past and present. ESP was defined by J. B. Rhine, a Duke University psychologist, as including telepathy, clairaudience, clairvoyance, psychokinesis, and precognition.

Telepathy is the ability of individuals to transfer thoughts or feelings from mind to mind without the use of sound or body language. Clairaudience is the ability to receive information from their inner or outer hearing. Clairvoyance is the ability to see objects or events that cannot be perceived by the senses. Psychokinesis (PK) is sometimes referred to as "telekinesis" or "mind over matter." It is the ability to move matter or energy through mental processes. Precognition involves extrasensory cognition of a future event (Clegg, 2013; Rogo, 1975).

Some in the field of parapsychology believe these ESP abilities are developments of our tendencies to be auditory, visual, or kinesthetic learners. For example, if your ability to learn is best through hearing information, you would be more inclined to develop clairaudience.

The seventh sense and more

Besides this sixth sense, scientists have described other abilities that are beyond the five senses. These senses include our sense of balance, our organic sense, and proprioception. Our sense of balance, or vestibular sense, is the sense that keeps us in alignment. That is the body's way of keeping us upright, like a cat's ability to land on its feet. It is believed this sense is due to a system of several structures in the inner ear. Our organic or interoceptive sense is what tells us when we feel hungry, thirsty, ill, or even have a change in heart rate.

A third sense, in this category of senses, is known as proprioception. Proprioception is how we know the location of parts of our body without the use of sight. If you close your eyes and move your arm, you will know where that arm is located and the direction in which it has moved without seeing the movement. Even if someone else moves your arm or leg, you immediately know where the body part has been placed.

In some sources, the above senses are in a category called *the seventh sense*, along with an ability to do remote viewing. In other sources, an ability to see the seventh sense is limited to a psychic ability for remote viewing. Remote viewing is a mental ability that enables a person to see or otherwise experience a target not accessible by normal senses because of distance or shielding. The book, The Seventh Sense, by Lyn Buchanan details the story of his life as a soldier in the military who worked on top-secret government and military projects using remote viewing.

In 1995, the CIA declassified and approved for release documents describing remote viewing research carried out at Stanford Research Institute in Menlo Park, CA. This research was carried out for two decades, from 1972 to 1985. As well as Lyn Buchanan, Russell Targ, a physicist and author, and cofounder of the Stanford Research Institute (SRI), authored books on the subject. Many of the psychical research centers have carried out research on remote viewing.

Development of psychical research

There are centuries-old reports of paranormal or extrasensory events. The first nonacademic but systematic investigations of apparitions and miraculous events were conducted by the Catholic Church. Initially, saints in the Catholic Church were chosen by public acclaim, starting with those who were martyred for their faith. This approach was changed in the tenth century when the canonization process was initiated. As part of the canonization process, besides other criteria, miracles had to be attributed to the person being considered for sainthood.

Members of the Catholic Church hierarchy were charged with investigation of apparitions and miracles. Visions of the Virgin Mary, such as those that took place at Lourdes, France, in 1858, and subsequent claims of miraculous cures, were and continue to be thoroughly investigated. After a three-and-a-half-year investigation, and the confirmation of thirty-five cases of inexplicable healing, in 1862, the Bishop Laurence of Tarbes declared the Virgin had appeared to Bernadette. The Lourdes Medical Bureau now investigates over 30 claims of cures a year. Most are ruled as lacking substance but a few are turned over to the International Lourdes Medical Committee for further investigation (The Medical Bureau of Sanctuary).

Apparitions of the Virgin Mary still occur during this time. According to Nelson (2000), there were over 300 reported apparitions in the 20th century. Psycho-physiological and psycho-diagnostic research was done on those who had visions at Medjurgorje, a village in the southwestern region of Bosnia and Herzegovina, formerly central Yugoslavia. The Italian doctors performed case histories, neurological exams, personality inventories, polygraphs, and other tests, even during the apparitional experiences. The results indicated the subjects do not show signs of any pathological states (Pandarakalam, 2001).

Lawrence (2014) interviewed a woman who reported seeing the image of Mary in the chapel in the village of Medjurgorje. While many pilgrims to this site see the apparition from inside the chapel, she was able to see an image from outside on the lawn. This woman said seeing the apparition left her with a wonderful feeling of peace and relief.

The investigation of apparitions and inexplicable healing attributed to a person being considered for sainthood continues. In 1983, Pope John Paul II changed the requirement from three miracles to two for canonization. These miracles must take place after the candidate's death as a result of prayers to that person. The beatification of Pope John Paul II was allowed to proceed when a French nun claimed that she was cured of Parkinson's disease. This "cure" was verified by medical doctors. Beatification, which requires verification of one miracle, is the first step in the canonization process. Another miracle is required for verification of sainthood (Fisher, 2007).

It was not until 1882 when the Society for Psychical Research (SPR) in London was formed that true research investigations of these phenomena took place.

One of the major issues of investigation, which still plagues this field, is methodology. It was important that the pursuit of knowledge about paranormal events used scientific methods. However, since the psychical researchers were investigating phenomena different from occurrences in the physical sciences, different approaches needed to be used. In some ways the psychical researches were analogous to the biological scientists trying to identify germs without a microscope.

Also the early psychical researchers were hindered by false claims of psychic abilities. Often they would find subjects were frauds, especially those who claimed to be mediums.

The founders of the SPR included many eminent men, well respected in London society. Edmund Gurney, Frederic William Henry Myers, William Fletcher Barrett, Henry Sidgwick, and Edmund Dawson Rogers were the founding members.

The SPR initially stated its purpose as being:

> To approach these varied problems without prejudice or prepossession of any kind, and in the same spirit of exact and unimpassioned enquiry which has enabled science to solve so many problems, once not less obscure nor less hotly debated (Grattan-Guinness (1982). p. 19).

The members of the SPR studied thought-transference (telepathy), mesmerism (hypnosis), mediumship, apparitions, and haunted houses. They were particularly interested in phenomena indicative of life after physical death.

One of the significant studies carried out between 1889 and 1892 was the survey of 15,000 to 17,000 non-institutionalized individuals in the United Kingdom (UK) by Henry Sidgwick. The subjects were asked if they could remember having one or more hallucinations. They found approximately 10% of the non-institutionalized population reported one or more hallucinations. The researchers also identified 350 firsthand reports of deathbed visions. At the time this study was being conducted in the UK, similar surveys were being done in Germany, France, and in the US led by philosopher and psychologist, William James (1842-1910). When the results of all these studies were put together through a meta-analysis, it was found 11.96% of non-institutionalized individuals experienced or witnessed hallucinations. These hallucinations were both visual and auditory. The final report from the SPR is called the Census of Hallucinations.

For a number of years, the members of the SPR studied mediums, often showing they were frauds. However, some individuals, such as Daniel Dunglas Home (1833-1886), were believed to have real paranormal abilities. Home was the most well-known medium of the nineteenth century. He showed remarkable ability in being able to levitate himself as well as objects. After many observations of his abilities, no one was able to show how he was able to do the levitations, although most believed trickery was involved. In one instance, he moved a table while standing at some distance. No one was able to determine how this occurred since no strings, wires, and so forth were found. William Crookes conducted numerous experiments from 1871-1874 without being able to detect fraud.

The SPR is still active in London. The members conduct research, hold events, publish *The Journal of the Society for Psychical Research* and *Paranormal Review*, and support an online and lending library.

William James (1942-1910), the notable psychologist, was involved with the London Society for Psychical Research from its beginning in 1882. In 1885, he helped form the American Society for Psychical Research (ASPR). Along with astronomer Simon Newcomb of Johns Hopkins; anthropologist Charles Sedgwick Minot of Harvard; Biologist, Asa Gray; Andrew White, President of Cornell; and Minister Phillips Brooks, James conducted research with mediums. Most were proven to be fraudulent except for Leonora Piper. So impressed was he about the accuracy of the knowledge she obtained while in trance, he referred to her as his own "white crow." "If you wish to upset the law that all crows are black, you mustn't seek to show that no crows are; it is enough if you prove one single crow to be white (James, 1896)."

Both the SPR and ASPR conducted research studies during which their subjects experienced what is known as veridical perceptions, the direct observation of the environment as it exists. In parapsychological terms this means the subject experiences accurately something in the environment they see, hear, or know, but that information is not through normal sense experiences. In the early days of both the SPR and ASPR, subjects gave information about the history of a person without previous knowledge of that person and/or reported the death of a person, whose death to the immediate family or community had not been reported.

In the US, Stanford University in 1911 became the first academic institution to study ESP and PK. This was followed by Duke University in 1930, which under the direction of psychologist William McDougall, conducted experiments involving subjects in ESP experiments. The Duke University efforts included quantitative statistical approaches, different from the qualitative or description approaches previously conducted.

J. B. Rhine formed an autonomous parapsychology laboratory within Duke and started the Journal of Parapsychology. He concluded in his first book, *Extra-Sensory Perception* (1934), after years of research, that ESP existed and could be demonstrated in a laboratory. Not everyone believed the results of the experiments carried out at the parapsychology laboratory. Claims of ways subjects could have deceived researchers were common from academics and other nonbelievers.

In 1957, Rhine proposed the formation of the Parapsychological Association (PA). The aim of the association was "to advance parapsychology as a science, to disseminate knowledge of the field, and to integrate the findings with those of other branches of science" (History of the Parapsychological Association).

In 1965, after Rhine's retirement, the administration at Duke broke links with the parapsychology laboratory. Rhine started the Foundation for Research on the Nature of Man in a building off the Duke campus but close by. In 1995, the FRNM was renamed the Rhine Research Center. In 2002, the building that held the Rhine Research Center was sold to Duke University and a new building, built for experimental work in parapsychology, was constructed. It is now known as the Rhine which houses the Rhine Research Center and the Rhine Education Center located at 2741 Campus Walk Avenue in western Durham about a mile west of the Duke Medical Center.

During the 1970s and 1980s, over 30 organizations worldwide involved in the advancement of parapsychology were formed.

Robert Thouless, a British psychologist and parapsychologist, in his book, From Anecdote to Experiment in Psychical Research (1972), applied Kuhn's theory of scientific revolution to the field of parapsychology.

Kuhn's theory of scientific revolutions contains many illuminations of the problems of parapsychology: Among others, it suggests why we should expect to have critics, and why they will not be convinced merely by increased weight of experimental evidence. He points out practitioners of normal science have always tended to resist new theories because these seem to throw doubt on what they are doing and on what they have already done. He also suggests that this resistance to change by normal science has its own value in emphasizing the fact of anomaly when a new finding does not fit normal expectations. But this resistance has always led a number of practitioners of normal science to refuse to recognize the necessity for conceptual change. They will not indeed abandon an old paradigm until a new paradigm is ready to take its place. We, in parapsychology, are far from the situation of being able to formulate a new paradigm. So we must expect incredulity to persist among our critics, and not expect that this incredulity will be overcome by mere increase of experimental evidence obtained under new conditions of stringency (p. 101).

Parapsychology has indeed struggled to create a valid identity within the scientific community. It is often referred to as "pseudoscience." Much research has been carried out by parapsychologists with results showing gifted subjects demonstrate psychic abilities at a statistically significant level. Even statistically significant results have not been enough to convince much of the scientific community of the existence of paranormal phenomena as anything more than fraud or products of vivid imaginations or psychological delusions.

Scott Rogo (1975) says this about the foundation of psychical research:

Although modern parapsychology, or psychical research, dates only from Victorian England, psi phenomena had been recorded and investigated for centuries before the scientific revolution. Despite the fact that the Age of Reason, Age of Enlightenment, and the Industrial Revolution all shunned what they thought to be crude superstition, no culture or era has been without tales and reports of what we today would call psychical phenomena (p. 28).

However, since 1975 when Raymond Moody's book, *Life after Life*, was published, paranormal or transpersonal experiences were documented as occurring in medical situations. These phenomena had been occurring for centuries, but Moody's book began the current investigation of these events. More sophisticated methods of resuscitation led to more individuals being brought back from the edge of death with possible glimpses of the afterlife. Healthcare professionals now became engaged in research of near-death experiences and other related phenomena. This research caused an explosion in the study of these transpersonal experiences and a new avenue of study of paranormal or transpersonal experiences.

The first researchers in the field were Raymond Moody, MD, PhD; Kenneth Ring, PhD; Bruce Greyson, MD; Melvin Morse, MD; and Michael Sabom, MD. Other researchers in the medical professions followed suit. Soon there began a body of research documenting the incidence of near-death experiences. Medical doctors and other health professionals have always been held in high regard thus increasing the credibility of this type of research. In Chapters 5 and 6 we will be discussing near-death experiences in more detail.

The most puzzling, at the same time interesting, occurrences were the veridical perceptions of patients while physically unconscious during near-death experiences. Anomalies, unexplainable by current science, were now being described in this literature.

Sabom (1982) studied over 57 cardiac patients who were clinically dead and brought back. Of those 57 patients, 32 had had an out-of-body experience (OBE) and 25 had none. All of the patients in the OBE group accurately described their resuscitation efforts. Over 80% of the members of the non-OBE group made serious errors in describing their resuscitation.

Ring and Lawrence (1993) published a report of three incidences of veridical perception by near-death experiencers. In the first situation a patient, when she became alert, reported seeing a red shoe on the northwest corner of the roof of the hospital. She had had a cardiac arrest during which she had a near-death experience. She was brought in unconscious and would have had no opportunity to be on the roof. She reported this occurrence to a nurse who reported it to the resident on duty. He was able to have someone from building services open the door to the roof of the hospital. He came back to the unit carrying a red shoe.

Around the same time, another patient remembered during her near-death experience seeing a nurse's plaid shoelaces. The nurse only wore them on the day the patient was unconscious while assisting with her having a cardiac arrest. In a third instance the patient remembered seeing a nurse's polka dot blouse during her near-death experience.

During the pilot phase of a study done in the Netherlands (van Lommel, van Wees, Meyers, & Elfferich, 2001) in one of the hospitals, a coronary care unit nurse reported a veridical out-of-body experience of a resuscitated patient. The 44-year-old man was brought to the coronary care unit in a comatose state. He immediately required artificial respiration, defibrillation, and heart massage. When the staff were ready to intubate the patient (put a breathing tube into his airway) they first removed his dentures. The nurse placed these dentures on the nearby crash cart. This is her report on the incident:

Meanwhile, we continue extensive CPR. After about an hour and a half, the patient has sufficient heart rhythm and blood pressure, but he is still ventilated and intubated, and he is still comatose. He is transferred to the intensive care unit to continue the necessary artificial respiration. Only after more than a week do I meet again with the patient, who is by now back on the cardiac ward. I distribute his medication.

The moment he sees me he says: "Oh, that nurse knows where my dentures are." I am very surprised. Then he elucidates: "Yes, you were there when I was brought into hospital and you took my dentures out of my mouth and put them onto that cart, it had all these bottles on it and there was this sliding drawer underneath and there you put my teeth." I was especially amazed because I remembered this happening while the man was in deep coma and in the process of CPR. When I asked further, it appeared the man had seen himself lying in bed, that he had perceived from above how nurses and doctors had been busy with CPR. He was also able to describe correctly and in detail the small room in which he had been resuscitated, as well as the appearance of those present like myself. At the time that he observed the situation, he had been very much afraid that we would stop CPR and that he would die. And it is true that we had been very negative about the patient's prognosis due to his very poor medical condition when admitted. The patient tells me that he desperately and unsuccessfully tried to make it clear to us that he was still alive and that we should continue CPR. He is deeply impressed by his experience and says he is no longer afraid of death. Four weeks later he left hospital as a healthy man (p. 240).

In our current paradigm, some would say the patient heard someone talk about the resuscitation procedure, the red shoe, plaid shoelaces, polka dot blouse, and where their teeth were placed. It is highly unlikely someone during the patient's critical state someone would have been talking about these events or descriptions. As these anomalies continue, the current paradigm becomes inadequate to explain these new occurrences.

The search for explanations of transpersonal occurrences continues. Those who support the facts, beliefs and theories of the current paradigm believe these transpersonal experiences to be due to the lack of oxygen, temporal brain lobe abnormalities, mental illness, and/or the influence of drugs. Others believe a new paradigm is necessary to explain these occurrences. Much is known about these events to guide the analysis and processing of these occurrences. We know there are several types of transpersonal experiences that occur to individuals who come close to death or are dying. What is also known is, these experiences occur in large numbers. It is estimated millions of individuals who come close to death, or are dying, have some type of transpersonal experience. In each chapter, incidences of each specific type of events are presented. What is also known is these experiences have a profound and mostly positive impact on the person and their family members.

CHAPTER 2

FRAMEWORKS FOR ASSISTING EXPERIENCERS

Keywords: Attribution theory, client-centered approach, frameworks, paradigms, Neuro-Linguistic Programming, spiritual emergency, Transpersonal Psychology.

"D r. Lawrence, would you come up to the unit this morning?" asked Betsy Hall, an RN from the medical stepdown hospital unit. "We have a sister of a patient who is beside herself because of her brother's visions. We don't know what to say to her."

"I'll be up around 11:00," I said.

When I got to the hospital unit I saw a woman who I estimated to be in her mid-thirties pacing the hallways. I thought maybe she was the distressed sister. I decided to talk with Betsy for more information before I talked to the sister.

"Hi, Betsy. So what is going on here? Is she the sister you want me to talk to?" indicating the woman I had seen.

"Yes, that is Marianne Hendricks. Her brother Jeffrey is being treated for AIDS. He is only 26. The medication he is getting is making him very sick. When he gets physiologically compromised, he has these visions. It is like he gets close to dying and then comes back. Sometimes he says he goes to 'heaven,' but other times he sees people and events here, particularly those involving his sister's son. She thinks he's going crazy. We figured you could help her understand what might be happening to her brother." This last statement was said with a big grin, like someone handing a hot potato to someone else. I laughed.

"Glad to help out and to talk with her. OK to use the conference room?"

"It is available, and thanks. Maybe after you talk to the sister, you could give us a mini-in service about what might be happening and what we should say to patients and their families?"

"Sounds like a plan."

"Ms. Hendricks? I'm Dr. Lawrence. The nurses tell me you have some questions about what is happening to your brother. Let's go into the conference room and chat."

"I think my brother is going crazy. He's telling me all these strange stories about going to heaven and seeing my son driving around here. I don't understand what is happening to him. It is bad enough he is so sick from the AIDS and having these terrible reactions to the medication. I can't deal with him becoming mentally ill, too. "I can tell you that what is happening to Jeffrey happens to many others, although maybe not in the exact same way. So far, there is no correlation between mental illnesses and seeing these visions. As best as I can tell, when your brother gets very sick from his medication, he has near-death experiences, known as NDEs, and out-of-body experiences not associated with NDEs. Those are common occurrences when someone is as sick as your brother. What specifically has you concerned?"

"He told me the other day, he saw my son in a car accident when he was driving my car. He also said not to worry, that my son was not hurt. At the time I told Jeffrey not to be concerned because my son was not driving my car. I came to find out, my son did take my car without permission and hit a fence. It was a minor accident and my son was fine. It freaked me out that my brother saw this happen when I didn't even know my son was out in my car."

"We don't know how your brother knew about the accident. What we do know is other patients report seeing events outside their rooms they should not be able to see. I talked to a patient the other day who said he could see the nurses in the break room making popcorn."

"So this happens to other patients and they are not crazy?" asked Ms. Hendricks.

"Yes, this happens to other patients. So far they seem to be in good mental health. These types of events are triggered by being physiologically compromised and being close to death. Many scientists are studying these experiences. What we know is they occur with considerable frequency but don't indicate psychopathology. Also, they are often a comfort to the person experiencing the event.

Feel free to talk with your brother about these experiences. He probably would appreciate being able to talk about them."

"I've been too freaked out to have him talk about what he sees. I'll listen more now that I know these things happen to other people, too."

Ms. Hendricks was visibly more relaxed as she walked to her brother's room. My job now was to develop a framework to help the nurses and other health professionals talk to the family members about these experiences.

The framework

The framework for nurses, other professionals, and family members to guide individuals experiencing transpersonal experience surrounding death was developed from approaches used in social psychology. While these approaches have historic roots, their development and inclusion into mainstream scientific inquiry is recent. The descriptions in this chapter present an overview of each approach. For more in-depth information, the reference section includes helpful resources.

The framework for assisting patients or clients who have these experiences is based on the following: 1) The work of Carl Rogers and his client-centered approach; 2) Attribution theory; 3) Transpersonal Psychology; and 4) Neuro-Linguistic Programming.

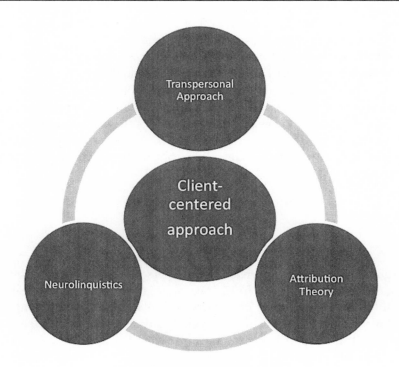

Table I. The Framework
Carl Rogers and his client-centered approach.

Carl Rogers (1902-1987) was a humanistic psychologist. His fundamental belief was that people were oriented toward being virtuous with
a desire to fulfill their potential (Boeree, 2006).

From this belief he developed a non-directive approach designed
with the client as the driving force for understanding their issues. A
client-centered approach involves creating an atmosphere of comfort
with empathy and no judgments about the client's behavior (Rogers,
1951). In a client-centered approach, the client is made aware the person with whom he or she is speaking does not have the answers to the
client's situation. Rogers advocated for unconditional positive regard as
the approach needed to create this environment. This enables a client
to freely describe their experiences without fear of rejection.

According to McLeod (2007), Rogers made a distinction between
unconditional positive regard and conditional positive regard. Unconditional positive regard involves accepting the person regardless of what
they say or do, even if they do something wrong or make a mistake.

Conditional positive regard involves accepting only the behaviors that are consistent with the desired outcomes of the loved one or therapist or healthcare provider. The positive regard is withdrawn if the person does not live up to the expectations of the other person.

During Rogers' time, in the 1940s and 1950s, it was popular for a therapist or counselor to advise clients and tell them ways to improve their lives. In healthcare, an authoritative approach is generally used and patients are directed on how to improve their health. When patients do not follow directives, they are judged to be "noncompliant" with little attempt to understand the patient's perspective (Ofri, 2012; Christensen & Hewitt-Taylor, 2006; Oudshoorn, 2005).

Rogers postulated more success would be obtained when clients identified issues and solutions instead of being told what to do (Rogers, 1951).

Wilkins (2000) offers us a description of a student's use of unconditional positive regard after being told to stop seeing a client because he was psychotic and exhibiting bizarre behavior.

> My student felt very strongly that she had a relationship with this client and that the point of counselling was not to "cure" the psychosis (which in any case seemed of marginal relevance to her), but to stay alongside her client as he travelled what was a traumatic and difficult path. She did not know that psychotic people were not susceptible to counselling interventions and that they were thought by some people to be incapable of forming a therapeutic relationship.
>
> So, with the agreement that she ensure her personal safety in a variety of ways, she continued to see this client and carried on responding to him in a person-centered way. While firmly rooted in her reality, she entered into his delusional world to some extent "as if" it were her own, and noticed that as she did, so his periods of rationality began to increase. He would still behave bizarrely in her presence, but every so often, his voice and demeanor would return to normal and he would thank her for staying with him through what he knew was a difficult episode for them both.
>
> This continued for some weeks until the client was once again able to encounter the world with confidence and to connect with people. He said to my student that it was the first time anybody had attempted to stay with him throughout a florid episode. He reported that even at his most delusional, he had been aware of her presence and that

her steadfast and accepting nature, and her obviously genuine desire to understand what it was like to be him, had been very comforting, reassuring, and helpful. His psychotic episode had been relatively short in comparison to his previous experience.

In our conversations during and after this therapeutic relationship, I was aware of my student's insistence that her client was worthy of deep respect and of his right to his fantasy world and odd behavior that is his right to be himself as he was at any time (p. 32).

Wilkins concludes an acceptance of the client's authority and self-expertise is a necessary component of unconditional positive regard.

According to Schneider and Langle (2012), there is a renewal of humanism in psychotherapy. Not only is humanism growing in its use, it has shown to increase effectiveness. There is also a trend for a more client-centered approach to become the norm in healthcare settings. According to Oudshoorn, "Nurses are challenged to develop a new way of seeing empowerment practice, and encouraged to focus on 'being with' clients, rather than 'doing to' them." It has recently been recommended in healthcare the term "noncompliant" be changed to nonadherent. Nonadherent is seen to be less judgmental and more open to inquiry with the patient as to difficulties staying with recommended medical treatment (Ofri, 2012).

With the event of improved resuscitation efforts, more individuals in the 1960s and 1970s reported NDEs. During that time, anyone who reported seeing otherworld apparitions or out-of-body experiences were often sent to mental health counselors for treatment. These events when reported by patients were called hallucinations and under that label fell under the psychopathology category in the minds of doctors, nurses, and other mental health professionals. Any image, sound, or smell that was perceived to be real by the individual but not experienced by others was determined to be caused by mental illness or the effect of a drug. The first individuals who reported an NDE were sent for psychiatric treatment and offered medications (Fracasso, Friedman, & Young, 2010).

As more research occurred in the field, it was found NDEs often occurred to individuals without a history of mental illness. Lawrence (1995) excluded individuals with a psychiatric diagnosis from her study of 111 patients who had previously been unconscious. From that group of subjects, 25% experienced some type of transpersonal experience.

Individuals initially were reluctant to report NDEs for fear of being labeled mentally ill. Some of the individuals Moody (2001) interviewed reported being told they were hallucinating. Others were told not to talk about their experiences because they were just imagining the events.

Moody (2001) reports the following conclusions from his interviews with NDErs in the early '70s.

> Despite their own certainty of the reality and importance of what has happened to them, they realize that our contemporary society is just not the sort of environment in which reports of this nature would be received with sympathy and understanding. Indeed, many have remarked that they realized from the very beginning that others would think they were mentally unstable if they were to relate their experiences. So, they have resolved to remain silent on the subject or else to reveal their experiences only to some very close relative (p. 78).

Individuals who have transpersonal experiences associated with being close to death or dying feel isolated when they are unable to discuss such deeply moving experiences. They often seek to understand the experience but lack guidance.

A client-centered approach with positive regard enables the individual to freely express their feelings and beliefs about their transpersonal experience. Even though there is no evidence that mental illness precedes these events, the isolation they feel can be detrimental. Family members, health professionals, and counselors who use empathy and positive regard while listening to the person's experience will find an increase in that person's willingness to speak and process the impact of the experience.

Attribution theory

In 1958, Heider proposed a theory of attribution. His belief was people tried to understand the behavior of others by identifying characteristics and coming up with a reasonable explanation or cause. Others (Harvey & Weary, 1985; Jones, Kannouse, Kelley, Nisbett, Valins, & Weiner, 1972) elaborated on this idea of attribution and developed a major research paradigm in social psychology.

Attribution theory deals with how the social perceiver uses information to arrive at causal explanations for events. It examines what information is gathered and how it is combined to form a causal judgment (Fiske & Taylor, 1991).

According to Forsterling (2001), we are all oriented toward a search for the cause of events. Not only do we experience an event, but we attempt to explain why that event occurred. If we see a man bend down to pick up a penny from a sidewalk, we will automatically come up with reasons why he did so. If the man is shabbily dressed and unkempt, we may believe he is poor. If he is well dressed, well kempt, we may believe he is tight with money or superstitious. If we wanted the penny, we may see the man as aggressive or competitive, beating us to something we wanted.

No matter what the event, we not only see it happening, we attribute a cause to it. How much thought we give to the event depends upon the significance of the event to us.

Initially attribution theory focused on how we as humans attribute cause to the behavior of others. These attributions were further distinguished between internal and external causes. This is consistent with our belief that behavior is internally as well as externally motivated.

If the man picking up the penny is thin and emaciated looking, we might believe he is picking up the penny and any other coin he sees in order to buy food. We attribute an internal motive for his behavior. If he was ordered to pick up the penny by his boss, we attribute an external motive for his behavior.

We also attribute internal or external motivation based on our perception of the status of the person. Generally, individuals we perceive as having high status we attribute more internal motivation and those with low status as being motivated by external explanations.

Besides what is perceived of the behavior, attributions are influenced by emotional and motivational drives. If someone's general orientation to life is to have high anxiety and fear, attributions of people are likely to be colored by that emotional orientation.

A person may see someone as achieving success because of their lack of anxiety. Others may see someone as behaving in a way that is threatening because they are anxious and fearful. A man walking toward an anxious person could be attributed to being dangerous because of their own fears, not necessarily by behavior associated with dangerous intentions.

In addition, Kelley (1967) describes how people contribute causality on how factors go together. We know, for example, poverty and hunger often occur in great frequency. When we see a person picking up a penny on the sidewalk who looks poor to us, we can attribute hunger to that person's motivation.

This is true not only for attribution of behavior of others but also of events. If a person sees a flash of lightning hit a tree and then the tree splits in half, the person will attribute the lightning as causing the tree to split. It is referred to as an antecedent event. The person does not just see the tree split, he or she will also see the lightning as causing the split since these factors are known by most people to follow each other. As a consequence, the person might fear lightning.

These background descriptions lead researchers to a general model of attribution.

Table II (Kelley & Michela, 1980 p. 459)

Attribution theory applies to individuals who experience transpersonal events and to the scientists who study these experiences. In the majority of cases, the person experiencing a transpersonal event believes strongly the event is real. If a dying person sees Uncle Fred sitting in a chair in the corner, he or she believes he is really there. If a person has a near-death experience, he or she will believe that while they were out of their body, what they saw was real. They will say it was not a dream or a hallucination. Individuals who had hallucinations because of a drug effect will say the transpersonal experience is totally different from that.

To the experiencers, these events were real. They continued to be who they had always been but could see beyond their normal world experiences during these transpersonal events. They would offer evidence to those who cared for them during their near-death episode. They would often tell doctors and nurses what they had seen during the event, often to the shock of the healthcare professionals. The individuals often recounted the resuscitation procedures performed on them.

While experiencers believe what happened to them and what they saw was real, they believed most health professionals and family members would dismiss these experiences as unreal and believe them to be "crazy." They would stop talking about the experiences because others attributed these experiences as a sign of mental illness, oxygen deprivation, or drug-induced delirium.

Since *Religious or Spiritual Problem* is a new diagnostic category (Code V62.89) in the *Diagnostic and Statistical Manual-Fourth Edition* (APA, 1994), it is important to be able to distinguish between spiritual emergence and spiritual emergency, the latter including severe disruption in functioning. There is limited attention and understanding of these experiences and differentiation of healing experiences from psychopathology (Allman, De La Roche, Elkins & Weathers, 1992).

In the case of negative or distressing near-death experiences, individuals who have them feel an additional burden. One subject said he did not want to talk about his hellish experience. Not only would people think he was crazy, they would also think he was bad (Lawrence, 1997).

Scientists who study these transpersonal phenomena attribute causes to them consistent with the current biological paradigm. Some believe it is lack of oxygen; others, an increase in endorphins; others, changes in brain chemistry or functioning; and still others, a psychological need. To date, no theory has adequately explained these transpersonal experiences. Two major obstacles cause many to reject these theories. Only about 10 to 15 percent of individuals who come close to death have some type of transpersonal experience. The scientific theories which say it is part of the dying process with low oxygen and increased endorphins have no explanation as to why just a small percentage of individuals have these experiences (Blackmore, 1993). The body physiology is generally consistent. Lack of oxygen should cause the same effect in most dying patients, not just 10%. In addition, there are no explanations for how individuals know events or conversations to which they have no access with their five senses.

Thus, it is natural for anyone who listens to an individual describing a transpersonal event to attribute a causal factor. In order to be the most therapeutic, it is important to suspend those causal beliefs and listen to the person's beliefs.

Neuro-Linguistic Programming

Neuro-Linguistic Programming (NLP) is the study of how our thoughts are processed. The focus is on how the mind inputs information from our senses and creates experiences. NLP is based on the theory that all thoughts are experienced as either pictures, sounds, smells, feelings, and/or taste (Hoobyar, Dotz & Sanders, 2013).

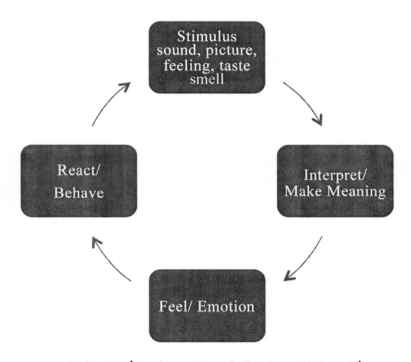

Table III (Hoobyar, Dotz & Sanders, 2013, p. 11)

This field of study started in the early 1970s by researchers interviewing and observing people in various activities. Much has been documented on how people process falling in love, grieving, learning, or just plain sleeping.

From some of this research we know the mind carries out some processes automatically when we have an experience. First of all, the mind generalizes how what is happening now with something that happened before. If you ride through a college town, your mind will automatically process what was similar to or different from other college towns you have seen or lived in. The same will happen in a store that is part of a chain like Wal-Mart. Your mind will automatically notice if items are located in similar sections or not. This ability to generalize can be useful and efficient. All Wal-Mart stores have some item placements in common. We can easily find those items in a store even though we have never been there before and adjust and recognize the differences.

Sometimes this tendency to generalize can have negative consequences. We may see someone who reminds us of someone who was nasty. We come to the erroneous conclusion that this new person is also nasty and develop a dislike for him or her.

Secondly, the mind has a deletion button. When we focus on certain tasks, sounds, or individuals, our minds delete extraneous information in the background. When we watch an interesting movie or become engrossed in a good book, we tune out our environment to some degree. Those who believe we have a conscious mind and subconscious mind will say the subconscious mind perceives all the information. In hypnosis or cognitive interviewing, some of that deleted or forgotten information can be retrieved.

Thirdly, the mind can distort what is actually present or the experience as it happened. We fill in our perceptions with our imagination. When we see a deer, for example, we may attribute Bambi-like qualities to it. We can also distort by generalizations. If we see a man walking tall and confident, we may think of him as intelligent, even if no evidence of intelligence is present.

Learning types

From NLP we have also learned about auditory, visual, and kinesthetic learners (Hoobyar, Dotz, Sanders, 2013). Several websites have a test, the VAK, to help determine what type of learner a person is. All of us have some degree of ability to take in information that we see, hear, or experience through touch or emotions. Generally we have one mode that operates more efficiently and thoroughly than the others. If you are a visual learner, you will learn best by activities such as reading and media presentations. Auditory individuals learn information best by hearing. These students will learn best by attending lectures. They use phones often to communicate. Kinesthetic learners like to manipulate objects or talk about emotions.

We use words that reflect our learning style even when the situation calls for words in a different style. Visual learners will use "seeing" words, i.e., "I can picture what you are saying." Auditory learners use "hearing" words, "Tone down the color in the room." Kinesthetic learners talk using "touch" words, "I grasp what you are saying."

Much of our miscommunication is assuming our learning style is what works best for the person with whom we are communicating. If we are auditory learners, we will use voice mail and leave messages in that modality. We become upset when our visual boss or visual significant other did not get the message. If we want to communicate with visual individuals, memos, text messages, emails are better than voice mail.

The early scientists who studied transpersonal events often limited the descriptions to one modality. The early researchers on deathbed communication, for example, described these events as deathbed visions. In fact, not only do individuals see apparitions, they also can hear voices or music or feel them and emotionally respond. In working with individuals who have these transpersonal events, it is important to listen to the descriptive words they use, be they visual, auditory, or kinesthetic. It is important to not generalize, delete, or distort the person's description or emotional response. It is important to elicit more information when we suspect generalization, deletion, or distortion on the part of the individual's description.

A transpersonal approach

Individuals who have transpersonal experiences are generally convinced they are real experiences. They also believe these experiences to be extraordinary and are elated to have had them. As mentioned earlier, others often try to discourage conversation about these experiences. Others often judge them as being indicative of psychopathology, or at the very least, temporary delusion. Some of these judgments are derived from the exclusion of spiritual and transcendent aspects of the human experience in many psychological theories of humankind.

Transpersonal psychology provides a school of thought that includes the spiritual and transcendent aspects of the human experience. Sometimes this school of thought is also referred to as spiritual psychology. The word transpersonal has been defined as "experiences in which the sense of identity or self extends beyond the individual or personal to encompass wider aspects of humankind, life, psyche, or cosmos (Walsh & Vaughan, 1993)."

25

William James first identified the concept of "transpersonal" more than 90 years ago (Taylor, G., 1997; Vich, 1998). The humanistic psychology (Abraham Maslow, Carl Rogers & Rollo May) and human potential movements (Erik Erikson, Aldous Huxley, Fritz Perl, Joseph Campbell, Robert Bly and Carl Rogers) of the 1960s laid the foundation for the development of transpersonal psychology (Davis, 2003). In 1969, the first issue of the *Journal of Transpersonal Psychology* was published. In 1972, the Association for Transpersonal Psychology was founded (Scotton, Chinen, and Battista, 1996). Transpersonal Psychology is being taught in a number of well-known institutions. Columbia University in New York (Otterman, 2012) and Sofia University in California have integrated transpersonal psychology into their clinical psychology programs. There is also Transpersonal Psychology Section in the British Psychological Society. Transpersonal psychology and research on near-death studies are linked in the *Journal of Transpersonal Psychology* through the writings of Kenneth Ring and Bruce Greyson (1993; 2000).

Transpersonal psychologists deal with issues such as peak and mystical experiences. They are not solely focused on events that cause psychological damage but include events that are uplifting, joyous, and filled with feelings of happiness and well-being, as well as feelings of intense love. Exposure to great art or music or an awe-inspiring natural sight, like the Grand Canyon, can bring about such an experience.

According to Lajoie and Shapiro (1992), definitions of transpersonal psychology commonly include states of consciousness, higher or ultimate potential, beyond the ego or personal self, transcendence, and spirituality. Art enthusiasts can be overwhelmed by the beauty of Monet's Water Lilies at the Musée de l'Orangerie Paris that completely fills two rooms. One woman was so moved, she had tears in her eyes. An artist wanted to stay in the room all day. Women report peak experiences at the times of the birth of their children.

Abraham Maslow in his book, *Religions, Values, and Peak-Experiences*, describes these peak experiences as leaving a permanent mark on the individual, usually changing him or her for the better. Also after these experiences, individuals have a definite sense of purpose, different from their previous orientation toward life. Here is a description of one of the individual's Raymond Moody interviewed during his research on near-death experiences:

> At this time – it was before I had gone off to college — I had grown up in a very small town, with very small-minded people, the people

I was associated with, anyway. I was a typical high-school fraternity brat. You just weren't "it" unless you belonged to my fraternity.

But after this thing happened to me, I wanted to know more. At the time, though, I didn't think I was a person who would know anything about psychology or anything like that. All I knew was that I felt like I had aged overnight after this happened, because it opened up a whole new world for me that I never knew could possibly exist. I kept thinking, "There's so much that I've got to find out." In other words, there's more to life than Friday night movies and the football game (p. 83).

According to Kasprow and Scotton (1999):

Transpersonal psychiatry does not promote any particular belief system, but rather acknowledges that spiritual experiences and transcendent states characterized by altruism, creativity, and profound feelings of connectedness are universal human experiences widely reported across cultures, and therefore worthy of rigorous scientific study. Inattention to these experiences and the roles they play in both psychopathology and healing constitutes a common limitation in conventional psychotherapeutic practice and research (p. 12-13).

On occasion, transpersonal or transrational experiences need to be distinguished from psychotic episodes. Lukoff (1985) states true transpersonal experiences are more likely to occur to individuals with good mental health functioning before the event, a stressful event with a sudden onset of reactions and a positive and exploratory attitude toward the experience. Even though these events are positive and life affirming, some individuals ignore the opportunity provided by these events and others grapple with the unknown journey before them.

Helping with the crossing

In Heckler's book, *Crossings: Everyday People, Unexpected Events, and Life-Affirming Change* (1998), he describes his interviews with individuals who had unexpected events. He first describes an interview with Karl, an enforcer for organized crime. He had become cold and violent carrying both guns and knives often in a drug-induced state. Instead of jail, Karl chose a religious-oriented detox program. Stone-deaf most of his life without any musical ability, he stood in front of the congregation one day singing perfectly in a full rich voice, "Old Ship of Zion." During the experience he heard a voice saying there was always hope and that was the message he was to share.

That event enabled Karl to rid himself of the drugs and eventually become a minister to the homeless. Some events are small: a sudden insight, a moment of peace, a vision of beauty. Others involve brushes with death, acquisition of fame or fortune, or both. As Heckler describes, "Something or someone comes hurtling through the trance of our everyday life, and startles us (p 2)."

Some individuals ignore these interruptions, not knowing what to do with them, moving on unaffected. Others accept the challenge and chose a new path, recognizing this initial awakening is just the beginning. In some cases the event is so powerful, the purpose and journey is clear to the experiencer. Family, friends, colleagues, mentors, and caregivers can influence the ease of the journey or present obstacles.

Individuals who chose to be more open minded see many more doors open with increased understanding of a larger world view. They often recognize they are on a journey and accept the challenges of their passage. As they proceed, the initial effect of the experience takes on a broader perspective that evolves into a generalized orientation toward life.

> Those who accept the challenge of this passage, who respond to the unusual (often with unusual choices) have learned to traverse an arcane territory. They have developed a working relationship with the unexpected and respond with skillfulness as it continues to enter their lives. For once accepted, the journey of awakening never ends, and one's relationship to the unexpected forever deepens (Heckler, p.197).

Lawrence (1997) describes the transforming passage of a man after his near-death experience. On his way home from the hospital on a cold winter day, he saw a man walking wearing clothes inadequate to keep out the winter chill. He asked his wife to immediately stop the car. When she asked why, he told her he wanted to give the man his warm jacket. The wife was shocked by his altruistic gesture but this was just the beginning of a new orientation toward life for this man.

Individuals who have transpersonal experiences surrounding death are typically moved spiritually and emotionally by them. They will often describe these experiences as the most profound ones they have had.

It is important to support the positive impact of these experiences and provide a supportive hand and the subsequent journey they embrace.

Overview of supportive guidelines
Foster a client-centered approach

Be empathetic using unconditional positive regard

Listen for the individual's causal explanation for the event

Bracket your causal belief for the event

Listen for the visual, auditory, or kinesthetic descriptions of the event

Determine if there appears to be generalizations, deletions, or distortions in the individual's descriptions.

Avoid making generalizations, deletions, or distortions of the individual's descriptions

Elicit the impact of the transpersonal experience

Provide support and discussion about the subsequent journey ahead for the individual

CHAPTER 3

NEAR-DEATH VISITS

Keywords: After-death communication, deathbed communications, near-death experiences, near-death visits, veridical perception

"Good morning, Mrs. Harris. I understand from the nurses you are having a visitor who is upsetting you. Would you mind telling me about this visitor?"

Mrs. Harris was pacing the floor of her hospital room when I walked in with the nurse. She was an older woman with short dark hair, peppered with gray. She had arrived at the hospital with acute respiratory distress but was now doing well. She had no respiratory complaints but was distressed about communications from her deceased mother. According to her chart she had no history of mental illness. Mrs. Harris had been fully functioning on her own before her respiratory illness.

"I know you are going to think I'm crazy, but my mother, who is dead, comes here in my room."

"Can you see her?" I asked.

"No, I don't see her. I feel her being here."

"Can you hear her?"

"It's a funny type of hearing. It's like I get a message in my head."

It seemed to me Mrs. Harris's mother might be communicating telepathically with her. Since she had no history of mental health issues and was oriented to time and place, I proceeded with more conversations about her mother.

"Mrs. Harris, what kind of messages are you getting from your mother?"

"She wants me to come and join her. My mother lived with me after my father died. She always depended on me for a lot. I just think she wants me to come be with her to take care of her again. Sounds, dumb, doesn't it?"

"No, I don't think it sounds dumb. I've heard other patients describe similar situations. How do you feel about what your mother is saying to you?"

"I don't want to go. I'm not ready yet. My mother lived a long life. She was 98 when she died. I want to spend more time with my children and grandchildren."

"Have you said that to your mother?"

"You think I should?"

"If that's how you feel, sure."

Mrs. Harris dropped her shoulders as some stress visibly left her. "OK. Next time I feel her presence, I'm going to tell her I'm not coming with her. You think she'll get the message?"

"Think about how you communicated with your mother when she was alive to get her to truly listen to you. I'll stop in tomorrow to see how you are doing. Is that all right with you?"

The next day, when I went to see Mrs. Harris, she was not pacing but sitting comfortably in bed reading a magazine.

"Good morning, Mrs. Harris. How are you today?"

"Doing much better, thank you. When my mother was alive, sometimes I had to be forceful with her to get her to stop being so demanding. Yesterday evening when I felt her presence, I said out loud, 'Mom, I'm not coming with you. It is not my time. Just leave me alone.' She went away."

It is not certain Mrs. Harris' mother was present in her room. It is equally not certain she was not in the room. We know the distress Mrs. Harris was feeling was real. Clinically, it was important to assist Mrs. Harris to help process and manage these visits.

Near-death visits (NDVs) were first described in Lawrence's book, *In a World of Their Own, Experiencing Unconsciousness* (1997). Some of the early descriptions of transpersonal experiences, initially referred to as near-death experiences (NDEs), were in fact NDVs. While descriptively different, NDVs have some characteristics in common with near-death experiences (NDEs), deathbed communications (DBCs), and after-death communications (ADCs).

NDEs and NDVs occur to people who are close to death but are not terminally ill. However, during NDEs individuals generally perceive themselves as being out of their body with the ability to see the world from a distant perspective and able to travel to a different realm. They see deceased friends and/or relatives existing in a perceived afterlife. A person who has a near-death visit will have contact with a deceased person in their own space, often a hospital room. They perceive themselves and their visitors only in an earthly realm.

Individuals who have DBCs are terminally ill. They know death is imminent. They communicate with deceased friends and/or relatives in their home. These communications are generally a source of great comfort. (Chapter 9 details these experiences.) Individuals who experience NDVs may be comforted by visits from the deceased but may also be distressed by them, as in the case of Mrs. Harris.

Someone who has an after-death communication (ADC) will see, hear, or feel the presence of a deceased friend or relative in their own space. One difference in those experiences is the person having the ADC is not close to death. Also, the communication experience is one of comfort, often ending the pain from the loss. Sometimes the ADC contains important information about life situations not typically found in NDVs.

Table I Comparison of the characteristics of the five main transpersonal experiences

	NDV*	NDE*	DBC*	ADC*
Location	this world	other world	this world	this world
Close to death	yes	yes	yes	no
Terminally ill	no	no	yes	no
Contact with dead Friends or relatives	yes	yes	yes	yes
Intent	comfort/or coaxing to transition	vision of afterlife	comfort/ transition	comfort/ information

*NDV = near-death visit
*NDE = near-death experience
*DBC=deathbed communication
*ADC=after-death communication

Types of perceptions

In an NDV, the visitors can be seen, heard, smelled, or sensed by patients who had come close to death. Sometimes the senses are altered as in the case of Mrs. Harris. She described hearing her mother by what is called telepathic communication. Telepathic communication is reported in many transpersonal experiences and involves the transmission of information without using known hearing channels. Most subjects will report telepathic communication as a type of hearing with the information occurring mind to mind, bypassing our normal hearing system.

It is also occasionally difficult for individuals to adequately describe the person they "saw." Lawrence (1997) reports the inability of subjects who had transpersonal experiences to describe the body of the person or specifically how they looked. Often the vision of someone is combined with the sensing of that person's presence.

Sometimes the characteristic of the person that existed during life had to do with a scent associated with the person. One of Lawrence's (1997) subjects sensed his father's presence but also could smell the chemicals with which the father had worked (p.132).

Veridical perception

In one instance of an NDV, a man saw his sister with his deceased mother in his hospital room. The sister had been ill and died, but her death had been kept a secret from this man because of his illness. The patient's wife had insisted the hospital staff and the patient's family keep the news of the sister's death from the patient. The man confronted his wife and told her he knew his sister was dead because he saw her in his room with his deceased mother.

Personality characteristics of visitors

During the NDVs, the description by the experiencers often includes personality characteristics of the visitor that was consistent with how he or she had acted in life. Lawrence (1997) describes another woman's experience (Gretchen) after her resuscitation in the emergency room.

I was on the stretcher in the hospital. My son, Bill, was walking beside the stretcher holding my hand. He told me not to worry, that everything was going to be all right. He was with me, and I kept saying, "What are you going to do about Christmas and the children?" He said, "When you are feeling a little stronger we will talk about it. You tell me what else you want done and I will do it." Just regular conversation.

When you were talking to him at this point, what was your reaction? asked Lawrence.

I thought, well, the only thing I thought was you can always depend on Bill. Bill would be right here for me.

Can you describe what you saw?

It was Bill. I could tell by his height and his build and his voice. It was very clear and very soft. He got very cross with me because I was crying, and he said, "You know I can't stand to see you cry. Stop the crying." It was like we were having a little conversation.

Did you think it strange to have this conversation?

I didn't see anything unusual at that. Bill always said he would be there when I needed him. Evidently that was one of the time he thought I needed him (p.132-133).

Mrs. Harris' mother had been demanding when she was alive. Bill had been a son that was dependable. He also did not like to see his mother cry during life. Those traits and characteristic behaviors were also exhibited during the NDVs.

Messages

Patients who have NDVs say the reasons their visitors are present are to provide comfort and/or to assist them to the "final frontier" as one of Moody's (2001) subjects said. This report from Moody describes a person very close to death who had an out-of-body experience but then saw his deceased friend in his hospital room.

Several weeks before I nearly died, a good friend of mine, Bob, had been killed. Now the moment I got out of my body I had the feeling that Bob was standing there, right next to me. I could see him in my mind and felt like he was there, but it was strange. I didn't see him as his physical body. I could see things, but not in the physical form, yet just as clearly, his looks, everything.

I kept asking him, "Bob, where do I go now? What has happened? Am I dead or not?' And he never answered me, never said a word. But, often, while I was in the hospital, he would be there, and I would ask him again, "What's going on?" but never any answer. And then the day the doctors said, "He's going to live," he left. I didn't see him again and didn't feel his presence. It was almost as though he were waiting until I passed that final frontier and then he would tell me, would give me the details on what was going on (p.46-47).

In this transpersonal experience that patient saw and felt the presence of someone close to him who would help with his transition after death, if that were to happen. In Mrs. Harris' case, her mother was almost demanding her to make that transition.

Lawrence (1997) reports another case by a subject named Ronald who, when he awoke from unconsciousness, saw his deceased brothers and father in his hospital room waving to him to come on. He, like Mrs. Harris, resisted the invitation to come on.

When you had the arrest and could see your father and brothers, were you out of your body? Lawrence asked.

No, I was still in my body . . . I felt that I was still myself, and I was still in my body, and I wasn't going to give it up. That was the resistance. At the time I knew I was resisting going with them. . . . I tell myself now that I didn't want to go because they were dead — that's my interpretation of it.

Gretchen's experience was different. Her son was there to provide support and comfort. There was no sense he was there to help with the transition after death.

Hallucinations, visions, and visitations

As we learn more about transpersonal experiences associated with near death and dying, we are able to define these experiences with more accuracy and separate them from other types of experiences that look similar. One of the major concerns for experiencers is their fear of "going crazy" because they associate transpersonal experiences with hallucinations which are often symptomatic of mental illnesses.

Oliver Sacks (2012), author of several well-known books such as *Awakenings, The Man Who Mistook His Wife for a Hat,* and more recently *Hallucinations,* believes about 10% of the population will experience some type of vision without signs of mental illness. He agrees in today's societies and in medical establishments, these visions portray ominous conjuring of severe mental or neurological disorders. Individuals often keep these experiences secret. He believes the majority of these experiences to be benign and perfectly normal.

Beyerstein (1996) also comments about the "bad press" associated with the word hallucinations. Hallucinations are associated with the belief these experiences are symptomatic of something pathological. If an experience is referred to as a vision, there is a sense of privilege associated with what is seen or heard. How the experience is named results in a positive or negative reaction. He has this to say about his assessment of transpersonal experiences based on his research.

> As the media revel in a growing parade of seemingly normal citizens claiming to have had contacts of varying degrees of intimacy with extraterrestrials, ghosts, and the like, it is tempting for clinicians to question the honesty and sanity of these self-professed "contactees." My study of brain mechanisms and consciousness has put me in contact with a large number of these contactees, and I am prepared to admit that the majority are not fools, and most do not show obvious signs of serious neurological impairment. Although I stop short of crediting the objective reality of their contacts with angels, ghosts, or aliens, I am willing to grant that most cope reasonably well and sincerely believe that their experiences were real events (p. 1).

Hallucinations

Hallucinations associated with medical conditions

According to Ryan, Caplan, and Stern (2009), a perception of an object or event without the presence of an external stimulus can justify the perception being called a hallucination. This is a common understanding in the medical fields. In the medical model framework, visual hallucinations can be caused by disturbances of brain structure, disturbance of neurotransmitters, and unconscious psychodynamic causes or a combination of all three (Asaad & Shapiro, 1986).

According to Beyerstein (1996), hallucinations can also be induced by severe stress, particularly those that are life threatening as seen in military experiences

Delirium

Patients who become delirious because of numerous medical conditions, i.e. septic shock, drug effects, also may experience visual hallucinations (Webster & Holroyd, 2000).

Alcohol withdrawal can lead to delirium tremens which is often associated with hallucinations of snakes and crawling insects associated with general agitation.

Dementia and seizure disorders

Visual hallucinations have been described in patients with dementia, particularly dementia with Lewy body disease, Parkinson's disease, and seizure disorders. Seizure disorders can be related to brain tumors.

Migraines

Individuals suffering from migraines also report experiencing an aura which may include 30 to 60 minutes of changes in their visual field. The changes are often a zigzag line which can be uncolored or colored.

Hallucinogens

Changes in visual perception due to drugs classified as hallucinogens technically do not fit the definition of a hallucination. The drugs alter perception of a stimulus present in the environment. True hallucinations often occur without an environmental stimulus.

Psychosis (schizophrenia/schizoaffective disorder)

The Diagnostic and Statistical Manual of Mental Disorders, Fourth Edition (DSM-IV) lists hallucinations as a significant diagnostic criterion for a psychotic disorder especially for schizophrenia. Reports on this affliction have shown auditory hallucinations to be the most common type of hallucinations reported by patients with other sense types occurring less frequently.

Qualitative differences between NDVs and hallucinations and visions

Place, Foxcroft, and Shaw (2011) describe a woman's experience with her voices associated with a psychosis and how they tormented her.

Night times are the worst time – that's their time. They work at night. It is always difficult to sleep as they keep me awake with their torture. They tear my skin in bed for hours, saying cursed things. They tell me how they are going to tear me apart and rape me, and I can feel them tearing at my skin and raping me. I can feel them actually doing it every night. I try to stay awake because if you go to sleep they come and take my spirit and I get tortured in hell while I'm asleep (p. 839).

Hallucinations, as this woman described, tend to be all encompassing and frightening with little control over them by the experiencer.

In a keynote address for the International Society for Psychological and Social Approaches to Psychosis, U.S. chapter (ISPS-US), Joanne Greenberg, author of *I Never Promised You a Rose Garden*, described her four diagnostic questions for determining if a person has had a hallucination or a vision.

According to Ms. Greenberg, a woman told her she had seen deceased family members, including her mother, sitting at the edge of her bed. She was afraid she had gone mad. She believes the answers to the following four questions were helpful to determine if the woman was having visions or hallucinations. Yes answers to the four questions indicated hallucinations. No answers were indicative of visions.

Ms. Greenberg asked the woman, when you see these dead people...

1. Do they look ugly? (No! the woman replied)
2. Are they angry? (No! the woman replied)

3. Do they demand something that you cannot provide? (No! the woman replied)
4. Do they make you feel guilty? (No! the woman replied)

Ms. Greenberg explains that this woman has had a vision.

Visions

According to Gersten (1997), a spiritual vision often involves experiencing seeing a light, God, angels, saints, and so forth. Gersten goes on to explain individuals with schizophrenia feel controlled by their hallucinations. He is in agreement these hallucinations are most often unpleasant in contrast to visions.

Well-known examples of spiritual visions occurred to St. Bernadette of Lourdes, France. She initially described seeing a beautiful lady in a grotto called Massabielle. This lady appeared to Bernadette 17 times and was said to be Jesus's mother, the Blessed Virgin Mary. The place of these visions is now a location of many pilgrimages, with over five million Christians of all denominations visiting each year (Martin, 2005, p. vii).

These spiritual visions are pleasant and elevating experiences. In addition, many of these visions lead to a different perspective toward life. They are transformative.

Lawrence (2014) interviewed a woman who had felt disconnected from God and spirituality. She was guided to make a pilgrimage to Medjugorje, in Bosnia and Herzegovina, where many had seen visions of Mary. Usually these visions occurred within the chapel built on the site where these visions first occurred. The woman was outside the chapel one morning and when she looked up, she could see a vision of Mary. She immediately felt a spiritual connection she had been seeking which brought tears to her eyes. She went home a transformed individual, much more spiritual and less materialistic. Since that day, she reported making 75 pilgrimages, often bringing others to Medjugorje.

Visitations versus hallucinations versus visions

NDVs are qualitatively different from hallucinations and visions. During the NDVs the individual having the experience is oriented to time, person, and place. He or she knows they are in the hospital or can identify their environment correctly. They can identify nurses, doctors, friends, and family members without hesitation. They know why they are in the hospital and what is happening to them. This is similar to individuals experiencing DBCs. What is different from typical patient experiences is seeing deceased friends and/or relatives in their hospital room.

The NDVs are generally pleasant and comforting but not necessarily transformative. The experiencers also can exert some control over the visits as in the case of Mrs. Harris. Once she told her mother she didn't want to go with her, the visits from the mother stopped.

We know they occur to individuals without a history of mental illness. Lawrence (1995), in her study of 111 patients who had experienced an unconscious episode, described several transpersonal experiences, including NDVs. Before being interviewed, all the research subjects were screened for a history of mental illness. No one who had a history of mental illness, drug, or alcohol abuse was admitted into the study.

So far, these NDVs have not included experiences with spiritual figures or saints or bright lights. Deceased friends and relatives are the only type of visitors described. At least while in the hospital, once the patient recovered fully from the initial emergency episode, the NDVs stopped. However, there have not been long term follow-ups of these patients. We do not know if any of these visits occur after hospital discharge.

A visitation is justifiably a better word to describe these visits than hallucinations or visions.

Table II Helpful communication with someone having a near-death visit

1. Assess the person's orientation to person, time, and place
2. Foster a client-centered approach by encouraging a description of the experience
3. Be empathetic and avoid any negative judgments
4. Ask the individual for their explanation for the event
5. Determine if the experience contained visual, auditory, or kinesthetic descriptions
6. Assess the emotional impact
7. Normalize the experience
8. Provide support and resources as needed

Table III Documentation of the near-death visit

1. The time and length of the occurrence
2. The type of experience – visual, auditory, or kinesthetic
3. Description of what occurred
4. Description of the emotional impact

CHAPTER 4

OUT-OF-BODY EXPERIENCES

Keywords: Dissociation, dissociative experiences scale, out-of-body experiences, physiological abnormality, reciprocal OBEs, spontaneous OBEs, temporal-parietal junction, veridical perception

It was a very long labor. I was exhausted. I told them I wasn't going to do it anymore. I had been in labor from eight in the morning until eight in the evening. It was really intense. I asked the doctor for some medication, but he said no, that I had to help myself. You know, "you have to work at it."

Of course, it never would have happened no matter how hard I worked, because the baby's head couldn't fit through my pelvis. The pain was really severe, and I remember thinking to myself, "I've got to get out of here." I mean, I was getting very nervous, and the next thing I remember, I was looking down on myself. I was on the ceiling in the corner.

You were on the ceiling?

I was looking down, and saw myself on the bed. It was pink. The room was a golden pink and very, very bright. I was in something pink and soft. I could look down and see my doctor and myself on the bed. He was sitting next to me, holding my hand. The nurse was on the other side, taking my blood pressure. I felt great. Light, very light. No pain at all. I could see myself and I wasn't frightened anymore.

Were they saying anything?

I couldn't hear them until another doctor came in. They started calling me. Like, "Heather, wake up," and the nurse had something she was putting on my lips. The doctor kept saying, "Wake up. We have to take you out of here," or something like that. I kept thinking that I couldn't go that I couldn't leave. I could hear but it was muted, like water in your ear. The new doctor examined me, and then they put me on something with wheels. That's the last thing I remember.

Did you know who that other doctor was? Did you see him again?

No, I didn't know him. He was just a doctor in a white coat.

Other than the fact that he had a white coat, was there anything else you remember about him? Was he tall or short?

He seemed thinner than my doctor. It seemed to me the other doctor was growing a little bald on the top of his head (Lawrence, 1997, 101-102).

Heather's experience is an example of an out-of-body experience (OBE), induced by pain and a physiologically compromised state. OBEs have been well researched in the general population and in relation to near-death experiences (NDE). Not as much is known about those that occur to hospitalized patients who are physiologically compromised or close to death, but not experiencing an NDE. Also this group of patients includes patients who have an OBE after an NDE.

OBEs in the general population

Generally an OBE is defined as a condition during which individuals perceive themselves to be conscious; perceive their environment as usual, but outside their physical body. Often the subjects can see their physical body and recognize they are no longer in it. During this state the subjects can move through physical matter and visit others in their homes or other places, even when at a long distance. Subjects who have repeated OBEs claim to be able to exert more control over their trips while out of their bodies (Monroe, 1985).

OBEs are common occurrences in the general populations with estimates of 10% to 20% of people having such experiences at least once (Alvarado, 1984; Monroe, 1985; Blackmore, 1982; 1984). These common, spontaneous OBEs can occur during rest, sleep, illness, and less frequently through drug use. Seeing their environment during an OBE is most common, with auditory sensations the next most frequent occurrences. During an OBE, it is not possible to feel objects or make them move. Individuals often report going through solid objects rather than around them. Occasionally they will report going through people they see or having those people go through them. While a person having the OBE can hear and see people in the environment, those people generally cannot see or hear them, although rare cases have been reported.

OBEs also are seen as interesting and able to be produced by the will of individuals using certain techniques. Many books are available on websites such as Amazon and Barnes and Noble on how to have an OBE. Graham Nicholls (2012), for example, describes some of his OBEs which are over 100, in his book *Navigating the Out-of-Body Experience: Radical New Techniques*. OBEs are not seen as part of a mental disorder in these books but as a skill to acquire.

OBEs while close to death

There are two types of OBEs that can occur to a person while close to death: spontaneous OBEs and those occurring in conjunction with an NDE.

In OBEs not associated with a progression to an NDE, the individual does not experience a wonderful feeling of love and peace, characteristically connected with NDEs. They also have more concern about being out of body and how to return to their physical body. In addition, individuals with a spontaneous OBE remain in their worldly environment, while those with an NDE will travel to what is perceived as life after death.

Lawrence (1997) reports the OBE of Mary, a 74-year-old woman who had come to the hospital because of a punctured lung that led to her respiratory arrest.

Well, I felt like I was rising above the bed. I was just leaving. I felt like I was rising — going up. I don't know what was around me. You know how when you ride - when you go up. It's just like when you push the button and go up. That's how I felt I was going.

Were you horizontal?

Yes, lying down. Just lying down and going up that way.

Could you tell if you were connected at all to your body? Was there anything underneath you?

No, it was too fast to think about what was happening. I think I was so frightened I woke myself up (p.98).

Pain or discomfort as in the case of Heather are often triggers for spontaneous OBEs in the hospital setting.

Here is another example of a patient experiencing pain after an operation.

I was exhausted and felt I could no longer bear the pain. I fell backwards on to the pillows. And then I seemed to be looking down at myself, I could see all about me and looking over towards the window I could see children playing in the garden next door. Yet that was something I couldn't possibly have seen from my bed. I looked so peaceful, and I can't describe the marvelous feeling I felt (Fenwick & Fenwick, 1996, p. 23).

Occasionally an individual learns they can induce an OBE when pain returns. Such was the case with a woman who was in severe pain due to an undiagnosed gall bladder problem.

I remember saying to myself, all right, take me, I can't go on any longer - here I am. I spent some time out of my body and then felt I had a choice of whether to go back or not. I chose to go back. For several weeks the same thing occurred, but I controlled the experiences. At the onset of pain, I relaxed and 'floated out' until it was 'safe' to return and the pain was gone. I was able to roam about the house, check that my baby was sleeping, look at the cat and dog, see my husband asleep. I could see my body sitting there waiting for me to return to it. I have

46

always felt that if I 'needed' to I could do it again - but only if I 'needed' to - and consequently have never been afraid of suffering acute pain. I have always felt guilty about not sharing these experiences as I feel if the techniques could be taught they could help people who suffer pain (Fenwick & Fenwick, 1996, p. 35).

Concern about others

Some individuals who reported a spontaneous OBE came back into their bodies because of concerns for others, particularly children. This is also noted in individuals who have NDEs.

An OBE in conjunction with an NDE.

It is common for individuals to experience an OBE during an NDE. Van Limmel (2001) reported 24% of the NDE subjects he interviewed post cardiac arrest described having an OBE in conjunction with their NDE. Ring (1980) stated 37% of the 102 NDErs he interviewed stated they experienced a body separation. Here's an example of a woman's experience from Lawrence's book. Notice the lack of concern about being away from her body and even wanting to go back to the light.

> I was up toward the ceiling. I watched the doctors and nurses around my bed, checking the equipment, putting paddles on my chest.
>
> How did you feel when you saw your body on the bed?
>
> Do you really want to know? All I could think of was to say to myself, "Honey, you need to lose weight."
>
> What did you look like up on the ceiling?
>
> I honestly don't remember. I just felt like I always did. Like it was me up there. My body didn't really matter. I remember feeling wonderful, totally at peace. I saw this light and felt totally loved. Then I was back in my body. I tried to go back and have the experience again. I heard the male nurse yell, and I hated him for resuscitating me again. I wanted to go back (Lawrence, 1997, p. 117).

47

Veridical perceptions and reciprocal cases

In both types of OBEs that occur close to death, individuals report seeing something or someone that is unknown to them and should not have been able to be experienced without the use of their normal senses.

In the case of Heather reported at the beginning of this chapter, she reported seeing a doctor come into the labor room while she was unconscious. She had not seen this doctor before, nor did she see him after the delivery. Lawrence (1997) reviewed Heather's medical record which described a consultation with an additional physician during her labor. There were no additional reports of the doctor consulting on Heather's case before or after the delivery. The nurses who knew both Heather's regular doctor and the consulting doctor, reported the consulting doctor as being taller and thinner than her regular doctor. The consulting doctor's hair was also thinning where the regular doctor had a thick head of hair according to the nurses.

Celia Green reported this OBE when she developed pneumonia after having an operation for peritonitis.

> The ward was L shaped; so that anyone in bed at one part of the ward could not see around the corner.
>
> One morning I felt myself floating upwards, and found myself looking down on the rest of the patients. I could see myself, propped up against pillow very white and ill. I saw the sister and nurse rush to my bed with oxygen. Then everything went blank. The next I remember was opening my eyes to see the sister bending over me.
>
> I told her what had happened; but at first she thought I was rambling. Then I said, "There is a big woman sitting up in bed with her head wrapped in bandages; and she is knitting something with blue wool. She has a very red face." This certainly shook her; as apparently the lady concerned had a mastoid operation and was just as I described.
>
> She was not allowed out of bed; and of course I hadn't been up at all. After several other details, such as the time by the clock on the wall, I convinced her that at least something strange had happened to me (Rogo, 2008, p. 2).

In this case, Ms. Green stayed within her hospital environment even though she left her own section of the ward. She, typical of OBEs not associated with NDEs, did not report the wonderful feeling of peace and love common with NDEs. She also did not move on to another place beyond the hospital environment.

Veridical perceptions are also common in the OBE segments of NDEs. A nurse reported a patient who had an NDE during her resuscitation. The patient floated above her body and, after watching the resuscitation efforts felt herself being pulled up through several floors of the hospital to the point where she could see the skyline of the city and the roof of the hospital. In the corner of the roof, she saw a red shoe. She was then pulled through a blackened hole and continued to have a typical NDE (discussed further in chapter 5).

The nurse mentioned the patient's experience to a skeptical medical resident. He had gotten a janitor to open the door to the roof. The resident came down holding a red shoe (Ring & Lawrence, 1993).

How the red shoe happened to be on the roof of the hospital was unknown. However, it was not the only shoe seen in an odd place by a patient during and NDE.

Kimberly Clark (1984) listened to the experiences of a migrant worker who had a cardiac arrest while in a Seattle hospital. During the arrest, Maria went out of her body and spotted a tennis shoe on the ledge of the third floor of the hospital. Maria was able to describe this tennis shoe in detail. Clark investigated the location of the tennis shoe and found it to be precisely where Maria said she saw it. Maria had also described the characteristics of the shoe from an external view, not able to be seen from inside the hospital room.

Out-of-body experiences after an NDE

In addition to having OBEs when in pain and close to death, patients also report OBEs after an NDE. Greyson (1983) studied 80 volunteers from the membership of the International Association of Near-Death Studies (IANDS) with a mailed questionnaire. The questionnaire contained items from the survey of psychic experiences developed by Palmer. Of the 80 mailed questionnaires, 69 were determined to be usable. All subjects had had an NDE in the past. When asked to compare the incidence of OBEs before having an NDE with the incidence after the

NDE, 11% reported OBEs before their NDEs and 43% said they had had an OBE after their NDE.

Lawrence (1997) interviewed a woman who had had an NDE while giving birth. After she was home, she would have OBEs while feeding her baby. During the first episode, she felt she was standing at the door to her bedroom watching herself feeding her daughter. When she reported these OBEs to her physician and her other similar incidences, she was put on medication and referred to a psychologist for therapy.

Incidence of OBEs

Olson (1988) interviewed 200 hospitalized subjects. Six reported having an OBE during the current hospitalization, with 25 others describing OBEs during their life. The subjects attributed stress (22), relaxation (6), and no specific reason (3), as the explanations for the OBE.

There have been many studies done to determine the incidence of OBEs in the non-hospitalized population. Palmer (1979) and Dennis (1975) studied 1,000 people in the town of Charlottesville, VA. They asked the following question of those survived: Have you ever had an experience in which you felt that you were located outside of or away from your physical body?

While 25% of students and 14% of townspeople said yes, further analysis was carried out. There was no relationship between age and incidence of OBE, however, there was a positive relationship between drug use and OBEs, predominately found in the student group.

Palmer and Green in their different studies found sex, age, race, birth order, political views, religion, religiosity, education, occupation, and income were all unrelated to the incidence of OBEs. However, Palmer did find meditation, mystical experiences, and drug experiences, increases the incidence of OBEs.

According to several researchers (Palmer, Green, Blackmore), experiencers view the OBE as positive. They state the experiences reduce their fear of death and their overall feeling of wellbeing improved. Most would like to have another OBE.

Perspectives on OBEs

The belief that some part of the body is able to separate from the body and travel, especially at the time of death, started in early religions. Early priests were the first to describe a belief in the existence of a soul or spirit that could separate from the body and exist independently. In Ancient Egypt (3200 BC to 30 BC), the vital essence of the person known as ka, would leave the body at the time of death. These Egyptians believed bodily death was not the complete cessation of life (Taylor, 2001).

In the poems of Homer (birth estimated between the 12th and 8th centuries BC), the soul is described as what departs from the body at the time of death. The Greeks believed the presence of a soul is what distinguished a living person from a deceased one (Taylor, 2000).

Hebrews

Initially the ancient Israelites did not see the "soul" as something separate from the body. They believed God blew the "breath of life" into man (Genesis 2:7). This life breath left the body at death and later (Ecclesiastes 12:7) this life breath became associated with the soul and returned to God at the time of bodily death.

Christians

Commonly, Christians believe there is an afterlife that the soul will enter. That afterlife can be positive if the soul goes to heaven or negative if the soul goes to hell.

Origen (ca. 185-254) was an early Christian scholar who started the development of an organized systematic theology. As an admirer of Plato, he wrote about the immortality of the soul. In his writings, he stated the soul had a life of its own. At the time of death, the soul would be rewarded with eternal life and blessings or punished with eternal fire (Chadwick, 1984).

Augustine of Hippo (ca. 354-430), also a well-known Catholic writer and saint, wrote about the immortality of the soul and death. He also believed the soul would continue to live on after life. Bliss for the soul was to be with God; with agony being separation from God.

Thomas Aquinas (ca. 1225-1274)' as put forth in *The Summa Theologica* taught the soul was a conscious intellect and will which could not be destroyed.

The philosophers

The ancient philosophers also described the soul as an entity separate from the body, continuing to exist after life. This is Socrates' (470-399 B.C.) explanation:

> Is it not the separation of soul and body? And to be dead is the completion of this; when the soul exists in herself, and is released from the body and body is released from the soul, what is this but death (Plato, & Grube, 2002).

Plato (ca.428-348 B.C. also believed the soul to be eternal.

The most prevalent idea in religions and philosophies, handed down through multiple generations, is the soul after bodily death takes on or is free to be in a higher form separate from the body. OBEs represent a slightly different phenomena. Individuals reporting OBEs may be close to death, like the individuals described in this chapter. Other individuals reporting OBEs are perfectly healthy. However, some means by which some part of individuals can exit the body and return is easily seen as related to a "soul" leaving the body at the time of death.

In a research study of 54 cultures, Sheils (1978) reported 46% of respondents believed most or all people could travel outside their physical body. Sheils concludes most cultures have some form of belief in OBEs.

Current explanations for OBEs

Current explanations for OBEs fall under two large categories: something leaves the body or nothing leaves the body. The category of nothing leaves the body has two subcategories: the perception of being out-of-body because of a physiological abnormality, and a perception of being out of body because of a psychological need or illness. The category of something leaves the body includes a mechanism by which someone can be out-of-body.

A physiological abnormality

Drugs

Tart (1971) in a study of 150 marijuana users found 44% claimed to have had OBEs. Since this is considerably higher than the typical 10% of the population that reports OBEs, Tart concluded marijuana use can facilitate OBEs.

Olaf Blanke (2004) and Michael Persinger (1992) conducted research to elicit experiences similar to OBEs. They both found stimulation of the right temporal lobe of the brain, particularly the right temporal-parietal junction (TPJ), can produce positions and visual perspectives similar to those having spontaneous OBEs. The TPJ area is known to be involved in the construction of the sense of the body in space. Blanke and his associates believe lesions in the TPJ region are associated with an OBE like phenomena.

Psychological need or illness

Murray and Fox (2005) tested the theory that OBEs occurred more often with individuals who would score high on measures of dissociation. A questionnaire was administered to 243 subjects, with 62 reporting at least one OBE. Those who reported a previous OBE scored statistically significantly higher than the non-OBE subjects on measures of somatoform dissociation, self-consciousness, body dissatisfaction, and lower on a measure of confidence in their physical self-presentation. The authors concluded that disassociation theory does explain the mechanism of OBEs.

One of the most popular measures of dissociation tendency is a tool known as the Dissociative Experiences Scale (DES) (Bernstein & Putnam, 1986). Subjects who already have had an OBE will, by virtue of the experience, answer many of the items indicating high dissociation. Some of the questions on the DES ask to score yes if they find themselves in a place and have no idea how they got there, experience a feeling of standing next to themselves, feel their body does not belong to them, and some find they are able to ignore pain.

To show the tendency toward dissociation as a predictor of OBEs, the person would need to have the DES administered before the OBE and not afterwards. Lawrence (1997), for example, placed an electronic message machine high on cabinets in an electrophysiology room where patients undergoing electrophysiology procedures were known to have OBEs and NDEs. Before patients had the procedure, Lawrence administered the DES to determine if high scores will predict an OBE or NDE. This prospective approach is needed before being able to say a tendency toward dissociation predicts OBEs.

Researchers have found, however, that dissociation in the form of OBEs is common in children during abuse situations. Lawrence (1997) described a subject in her study whose mother physically abused her. During these episodes the subject would go out of her body and not feel any pain but could watch what was happening to her. Severe pain can be a trigger for OBEs.

Myers, Austin, Grisson, and Nickeson (1983) studied the personalities of individuals who reported OBEs. The researchers found typically these individuals to be responsible, honest, curious, inquisitive, adventure-seeking, clever, intellectual, analytical, social, and scoring low on conformity scales.

Something leaves the body

To date, there are no scientific explanations or theories that explain a projection leaving the body when the body is still alive and functioning. A paranormal interpretation is an etheric or spiritual body leaves the physical body. This body is able to travel within the spirit world (the astral plane) and also able to travel to other places in the physical plane. How this is able to happen is not understood even though reports are well documented.

Ring and Cooper describe an OBE that occurred to a blind person. He was able to determine the color and pattern of a tie while out of his body, an experience inconsistent with the biological understanding we have of the functions of the body.

Approximately 10 years after becoming blind, Frank was going to be driven to a wake by a friend. This is how Frank remembered the incident:

> And so I said to her that morning, I said: 'Gee, I haven't got a good tie to wear. Why don't you pick me up one?' She said, 'Yeah, I'll pick you up one when I get down to Mel's [a clothing store].' So she picked it up and dropped it off and said, 'I can't stay. I've got to get home and

get ready to pick you up to go to the wake.' So I got dressed and put the tie on. She didn't tell me the color of the tie or anything else. I was laying down on the couch and I could see myself coming out of my body. And I could see my tie. The tie that was on. And it had a circle on it—it was a red—and it had a gray circle, two gray circles on it. And I remember that (p. 120).

Shocked by Frank's description, the friend, when she came to pick him up, did confirm the tie was exactly as he had described.

Table I Helpful communication with someone who has had an OBE

    1. Establish a client-centered rapport
    2. Hold in reserve your causal belief about the event
    3. Encourage communication about the experience
    4. Listen to the client's description of the event with empathy
    5. Determine if the experience was visual, auditory, kinesthetic, or a combination
    6. Determine the client's explanation for the experience
    7. Validate any veridical perceptions
    8 Normalize the experience
    9. Assess the emotional impact
    10. Provide resources as needed

Table II Documentation of the out-of-body experience

    1. Description of the state before the OBE
    2. The time and length of the occurrence
    3. The type of experience – visual, auditory, or kinesthetic
    4. Description of what occurred
    5. Description of the emotional impact

CHAPTER 5

NEAR-DEATH EXPERIENCES

Keywords: Beings of light, distressing near-death experiences, grim reaper, life review, near-death experiences, out-of-body experience, tunnel experience, veridical perception,

Louis was in the operating room having open heart surgery when his near-death experience occurred.

I was prepped for surgery. The doctor was looking at me and he says, 'You are going to feel a little pinch.' I felt the pinch and I'm waiting for him to tell me something more. I realize I'm no longer there. He didn't have to tell me, I could see him. I'm up at the ceiling looking down at him and the two doctors and a nurse assistant. I guess an anesthesiologist. I could look through those people I didn't choose to see what they were doing. I could look through them and see the doctor's boots.

"You could see through the people?"

I saw them and I looked at them, but then my vision penetrated through the corner of the stretcher. I told the doctor he wore glasses. I never knew he wore glasses. Anyhow, I became very uninterested in what they were doing.

"What were your reactions to being out of your body and seeing your body on the operating room table?"

Kind of a "who cares" attitude. I assumed the real me was up here. What I was looking at was something I use to travel in-like a Stop and Shop grocery bag or something similar. It just wasn't me because the real me was up watching. I didn't feel any compassion. I had no feeling for what was there. I was at first curious as to what they were doing.

...I looked upward and everything seemed to be brighter. I thought myself into an ascent. It wasn't swift, because I was unsure of where I was headed....In front of me was a brown ceramic wall. Immediately upon hitting that barrier, I started to feel a love, a joy, a real euphoric feeling that I had never had. I felt loved. I felt as if I were really loved for the first time. When I turned my head I saw three figures – one was my deceased bother-in-law. I didn't know the other two guys.

"What did you brother-in-law look like?"

Exactly as I knew him in his healthier days. He died of a heart problem. He looked pretty healthy.

....I don't know why but I had a need to get to the wall. On the other side was the most beautiful geography. Very rich brown, yellows. Everything was very rich looking.

Louis then met with his mother, who had died when he was seven. She told him he had to go back, which he reluctantly did (Lawrence, 1997, p. 117-120).

Of all transpersonal experiences associated with dying, the near-death experience (NDE) is the most researched phenomena. Because there is so much information about NDEs, two chapters in the book are devoted to these experiences. This chapter includes descriptions of both pleasurable and distressing NDEs and all their components. The information in Chapter 6 includes the aftereffects of NDEs, theories about the causes, and interventional approaches.

Descriptions of NDEs have been reported for centuries and illustrated in well-known paintings. Drawings of souls entering a tunnel toward a light was first conceived as an illustration of "empyrean" by

Hieronymus Bosch, an early Netherlandish painter, who lived from c. 1450 to 1516. The painting is entitled *Ascent to Empyrean*. The word empyrean is used to designate the dwelling place of God (Falk, 2008).

In 1861 Gustave Doré illustrated the Empyrean in Dante Alighieri's epic poem the *Divine Comedy* (2011). There is a similar depiction of a tunnel with the light in the distance at the center.

It was Moody's book in 1975, *Life after Life*, which stimulated the interest in current day descriptions and research in NDEs. Because of better resuscitation efforts, more individuals were reporting NDEs. These experiences were a surprise to the experiencers who generally had no knowledge of out-of-body experiences or other experiences labeled paranormal.

During these early years of NDE research, the International Association of Near-Death Studies (IANDS), the brain child of John Audette, was founded in 1978 and incorporated in Connecticut in 1981. The formal organization was co-founded and co-created by Audette, Moody, Ring, Greyson, and Sabom. Ring was a professor at the University of Connecticut (UConn) at Storrs, and Greyson worked as a psychiatrist at the UConn Health Center in Farmington.

One of the first formal NDE conferences was held in the 1980s at UConn through the School of Nursing continuing education program. Ring was instrumental in starting the first journal dedicated exclusively to near-death studies, called *Anabiosis*, later called the *Journal of Near-Death Studies* with Bruce Greyson as the first editor. A less formal newsletter, *Vital Signs*, was printed quarterly. As the word spread about this phenomena called near-death experiences, other researchers joined the ranks of those attempting to answer the questions of the NDE. IANDS continues to this day to be a resource for researchers and experiencers.

Ring was one of the early researchers to describe the five-stage continuum of an NDE:
The stages were:
1. Peace
2. Body separation
3. Entering darkness
4. Seeing the light
5. Entering the light

Ring stated not all experiencers reached all the stages. Stage 1 was experienced by 60% of NDErs and stage 5 by only 10% (Ring, 1982). It is estimated between 10% to 15% of all who come close to death with have an NDE.

Other researchers (Greyson, 1983) added to his description to include additional steps. To date the description of a positive NDE includes the following stages, although not necessarily occurring in order or by everyone with the same depth:
- A sense/awareness of their body being dead.
- A sense of peace, well-being, and painlessness.
- An out-of-body experience. A perception of one's body from an outside position often observing their body being resuscitated with general lack of concern.

- A "tunnel experience" or enclosed experience with a moving upward.
- Visions and/or communication with a powerful light.
- An intense feeling of unconditional love and acceptance.
- Encountering "Beings of Light" and/or reunited with deceased loved ones.
- Enhanced sense experiences; beautiful flowers, trees, hearing music unlike any previous sounds.
- Experiencing a life review.
- Receiving knowledge about one's life and the nature of the universe.
- Approaching a border or a decision by oneself or others to return to one's body, often accompanied by a reluctance to return.

Distressing NDEs

Not all NDEs are experienced as positive. There are also descriptions of distressing NDEs. In 1996, Greyson and Bush reported on 50 cases of distressing NDEs. They classified these NDEs into three categories;

1. Same features as the pleasurable type but feeling out of control and frightened.
2. Feeling completely alone in an absolute void.
3. Hellish imagery, demonic beings, frightening creatures, ugly landscape, loud, unpleasant noise.

A fourth type was added by Rommer (2000) which describes being harshly judged during a life review.

Lawrence (2012), in a book review of Bush's book on distressing NDEs, Dancing Past the Dark, questions if visions of a grim reaper could also be included under the classification of a distressing NDE.

Unique to distressing NDEs, is the occurrence of being an observer rather than a participant in the experience. Some individuals report being shown hellish imagery and receiving a charge to share what they have seen. In the pleasurable NDEs, the experiencers are there as full participants in the occurrences.

Pleasurable NDEs

Aware of their body being dead

In some respects those who experience an NDE do not actually perceive themselves as dead. They come to the realization their body is dead but they still feel like themselves. What they recognize is the change. Also, most are not concerned with their dead body. The body is usually seen as a covering they were in, not their real selves.

One of Moody's (2001) subjects reported seeing his body tangled up in his car after an accident. He had no feelings toward his body. He himself was alive and the body seemed of no consequence.

A woman recalls her NDE from a near drowning at age 10 and her reaction to her body.

> I focused on the body below as it continued to be pummeled by the water rather turbulently, and I realized it was mine. I felt like I owned it as a child owns a novelty toy; to be played with and easily discarded. However, I didn't remember who the people were standing around the perimeter of the body, and it didn't matter to me at all. I could care less who they were. In fact, there was no emotional connection to my body, or to my mom and brother. I doubt I would have cared about them even if I had remembered who they were at that moment. I remember feeling such acute amusement towards my body, watching it flap around like a piece of meat being ripped apart by some hungry animal (IANDS, 2002-2004, Confirmation of eternity).

While not concerned about their body being dead, many NDErs are aware they are in a different, unknown state. Some experience an awareness of newness and are unsure of what to do next or what was going to now occur. One of Moody's subjects realized she was dead and wasn't sorry but could not figure out where she was supposed to go. She decided she was going to wait "until all the excitement died down" and her body was gone to consider her next steps (p.32).

Also the NDErs learn what they can and cannot do in this new state. Soon they recognize no one who is physically alive can see or hear them. In this new state, they cannot move objects. It is for some difficult to describe their current state in physical terms. One of Moody's subjects described trying to move a person's hands who was carrying out CPR. He could not feel the pressure against the person's hands. In addition, it was difficult for him to determine if his hands were going through or around the live person's hands.

The new form of their person is often difficult for them to describe. Some say they felt whole but had no shape. Others said they were light or energy. Many did not remember or notice what form they took. One person described himself in the following way:

> Then I took an inventory of what I had brought with me. This was bizarre. I had my head, my right arm, and my left leg. That's all I took with me, but I felt total. I felt connected but there was space in between my arm and my head (Lawrence, 1997, p 119).

Regardless of their perception of themselves, they were not concerned with their form. They felt who they were went on and they were themselves.

Initial feelings of peace, well-being, and painlessness

Often NDErs experience a wonderful feeling of well-being and painlessness at the beginning of an NDE. There may be a description of an initial struggle with pain and fear caused by the precipitating event. That soon dissipates into feelings of comfort and painlessness.

The following narrative is an example of an NDE during drowning that occurred around 1795. The NDE happened to British Rear Admiral Sir Francis Beaufort which he described in a letter to his physician, Dr. Wollaston. Beaufort was a young sailor on one of His Majesty's ships in Portsmouth Harbor, England. He did not know how to swim. While first sculling about in a small boat he tried to fasten the boat to the ship, lost his balance, and fell into the water. This accident was seen by others on the boat but it took time for them to reach him. He thrashed about but soon sank under the surface of the water.

> From the moment that all exertion had ceased – which I imagine was the immediate consequence of complete suffocation – a calm feeling of the most perfect tranquility succeeded the most tumultuous sensation. It might be called apathy, certainly not resignation; for drowning no longer appeared an evil; I no longer thought of being rescued, nor was I in any bodily pain. On the contrary, my sensations were now of rather a pleasurable cast, partaking of that dull but contented sort of feeling which precedes the sleep produced by fatigue. Though the

senses were thus deadened, not so the mind; its activity seemed to be invigorated in a ratio which defies all description; for thought rose after thought with a rapidity of succession that is not only indescribably, but probably inconceivable, by anyone who has been himself in a similar situation (De Morgan, 1863, p. 176-178).

Here's another similar description from a man experiencing a heart attack.

I was walking and felt these pains. I said to myself, I'm having a heart attack. I remember praying to Jesus to take the pain away. Then I felt this relaxation, this feeling of contentment and euphoria like nothing I've ever experienced before. There was no pain. It was wonderful (Lawrence, 1997, p. 114).

Out-of-body experience and veridical perceptions

Not all NDErs report an out-of-body experience (OBE). Some feel peace and well-being and move into a tunnel or some similar enclosure. Those who have an OBE associated with their NDE often report seeing their bodies being resuscitated. As previously mentioned they are not concerned with their bodies.

The following is a description of a woman who had an NDE during labor.

I heard them talking about the baby's heart rate being low. The next thing I knew I was above everyone. I watched them scurrying frantically, checking my blood pressure, giving me oxygen (Lawrence, 1997, p. 122).

NDErs often observe resuscitation actions and activities with surprising accuracy. Sabom (1982), an Atlanta cardiologist, conducted a study of 57 individuals who had undergone resuscitation. There were two groups of subjects: 32 people had an NDE with an OBE and 25 had no OBE. Sabom compared the descriptions of the resuscitations by the individuals in the two groups. None of the individuals in the OBE group made major errors in describing their resuscitation while 23 of the 25 in the non-OBE group made major errors.

NDErs also seem to notice objects or situations that are out of place. One person saw a shoe on the ledge of the hospital (Clark, 1984) while another saw a red shoe on the roof of a hospital (Ring and Lawrence, 1993). One patient noticed his doctor wore glasses during his surgery which was a surprise since he had not known this about his doctor.

Colton was only four years old when he had an NDE after an appendectomy. It took time for his parents to recognize this occurrence. One of the convincing statements was Colton's description of what the parents were doing while Colton was out of his body. He said to his father, "You were in a little room by yourself praying, and Mommy was in a different room and she was praying and talking on the phone (Burpo, 2010, p. 61)." His father states no one, not even his wife, knew he was in that little room.

A tunnel or enclosed experience

Some individuals have NDEs that just include a wonderful feeling of peace and comfort and an OBE. Those who go further will go through a tunnel or some type of enclosure. This enclosure is generally described as dark and confining although not frightening. This tunnel is experienced as the next direction to take in this new state. For some NDErs there is often literally the light at the end of the tunnel.

An intense feeling of unconditional love and acceptance.

As they leave the tunnel some find themselves near or engulfed by a bright, powerful light. At this point a number of different experiences may happen. Often there is an overwhelming feeling of peace and love, of total acceptance. One of the individuals who submitted her account to the International Association of Near-Death Experiences (IANDS) describes this wonderful feeling.

> I'm standing in a place of love. It's completely enveloping, and I'm thoroughly immersed in feelings of loving acceptance, calmness, and of being home (of belonging). There's a glow of golden light ahead of me in the distance, and I need and want to get there. But as I take a step forward, a golden being blocks my way. Humanoid in shape, there are no features, no clothes, nothing but a glowing being who exudes an

overwhelming sense of calm and agape. The right hand of the being is raised palm outward in a stopping motion, and in my head I hear, "You must go back." I'm devastated. I don't want to go back. I want to stay in this place of love (IANDS, Blocked by a Golden Being).

Life review

Others may have a life review. It is estimated only in about 20% of NDEs is there a life review. Typically this review is not a judgment about their lives but a review and perspective of what has happened during their lifetime. On occasion not only does the person feel their own emotions about their life, they may feel the emotions of others involved in different aspects. Later this review helps the person come back with a clearer purpose of their existence.

The following is a life review as described by Barbara Harris Whitfield (1990).

God was totally accepting of everything we reviewed in my life. In every scene of my life review I could feel again what I had felt at various times in my life. And I could feel everything everyone else felt as a consequence of my actions. Some of it felt good and some of it felt awful. All of this translated into knowledge, and I learned — oh, how I learned! The information was flowing at an incredible breakneck speed that probably would have burned me up if it weren't for the extraordinary energy holding me. The information came in, and then love neutralized my judgments against myself. In other words, as we relived my life, God never judged me. God held me and kept me together. I received all information about every scene — my perceptions and feelings — and anyone else's perceptions and feelings who were in the scene. No matter how I judged myself in each interaction, being held by God was the bigger interaction. God interjected love into everything, every feeling, every bit of information about absolutely everything that went on, so that everything was all right. There was no good and no bad. There was only me and my loved ones from this life trying to be, or just trying to survive (p.24).

Meeting with deceased friends and/or relatives

If they move on from here, a person may see deceased friend and/ or relatives. When asked to describe these deceased individuals, the NDErs often say they were like they were in life but details about their form, shape, age, are noticed by only a few. The communication with these deceased individuals is telepathic. Hearing is perceived as being in their mind and not obtained through ordinary hearing.

Around me, as the tunnel began to lighten, there were presences. They were not people, and I didn't see anything but I was aware of their minds. They were debating whether

I should go back. This was what made me so safe; I knew that I had absolutely no responsibility to make any decision. This is an almost unknown situation for me, and it was wonderfully liberating. I also knew I could not influence what decision they made, but that whatever it should be it would be right. There was total wisdom and goodness in them. I did not hear voices or words, so I don't know how I was aware of this discussion, but it was not only one presence: it was as if there were many minds gathered on each side into one, and these two debated the decision about me. I didn't know the outcome, but I was intensely interested and peaceful (Fenwick & Fenwick, 2001, p.44).

Enhanced sense experiences

At this time an NDEr may see beautiful flowers, trees or other scenes with an intense beauty unparalleled rolled in their ordinary life. If they hear music, it is equally exceptional.

I stood there in this gorgeous meadow and I remember that the light there was different from the light here on Earth. Though it was not that brilliant white light in which I was involved, it was a more beautiful light. There was a goldenness to this light. I remember the sky was very blue. I don't recall seeing the sun. The colors were extraordinary. The green of the meadow was fantastic. The flowers were blooming all around and they had colors that I had never seen before. I was very aware that I had never seen these colors before and I was very excited about it.

I thought I had seen all colors. I was thrilled to death of the beauty that was incredible. In addition to the beautiful colors, I could see a soft light glowing within every living thing. It was not a light that was reflected from the outside from a source, but it was coming from the center of this flower. Just this beautiful, soft light. I think I was seeing the life inside of everything (Williams, 2014).

Approaching a border or a decision by oneself or others to return to one's body, often accompanied by a reluctance to return.

Going further into the experience the NDE may reach a barrier. The barrier may be water, a wall, or some other type of object that makes them realize this is a place of crossing. If they cross this barrier they realize there is no return to their previous life.

I can remember some kind of meadow or stream flowing through it. I don't remember flowers or trees or anything like that. I do remember this stream with some kind of crossing. There was a point where if I went past this, I was not coming back. I don't remember a voice but I do remember somehow being told I couldn't cross the stream. It wasn't time for me yet. I don't know if it was telepathy but I thought something like, 'I don't want to go back. Can I stay for a while?' They said, 'OK,' they let me stay there and just kind of wander around. It was peaceful. It was quiet. Not harsh or bright. It was a nice place to be, and I was very happy there. I suppose something in me knew I had to go back, that I was eventually going back (Lawrence, 1997, p. 115).

The Being of Light or their deceased friends or relatives may tell them they must go back or they may decide themselves they have someone for whom they must see to. It may be a spouse a child from whom they must return. Most frequently the person does not wish to come back. They feel wonderful in this state. As above, some have bargained for more time before going back. Some also recognize being brought back by the resuscitation efforts and express anger at their resuscitation and return.

Enhanced experience by the blind.

Ring and Cooper (1997) investigated the experiences of 31 blind individuals who reported having an NDE. Their blind subjects reported a classic, pleasurable NDE similar to those described by sighted subjects. Most also reported seeing during their NDEs and OBEs. Ring and Cooper were also able to corroborate some of the information obtained by these blind individuals that could not be obtained through ordinary means. This is the story of Vicki, who was blind from birth.

> I knew it was me ... I was pretty thin then. I was quite tall and thin at that point. And I recognized at first that it was a body, but I didn't even know that it was mine initially. Then I perceived that I was up on the ceiling, and I thought, 'Well, that's kind of weird. What am I doing up here?'

> I thought, 'Well, this must be me. Am I dead? ...'

> I just briefly saw this body, and ... I knew that it was mine because I wasn't in mine (p.110).

Receiving knowledge about one's life and the nature of the universe

Some NDErs go to a place where they receive information. They feel in this place they have answers to many situations and complete understanding. Most report the general purpose of life is love and knowledge. Their memory of the information they were given does not come back with them in total. Bits and pieces of information come to them as their regular life progresses.

> From this bubbling energy a kind of brown wavy motion comes right up. It kept coming. It turned out to be my mother who died when I was seven years old. She was cloaked in brown – her favorite color, I later found out from my aunts. My first thought was 'Are you my mother?' She retorted back telepathically, 'You are my son.' That was the answer. She started giving me knowledge. She gave me formulas. She gave me the cure for all of the nation's catastrophic ills. I accepted

everything. How many things she told me I just can't remember because of restrictions when you get back down here (Lawrence, 1997).

Description of distressing near-death experiences

Not all NDEs involve positive experiences. There are also descriptions of distressing NDEs. In 1996, Greyson and Bush reported on 50 cases of distressing NDEs. They classified these NDEs into three categories: same features as the pleasurable type but feeling out of control and frightened; feeling completely alone in an absolute void; and hellish imagery, demonic beings, frightening creatures, ugly landscape, loud, unpleasant noise.

While the incidence of pleasurable NDEs is estimated to be between 10% and 15% of all who come close to death, a clear estimate of distressing NDEs is difficult to obtain. The range of the number of NDEs that are distressing is estimated between 1% to 15% (Gallop, 1982; Greyson & Bush, 1996). It is not unusual for researchers to find no one with distressing NDEs in their sample. It is believed more subjects will be reluctant to report distressing NDEs because it may indicate they are living an immoral life.

As with pleasurable NDEs, distressing NDEs can occur equally to both genders, ages, socioeconomic levels, educational levels, religious affiliations, and belief systems. There is no evidence that the type of life one lives relates to the type of NDE experienced. Also suicide attempters most often have positive NDEs, contrary to the tenets of many religions.. Greyson interview 16 suicide attempters and found all had had a positive NDE. Rommer (2000) also found no relationship between the moral acts in a person's life and the type of NDE.

In 2012, Nancy Evans Bush published the first comprehensive description of disturbing NDEs and their interpretation entitled *Dancing Past the Dark: Distressing Near-Death Experiences*. The book contains many firsthand accounts by experiencers.

Here are some examples of individual experiences:

Nothingness

My first thought was, "I must be dead. This is what death must be." But it certainly wasn't blissful. Just nothingness. I felt like a piece of protoplasm floating out on the sea. I thought, "Maybe I'm lost, maybe I'm not going to heaven (Gallup, 1982, p. 80)."

Same features as the pleasurable type but feeling out of control and frightened

Both my eyes were completely swollen shut, and I was having difficulty breathing...After a few minutes my body began to shake violently. I then experienced a sensation of floating above the room. I saw a clear picture of myself lying on the table. I saw the doctor and the nurse, whom I had never seen before, and my husband standing by my body. I became frightened, and I remember strongly feeling I didn't like what I saw and what was happening. I shouted, "I don't like this!" but I was not heard by those in the room. After a while one eye opened a little [and] I saw that the room and the people were exactly as I had seen them during my floating sensation (Bush, p. 29).

Hellish imagery; demonic beings, frightening creatures; ugly landscape; loud, unpleasant noise

I was over at a friend's house having a good time. We were low on beer, so I went to get some. I remember my buddy's wife asking me not to go. I had been drinking a lot. I got on my motorcycle and wiped out a few miles down the road. I had this sensation of going down there into a hole. There was fire down there and figures. My father who had died was there. He told me it wasn't my time. Then he and I went up through a tunnel toward a light. I felt totally transformed. My father told me I had to go back. The next thing I remember I was in the hospital.

How did this experience affect you?

I stopped drinking. I go to church now. It totally turned my life around (Lawrence, 1997, p. 121).

Additional findings

While there is a commonality to most NDEs, each person's NDE has unique qualities. Not everyone has all the experiences mentioned above. The depth of the experience will vary with more individuals describing the earlier stages. Also individuals interpret what they see according to their culture and religious background. Even though different individuals may see a bright light, not all will see the light as representative of God.

Discussion about NDEs continues in Chapter 6. Guidelines for helpful communications are presented there.

CHAPTER 6

NDE AFTEREFFECTS, EXPLANATIONS, AND SUPPORTIVE MEASURES

Keywords: aftereffects, consciousness, psychic, Psychic Experience Inventory (PSI), spiritual, spiritually transformative experiences

The moment I left the hospital, I began to leave my husband and the life we had fallen into. The decision was clear. It was just a matter of how. I felt that I made a powerful decision when I said, "All right, I'll come back (from the NDE)." I realized that I knew what the light was. It was the realization I had choice and free will. I began to meet people who could answer some of my questions. I just seemed to gravitate to them ...

I began to think that I needed to have that profound experience of the light and the healing in order to make the choice to leave my circumstances. The fast life had been very powerful for me and the most attractive thing to me at the time. After that, I began to seek out healers of all types. I began to go to conferences and gatherings in order to hear other stories and get more of a sense of what had happened to me. I began to read spiritual texts and I learned massage (Heckler, 1998).

Most individuals who have an NDE will experience aftereffects. The most common aftereffect includes a tendency toward spirituality with a concurrent movement away from materialism. Also, NDErs lose their fear of death, believe in a life purpose, and the importance of human relationships. Some but fewer NDErs experience interference with electronic devices, have increased psychic abilities, seek knowledge, and have heightened sense experiences. It is common for NDErs to experience challenges integrating these new life perspectives and abilities into their previous life patterns. They have changed, sometimes dramatically. The other people and situations in their lives have remained the same. A small number of NDErs also have reported being healed or cured of an illness after their NDE.

More spiritual, less religious, less materialistic

Being more spiritual, less religious, and less materialistic is a spontaneous occurrence after the NDE. This is not the type of change that occurs over time after contemplation. It is a transformative experience that changes the core of the person's belief system. When they come back into their body, experiencers believe they have a clearer understanding of spiritual beliefs. They generally believe firmly in a higher power and an afterlife. In most instances their NDEs combine with their religious or cultural background to produce a strong belief in the reality of what they saw, felt, and/or heard.

Nearly dying changed me. I no longer saw the world the same way. I saw people as connected; all part of the same Source, but living different experiences. I understood how much of our experience is about choice, even when we decide to die. Every experience had purpose and helped us on our path to fulfill what we came here to do. There is no right or wrong, good or bad. It is only our perceptions that make it one way or the other. There is no one true religion or path to heaven. Whatever speaks to our hearts individually is the right path for us. All roads lead back to Source. This created a tremendous growth experience for me. Some people would ask about my experience and listen with genuine interest, for others it was too much to take in (IANDS, 2013).

Increase in psychic abilities after an NDE.

Ring (1984) created the 14-item Psychic Experience Inventory (PEI) designed to measure the frequency of psychic experiences reported by NDErs. Ring found 58% of NDErs had a score of eight or higher on this inventory. The PEI measures such paranormal experiences as telepathy, synchronicity, clairvoyance, precognition, déjà vu, and out-of-body experiences.

Sutherland (1989) studied 40 NDErs regarding the incidence of psychic phenomena before and after an NDE using a modified version of the PEI. Sutherland found there was no difference in psychic experiences in those having an NDE and the general population before the NDE. However, there was a statistically significant difference in the incidence of psychic experiences in the NDE population after the experience.

Table I Reports of Paranormal Experiences and Beliefs Before and After NDE

	General population	before NDE	after NDE
Clairvoyance (n* = 37)	38%	43%	73%
Telepathy (n = 39)	58% - 36%	46%	87%
Precognition (n = 37)		57%	89%
Deja vu (n = 37)		76%	84%
Supernatural rescue (n = 37)		38%	78%
Intuition (n = 37)		60%	95%
Guidance (n = 38)	43%	37%	92%
Dream awareness (n = 37)	42%	43%	76%
Out-of-body experience (n = 39)	14% - 12%	18%	51%
Spirits (n = 38)	27% - 26%	24%	68%
Healing ability (n = 37)		8%	70%
Perception of auras (n = 36)	5%	14%	47%

*n indicates number of subjects

(p. 99)

Lawrence (1997) interviewed one NDEr who after his NDE experienced profound telepathic ability. When on an elevator, he could telepathically hear the thoughts of those in his presence. As he walked by the desks of co-workers, their thoughts were also transmitted to him. He sought help to shut out this ability from some of the parapsychology groups because of his inability to focus on his own work and interactions. Another woman Lawrence interviewed had a near-death experience after an operation. The woman started receiving psychic visions. Her clairvoyant abilities were so strong she started seeing clients for psychic readings. She also worked with the police to help locate the body of a person, assumed to be dead.

No fear of death

Moody (2001) describes a number of subjects who reported they have lost their fear of death after their NDE. He believes they no longer fear death because the NDE shows them life exists after bodily death.

"But since this experience, I don't fear death. Those feelings vanished. I don't feel bad at funerals anymore. I kind of rejoice at them, because I know what the dead person has been through (p. 89)."

It is one thing to say you are not afraid to die when you have just been resuscitated. It is another to not be afraid when you are on a hospice program years later. Lawrence (1997) interviewed three hospice patients who had NDEs years before becoming terminally ill. All stated they no longer feared death. One patient agreed to be videotaped. He had had a nose bleed eight years previous. The bleed was severe enough for him to be admitted to a hospital. During the night, he had an NDE where he proceeded through a purple/pink tunnel, described as exquisitely beautiful, unlike any colors he had seen before. He felt an overwhelming feeling of peace and love. A figure, who he interpreted as Jesus, stood at the end of the tunnel in a long purple robe. He told him he had to go back, it was not his time. The patient said he did not want to go back. Now on the hospice program, he was not afraid to die. In fact he said, "I can't wait."

He believed what he experienced during his NDE eight years previous would happen again. The patient died three weeks after the interview, after which Lawrence spoke with his wife. She reported that patient died peacefully and smiling. His hands were raised toward the ceiling with the patient reporting seeing hands coming down toward him.

Electromagnetic issues

Many NDErs also notice their presence interferes with electronic equipment. Some noticed if they stood too close to the conveyer belt in grocery stores, the system did not pick up the transmission from the barcode on the food items. Clocks may not work properly, computers become erratic, and even televisions become filled with static (Ring, 2000). They may not be able to communicate on their cell phones (Bonenfant, 2005). It is estimated approximately 70% of NDErs will experience electromagnetic issues (Fracasso & Friedman, 2012). Nouri found NDErs had a higher than a comparison group number of electromagnetic issues even before their NDE. There was still a statistically significant difference between the incidence of electromagnetic issues before and after the NDE for experiences (Nouri, (2008).

The following is a description by a subject interviewed by Ring (2000).

I have a difficult time as many computers malfunction and lights blow when I walk under them. This has happened for years, and I tried to ignore this was happening. I simply cannot wear a watch for long before it breaks down. I went to a department store and walked in front of their brand new computer and it quit working ...When I held a fluorescent light in my hands, the entire bulb lit up, like it was turned on. It seemed like there was a lot of static electricity (p.159).

Healings after an NDE

Dr. Penny Sartori (2006) in her study of NDEs occurring to patients in intensive care units describes the healing of a man who had a contracted right hand from birth. Before the NDE he could not fully open his right hand. After the NDE he could open it fully, which should not have been possible without surgery if even that could have corrected the contraction completely.

A man had an NDE during a Catholic healing service when he fell, commonly referred to being "slain in the spirit." He had a typical NDE and when he could hear his family calling him to come back, he returned to his body. He had had heart damage with EKG changes from a heart attack before the NDE. After the NDE his EKG was completely normal, according to his physician (Lawrence, 1997).

Explanations

There are many theories and beliefs about how and why NDEs occur. It is important to distinguish between scientific theories, non-scientific ones, and beliefs. In a non-scientific context, theories are described as unproven ideas or beliefs. They are more speculative. In science, theories are based on results of tested hypotheses, facts, and logical reasoning. These theories continue to be tested to further establish their validity.

Religious beliefs and knowledge, while not based on scientific theories, are gained from religious leaders, texts and scriptures like the Bible, the Torah, the Quran as well as from revelation. The Ten Commandments, for example, were revealed to Moses and guide many religious practices. Personal religious beliefs often come from religious upbringings, family values, and books.

Belief-based explanations

Those who have an NDE are convinced, based on their experience, their consciousness, soul, or true self existed when their body died or was close to death. The core of the NDE is largely consistent regardless of gender, age, culture, and religious background. How the experience is interpreted varies depending on the person's belief system. A person with a Christian background might refer to a God like figure as Jesus. Buddhist experiencers have seen the personage of Buddha and Hindu experiencers, Krishna (Rawlings, 1978; Ring, 1980).

The NDE is generally consistent with the belief in the afterlife described by many religions. Generally leaders of organized religions have been noncommittal about NDEs with a few exceptions. Historically the study of consciousness has been relegated to departments of theology and philosophy and not available for study by the physical sciences. In his book, *Revealing Heaven: The Christian Case for Near-Death Experiences*, John W. Price (2013), an Episcopal priest admitted he was a skeptic. At first he told NDErs not to talk about their experiences. His position as a hospital chaplain with hundreds of stories by experiencers changed his views. He sees where NDEs can challenge some religious beliefs. Some individuals, who would be seen in some conservative religions as being damned for eternity, such as atheists, suicide attempters, criminals, have reported positive near-death experiences and not distressing ones.

Some types of NDEs also challenge some religious beliefs. Some religions believe it is morally wrong to commit suicide. It has been shown those who have attempted suicide often have positive near-death experiences (Greyson, 1986). Also pleasurable NDEs are not always occurring to those who have led morally good lives and distressing NDEs not always occurring to those with morally bad lives.

NDEs are generally transformational, leading to experiencers assessing their life choices. They have been known to change the life patterns of those who led immoral lives before the NDE. Some religions view the NDE as an opportunity for the individual to improve their lives.

The man described in chapter 5 who had been drinking a lot until he was in a motorcycle accident that changed his life. He had both a hellish and positive NDE. He stated he gave up drinking and now goes to church, a large transformation for him.

In an interview for the National Catholic Register, Father Gerald O'Collins, Professor of Systematic Theology at the Prestigious Gregorian University in Rome, believes NDEs to be a good thing but more supportive of Jesus's victory over death rather than a major argument for life after death. However, he added, "Some people have quite a big change in their lives for the better after one of these experiences (Burnell, 2001)."

Old paradigm explanations

As described in Chapter 1, according to Kuhn (1970), when anomalies occur in an area of investigation, scientists will use the current paradigms to attempt to explain these incongruities. In the case of the NDE, scientists are using physiological and psychological understandings of the human body to identify the causes of various components of the NDE.

Some neurological research has shown components of the NDE can be simulated through the triggering of areas in the brain (Persinger, 1983). Out-of-body like experiences can occur by stimulating the right temporoparietal junction (TPJ) of the brain (Blanke & Mohr, 2005). The TPJ is the meeting point of the temporal and parietal lobes. At this juncture point information from the thalamus, limbic system, visual, auditory, and somatosensory systems is integrated. It has also been long thought to be important for a person to discriminate self from others. The nearby angular gyrus, during electrical stimulation, can create a sense of someone being present (Britton & Bootzin, 2004).

Certain diseases can produce effects also seen in the NDE. Glaucoma, with its loss of peripheral vision, can result in tunnel-like vision. Vivid hallucinations, usually frightening, can occur to individuals with Alzheimer's or Parkinson's disease. Pilots exposed to G-forces who experience hypotensive syncope can have tunnel-like visual changes. Retinal ischemia due to low oxygen levels at the time of death or near death, has been described also as a cause of tunnel vision (Blackmore, 1996; Mobbs & Watt, 2011;Whinnery and Whinnery, 1990).

The feelings of joy and love have been attributed to endogenous opioids released at the time of death or near death (Molina, 2003). Also the neural transmitter, endorphin, has been known to lead to a euphoric feeling. Studies of ketamine can induce hallucinations, out-of-body experiences with positive emotions like euphoria (Jansen, 2001).

Psychological approaches

Early in the description of NDEs, some of the visions were described as hallucinations, consistent with mental illness. Researchers (Greyson, 2000) identified that mental illness was not any more prevalent among NDErs than the normal population. Some have described these experiences as disassociation approaches to protect individuals due to the fear of being close to death.

The most consistent rebuke to these theories has been the limited number of individuals who have NDEs—estimated to be 10% to 15%—when close to death. If lack of oxygen explained components of the NDEs then given the consistency of human physiology, most individuals suffering from lack of oxygen would have these experiences. Also complete brain anoxia is not compatible with any level of consciousness existing within the body.

In addition, these explanations do not address the numerous incidents of veridical perception during NDEs. Many have described people or clothing or scenes, given their physical condition, they could not have seen through ordinary senses.

Lawrence (1997) describes intrapersonal communications of patients who were unconscious and unable to interact with their external environment. Somehow they were able to "talk to themselves" as it were. How that can occur during an unconscious episode is also a scientific anomaly.

Evolving new paradigm

The NDE experience suggests consciousness exists even without brain function. How this happens is unknown. Chris Carter in his book, *Science and the Near-Death Experience: How Consciousness Survives Death* (2010), describes the need and difficulty in the movement away from a materialistic and reductionistic explanation of consciousness.

> Materialism – the belief that consciousness is produced by or is the same thing as the physical brain – is one of those beliefs that have already been proved false by science. However, although science has in fact already established that consciousness can exist independent of the brain and that materialism is therefore empirically false, it will take another generation before these facts are recognized by mainstream academia. Old paradigms never go gently into the night: they go screaming and kicking. And the defenders of materialism are indeed screaming and kicking even more loudly, perhaps because of a total lack of evidential support of their respective ideology (p. x).

Facco and Agrillo (2012) in their article in the *Journal of Frontiers in Human Neuroscience* also discuss the inadequacy of our explanations of how an NDE can occur to date. They see the NDE as challenging the heart of neurobiological axioms. They advocate for removing "... the ongoing cultural filters and include consciousness, spirituality, and the highest mind expressions in neuroscience in a free, secular, and scientific perspective to overcome old prejudices (p. 8)."

Consciousness is now being studied by many disciplines including departments of psychology, neuroscience, medicine, and physics to name a few. The incidence of transpersonal experience occurring to patients near death has captured the attention of researchers from professions with strong backgrounds in biological sciences with openness to the integration of transpersonal experiences into their research. Eban Alexander (2012), a neurosurgeon and an NDE skeptic before his own NDE, and others (Greyson, 2010; Facco & Agrillo, 2012) are challenging the use of the reductionists paradigm to explain the NDE.

New theories are evolving using new or previously untested ways of explaining nonlocal consciousness. There are theories involving quantum physics that attempt to explain how nonlocal consciousness and connection can occur during an NDE (van Lommel, 2006; 2011). Fenwick (2010) suggests there might be a quantum mechanical explanation. He hypothesizes consciousness becomes separate from the brain at the time of death and a non-local consciousness evolves. Human consciousness, theoretically, is thus partially measurable as an electromagnetic energy field according to some scientists (Fracasso & Friedman, 2012). There is currently a journal called *NeuroQuantology*, which is an interdisciplinary journal of neuroscience and physics. What is now in place is a search for a new paradigm that more fully explains the NDE.

Caring for the NDE experiencers

From an interdisciplinary conference on clinical approaches to the near-death experiencer sponsored by IANDS (during which the author was in attendance), a number of guidelines and interventions were developed to assist NDErs. Some of the interpersonal challenges identified include: a sense of separation from those who have not had a similar experience, a pervasive fear of ridicule or rejection, difficulty in integrating attitude changes with expectations of others, and difficulty in maintaining customary life roles that no longer have same importance.

General guidelines for caregivers include exploring own attitudes toward NDEs, provide respect (positive regard) toward the person and experience, avoid labeling, assure confidentiality, encourage expression of emotions, avoid regarding the NDE as a symptom of pathology, and provide reflection back to the NDErs' statements.

In some cases NDErs can develop a sense of being special because of the NDE descriptions in the media, being studied by researchers, and possibly from expectations of family and friends. These expectations can become burdensome and slow down positive life integration (Greyson & Harris, 1987).

In 2006, under the auspices of IANDS, 25 NDErs agreed to meet and share the issues they dealt with after their NDE. They identified six categories of challenges: processing a radical shift in reality; accepting the return; sharing the experience; integrating new spiritual values with earthly expectations; adjusting to heightened sensitivities and supernatural gifts; and finding and living one's purpose (Stout, 2006).

Near-death experiences, both negative and positive, create numerous changes in an NDEr's belief system, abilities, and interests. According to Dr. Regina Hess, from the American Center for the Integration of Spiritually Transformative Experiences (ACISTE), these NDEs are spiritually transformative.

An experience is spiritually transformative when it causes people to perceive themselves and the world profoundly differently: by expanding the individual's identity, augmenting their sensitivities, and thereby altering their values, priorities and appreciation of the purpose of life. This may be triggered by surviving clinical death, or by otherwise sensing an enlarged reality (Hess, 2013).

Additional surveys have identified other challenges when dealing with emotional responses, such as anger about being sent back, mourning the loss of one's life or identity, and feeling different from others (Stout, et al., 2006; Sutherland, 1990).

Goals

While adjustments to NDEs can be positive or negative, by far these experiences lead to general greater well-being, more stability, more purpose to their lives and increase in creative expression (Greyson & Ring, 2004; Ring, 1984; Sutherland, 1989). At the same time, some research shows the divorce rate amongst NDE experiencers is significantly higher (64%) when compared to others (19%) who have come close to death but did not experience an NDE (Christian, 2005).

Assessment

Table II Aftereffects from an NDE

1. Emotional adjustment to a transformative experience
2. Increase in spirituality
3. Decrease in materialism
4. Increase in psychic abilities
5. Electromagnetic issues
6. Loss of the fear of death leading to a different response to death of others
7. A strong sense of life purpose
8. Search for knowledge and understanding
9. Changes in personal and professional relationships

Table III Helpful communication with someone after an NDE

1. Foster client centered communication about NDEs and any aftereffects
2. Ask about the client's experiences
3. Determine if the experiences included visual, auditory, or kinesthetic aspects of a combination.
4. Ask the client's explanation for the NDE and aftereffects
5. Assess immediate concerns
6. Assess the emotional impact
7. Normalize the experience
8. Provide resources

Table IV Documentation of the NDE

1. The person's physical and mental condition at the time of the occurrence
2. Description of what occurred
3. Immediate emotional response to the occurrence
4. Occurrence of aftereffects

CHAPTER 7

ANGELS, GRIM REAPERS, AND SHADOW FIGURES

Keywords: angels, grim reaper, shadow figures, entities, near-death, religious figures

One time when the angels were with me in my hospital room, my daddy asked me if I wanted to sing with them. I said, yes, so we played a worship song - I couldn't sing with my mouth but I was singing with the angels - they could hear me. This was in the days when I had to talk to people with special signals - but I didn't need to talk that way to the angels!

People have told me that after I am with the angels my face is glowing – like a thousand Christmas mornings. It's funny that I could usually only smile with just one corner of my mouth, but that my smiles after the angels' visits were huge (Malarkey & Malarkey, 2010, p. 87).

These are the words of Alex Malarkey who, when he was six years old, suffered a car accident that left him paralyzed and near death. During that time Alex had many encounters with angels who took him to the gates of heaven.

Angels are one type of other worldly beings reported appearing to individuals, particularly children, during an NDE. Angels, grim reaper figures, and shadow people appear to individuals during NDEs and other times when someone is close to death. Less frequently, they appear to others not close to death. To date we have limited knowledge about the frequency of their appearance. The appearances tend to be under-reported because of their mystical or paranormal classifications.

According to Karlis Osis (1961) in a study of deathbed observations by physicians and nurses, out of 122 patients who had some type of communication with an apparition, 28 (23%) saw a religious figure. The religious figures could have been an angel, devil, Jesus, God, saints, the Virgin Mary or unidentified figures.

Angel appearances during NDEs

During an NDE an angel sometimes appears with wings and some-times without. Usually they are glowing and full of light. Sometimes a being of light is seen as God and sometimes as an angel. The angel can be there as an escort during this transition from life to death or to provide a message, often saying the person must go back (Lundahl, 1992). The angel may describe themselves as a guardian angel who had been with the person during their lifetime. Moody cared for a nine-year-old boy he calls Sam, while a resident at a Georgia hospital. Sam suffered a cardiac arrest because of a serious adrenal gland disease when he saw angels.

> I was chatting with him about his illness when he shyly volunteered, "About a year ago, I died." I began to coax him about his experience. He told me that after he died, he floated out of his body and looked down as the doctor pushed on his chest to restart his heart. Sam, in his altered state, tried to get the doctor to quit hitting him but the doctor wouldn't pay any attention. At that point Sam had the experience of moving upward very rapidly and seeing the earth fall away below him. He then passed through a dark tunnel and was met on the other side by a group of angels. I asked him if these angels had wings and he said no.

> They were glowing, he said, luminescent, and all of them seemed to love him very much. Everything in this place was filled with light, he said. Yet through it all he saw beautiful pastoral scenes. This heavenly place was surrounded by a fence. He was told by the angels that if he went beyond the fence he wouldn't be able to return to life. He was then told by a being of light, Sam called him God, he had to go back and reenter his body (Moody & Perry, 1988, p.58-59).

Elizabeth was an angel who accompanied Katie, a seven-year-old girl who had nearly drowned. Katie told her story to Dr. Melvin Morse.

> She remembered nothing about the drowning itself. Her first memory was of darkness and the feeling that she was so heavy she couldn't move. Then a tunnel opened and through that tunnel came Elizabeth. Elizabeth was tall and nice with bright, golden hair. She accompanied Katie up the tunnel where she saw her late grandfather and met several other people... Finally, Elizabeth, who seemed to be a guardian angel to Katie – took her to meet the Heavenly Father and Jesus (Morse, Perry & Moody, 1991, p. 5 and 6).

Adults less frequently report seeing angels. Lorna Byrne, author of Angels in My Hair, depicts her experience during a miscarriage in her third month of pregnancy. During this time she felt her soul and that of her baby's rising. She went through a tunnel made up of shiny white angels. At one point, a lovely angel told her she could go no further. The baby's soul was to stay in heaven but she must go back. Even though she was reluctant to return, she knew it was what she needed to do (Byrne, 2013).

Appearance of angels during deathbed communications

William Barrett (2011) describes the experience of a three-year-old girl named Lily. Lily's aunt, Louise, died in 1896. She was fond of Lily and had asked before the surgery if Lily could come and stay with her in the country. After Louise died, Lily reported seeing her from a window with her hand stretched out calling to Lily. Lily's brother described the following events.

> I was then eleven-years-old and my sister said, 'What! Don't you see Tata?' as she called her aunt. Of course I could see nothing. For some months nothing further was seen by the child, the visions ceased. Towards May 20th, little Lily fell ill and, when in bed, she looked up to the ceiling saying that she saw her aunt calling her, surrounded by little angels.
>
> 'Mother, how pretty,' she said. From day to day her illness increased, but she always repeated, 'My aunt has come to fetch me; she is holding out

her arms to me,' and as her mother wept, she said, 'Don't cry, Mother, it is very beautiful, there are angels round me (p. 38-39).'

Lily died four and a half months after the death of her Aunt Louise.

More recently, Senator Mark Kirk from Illinois, in an interview following his stroke, reported seeing angels at the foot of his bed. There were three angels standing there asking if he wanted to come with them. He told them, no, that he would hold off for a while (Lester, 2013).

On occasion, those who are present at the time of a loved one's death may also see these angels and even take a picture. This picture was taken of a hallway at a hospital in Charlotte, NC when a young girl was taken off life support. A nurse reported seeing a man in the hallway, although when she pushed the button to allow him entrance, no one was there. After this happened a number of times, the mother of the young girl was able to take a picture of an angelic figure. The girl recovered and was able to go home (Do Angels Exist?, 2008). There are numerous reports of pictures of angels similar to this one.

Background and explanations

In theological descriptions, angels are often seen in a human form with wings on their backs and halos around their heads. A bright light often surrounds them. These angels are described as being messengers from God delivering information. In the New Testament, for example, angels brought messages to Mary, Joseph, and the shepherds. Angels proclaimed the birth of Jesus in the "adoration of the shepherds" in Luke 2:10. They also are depicted as guardians of individuals. In some religions, children are told they have a guardian angel who is with them during their lifetime.

In 2008, the Baylor University Institute for Studies of Religion conducted a comprehensive poll of almost 1,700 individuals across the US about religious beliefs and practices. Two of the questions asked were: "Do you believe you have been protected from harm by a guardian angel? Do you believe you avoided an accident through the agency of a guardian angel?" The pollsters found 55% of this sample of Americans said they were protected from harm by their guardian angel. In addition 45% reported having at least two religious encounters (Stark, 2008).

Schutzengel (Guardian Angel) by Bernhard Plockhorst

Emma Heathcote (2002) collected 50 accounts of angel sightings from individuals in the UK. She describes numerous descriptions by ill persons and their families of angels being present in their hospital rooms.

Explanations

Woerlee (2005), an anesthesiologist, believes there are biological explanations for visions of angels. He hypothesizes these visions can be caused by deja vu phenomena, temporal lobe disturbances, and possibly widening pupils due to terror, oxygen deprivation, or extreme relaxation.

Buddhists use the word devas to describe celestial beings, referred to as angels in other cultures and religions. They, like many Christian religions, believe devas are spiritual beings. They also believe they are emanations of light or energy. Some traditions believe the energy frequency of angels is generally such that normally humans cannot see them. When the energy frequencies of the angels match those of individuals which can occur at the time of stress or near-death, they become visible to us.

The Grim Reaper

> I was running down the hall to get to my patient's room so I could relieve the nurse in charge. I ran past this room, across from the central floor nurses' station, and had run past five rooms before it registered what I saw. I did not believe it! I went back down the hall and stopped at the room. I glanced into it. On the bed was a little grey-haired lady dressed in lace, propped up with pillows.
>
> Beside the bed stood this tall figure dressed in a monk's robe with its head covered. It looked up at me when I appeared in the door. His face was a skull with tiny red fires for eyes. His hands, skeletal, were patiently folded over each other inside the dark sleeves. My impression was he was very patient, waiting (Chorvinsky, 1997, p.8).

This was a report by a nurse who saw the Grim Reaper while working in a hospital in Texas. Another nurse's report to Chorvinsky (1992) was of an encounter in a long-term care facility. In that episode, both a registered nurse and a licensed practical nurse saw a black-robed figure with a hood standing at the foot of the bed of a dying patient. Another nurse joined them but could not see the figure. The figure waiting patiently at the foot of the bed but was not threatening to the observing nurses. The patient died the next night.

More commonly, it is the ill or dying person who sees the figure. In many cultures, the reaper is seen as the personification of death. If the Grim Reaper is nearby, it is the sign someone will die soon. While individuals do report death occurring when the Grim Reaper is near, sometimes a person is saved because of the visitation.

> I was ice-skating alone on a pond when I fell through the ice. I couldn't find the opening and I was panicking and starting to pass out from the cold water which was flooding my lungs. Suddenly, I felt something poking at me and I grabbed it, and felt myself being pulled through the water and up through the opening in the ice. When my head came out of the water, I couldn't believe my eyes! I was terrified! I saw a hooded, black-robed corpse. The stick that I was grabbing onto was actually the blunt end of a very large, silvery scythe (Chorvinsky, 1997, p. 11).

This occurrence happened when the man reporting the incidence was eight years old. He also reported the entity spoke to him to tell him not to be afraid that he was there to protect him and that it wasn't his time to die. The entity also provided him with enough warmth to walk the mile home in the 14-degree weather. After this incidence he lost his fear of death.

Another incident occurred to a man who had been on the couch late one evening watching television. He saw the cloaked figure, realizing someone was close to death. He ran upstairs and found his wife had attempted suicide. He was able to call an ambulance in time to save his wife (Chorvinsky, 1992).

This entity has also been seen as a trickster. During a near-death experience, Louis reported seeing the Grim Reaper who tried to create a tunnel with a light.

> Immediately, I was engulfed in total, pitch black, the total absence of any color. I was scared. It was totally foreign to me. Then this entity came out from the blackness toward me, looking like what we'd call the Grim Reaper.

> What did he look like?

> Skeletal. Yellowish and it had moving robes. Now I could have been conditioned to see something like that but I never saw a Halloween costume that spooky. And there was a hand coming from the darkness, motioning for me to come toward it-toward the entity.

> What was your reaction?

> I was frightened. But I was also thinking, well he's the only thing I can identify here. The rest is total blackness. So I thought that maybe I should pay attention to his directions, until I began to feel that he was trying to trick me into doing something other than what I'm supposed to do ...

> Then he swirled his hand in the air ... and made kind of a light area, like a tunnel. And he said, 'Go in there.' and I said 'No.' That wasn't what I was supposed to do. I think anyone with the IQ of a turnip would have known that it wasn't a real light. He just made a hole there, and out of nowhere, he produced some yellow, acrid-looking stuff that he threw in the hole and swirled it around. And he said, 'You have a golden light. Go to it now.' But I refused.

And when I refused, the darkness left, and I was in a dim lit up area (Lawrence, 1995, p. 142-143).

Sometimes this grim reaper is seen as not only representing death but also representing evil. If angels come to help us with a life-to-death transition, they are seen as transitioning us to a heavenly environment. Not so with the Grim Reaper. Ralph had an encounter with the Grim Reaper after being admitted to the hospital because of a heart attack. He reported suddenly feeling very cold, below freezing.

At the foot of my bed on the right side was a dark, gray, cloaked stranger. He had no face.

How did you know it was a he?

I don't know. I just knew. The other thing I knew was he didn't think I was bad enough or sick enough to go with him (Lawrence, 1997, p. 141-142).

Wagner (2005) reports a description of the Grim Reaper by a six-year-old girl that also personified evil. This young girl woke up in the middle of the night to go to the bathroom. On her way there she saw an entity dressed in a black cloak and a hood. Its face had a greenish tinge with black eyes that projected evil. The entity also grinned at her, but it was an evil grin (p. 11).

Background and explanations

From the time of ancient Greece, there were personifications of death. The vision of death varied over the centuries and in different cultures. Sometimes death had wings. Most of the time the person-ifications of death were male but, in Norse mythology, the Valkyries were beautiful women who escorted souls of brave warriors to Valhalla, their afterlife. A darker figure is Charon, the ferryman who accompa-nied departed souls across the River Styx, representing the transition from this world's life to the afterlife. Charon's description in the paint-ings of various cultures across centuries changed from a rough look-ing seaman, to a haggard, unkempt old man with a long beard, to the popular culture depiction as a skeletal figure, in a long hooded robe, much like the Grim Reaper.

The Grim Reaper is depicted not only in paintings but also in literature. In *A Christmas Carol* by Charles Dickens, the ghost of Christmas yet to come is a cloaked skeletal figure who reveals to Scrooge an undesirable death. Even in *A Christmas Carol*, the ghost is negotiable. He is a harbinger of a death which can be altered if Scrooge changes his ways.

Are these experiences only dreams? Are the hooded beings an archetype from the collective human unconscious? At this point in time, there is little scientific investigation of apparitions of the Grim Reaper. A search of various medical and psychology databases revealed no investigation of visions of the Grim Reaper. Lawrence (1997) reported three out of 111 subjects who had experienced unconsciousness saw the grim reaper. What is known is numerous individuals, of all ages from different centuries and cultures, have reported seeing the Grim Reaper or a facsimile. How that occurs is unknown.

Shadow people and hellish entities

> After being injured by a car, Scott next found himself facing the entrance to a vortex like tunnel in a 'bad dark place.' He described the tunnel as looking like a tornado lying flat on the ground. As he was drawn further into the tunnel he found himself face to face with the devil. The devil spoke to him in a deep raspy voice saying, "You're bad," and made an attempt to grab him. At that point Scott was completely terrified. He felt subconsciously the devil was trying to suck him away from God. Scott said, in some way he could feel a strong negative force emanating from the devil. Scott described the devil as being composed of rotting, putrefied flesh and covered with sores and slime. The devil projected the impression of a being who was both mentally and physically ill (Bonenfant, 2001, p. 89).

Scott was eight years old at the time of this distressing aspect of his NDE. Scott moved out of this dark tunnel and went on to see a brilliant light that he felt was God where he felt safe. Another smaller light moved toward him in an angelic form. She took him to a dark but comfortable place where he was safe from the devil. While Scott's description was of a devilish entity, others do see dark shadow figures.

A woman's husband who was dying from end-stage liver cancer reports her husband saw shadow people at the edge of his room. In his case he said there were 12 to 20 of them. He asked her to take a trip, hoping being away would cast off the shadow figures. He again saw them in the hotel at which they were staying. They moved to a relative's house but still the shadow figures found them. The husband could not tell if they were good or bad entities, but he knew he was afraid of them.

The woman addressed the spirits, even though she could not see them, and told them her husband was a child of the light and a child of God. She also said her home was a home of peace and love and told them there was no place for them there. She went on to say, that in the name of the Father, Son, and the Holy Ghost they needed to be gone.

The husband's body jerked and as soon as she finished her discourse. He announced the spirits were gone as soon as she finished. He said the spirits were keeping him here, maybe for fear he would have to go with them when he died. He died two days after the shadow people were banished (Offutt, 2009).

Background and explanations

Shadow people have been written about in literature for a number of years. They were also shown in the movie, *Ghost*. When the villains in the movie die, their spirits are dragged away by a gang of shadowy demons. It is presumed they are taken to hell. While entities that emit brilliant light are seen as representatives of God or a heavenly place, the dark shadow people are seen as representing evil and hellish places.

In Jason Offutt's book, *Darkness Walks: The Shadow People Amongst Us* (2009), he lists eight categories of shadow people: benign shadows, shadows of terror, red-eyed shadows, noisy shadows, angry hooded shadows, shadows that attack, shadow cats, and the hat man. Each of these shadow types look and act differently according to the dozens of eyewitnesses he interviewed. He himself as a child saw shadow people.

We have here again a situation where individuals have visions of these shadow people but there is little agreement about them being ghosts, hallucinations, or some type of entity. Religious officials may believe they are demons. Others see them as ghosts, operating in a different dimension. These shadow people generally are seen as dark and, while in a humanoid shape, lack detailed features, much like seeing a shadow.

Some speculate they are imagined by the individuals who see them. Some believe they are seen out of the peripheral vision of an individual's eyes. With peripheral vision, an individual recognizes patterns but with less detail than provided by central vision. This corner-of-the-eye phenomenon can occur during which the brain incorrectly interprets shadows or texture into something familiar, like a person. While this may be an explanation for some individuals seeing shadow figures, others claim to see them while looking straight ahead.

Others report that the hypnogogic state can create an opportunity for the vision of shadow people. This is the time between waking and sleeping when the person is becoming aware of their surroundings. It is a natural hypnosis state. Generally images are not clear for a few moments and can be interpreted as shadow figures.

Changes in the body's electromagnetic fields, particularly when someone is close to death, can induce visions of shadow figures. The opportunity for this to occur is enhanced by the use of narcotics.

Since there is little research on shadow figures other than descriptive reports, there is no definite answer to why they occur and their frightening nature, even with young children.

Assisting those with these visions

It has been particularly difficult in the past for individuals to describe visitations from entities that lack human existence. Reports of angels are now more common with less negative reactions associated with descriptions of their presence. Lorna Byrne's book, *Angels in My Hair*, is a bestselling book, translated into 26 languages. There is no book about sightings of the Grim Reaper although there are books about shadow people. Like the NDErs, it is more accepted to report sightings of positive images associated with goodness than dark images associated with hellish encounters.

It is important to provide positive regard for all who report both positive and dark images when talking with individuals who have had these experiences. While there is little scientific understanding of the reasons for these apparitions, we know they occur to many people. It is important to normalize these experiences for any individual to whom they happen.

Each person will interpret these experiences based on their frame of reference. Some are joyous and some are frightened. Like with near-death visits, angels, grim reapers, and shadow people seem to respond to being told the person does not wish to go with them at this time.

Many have reported these apparitions vanish when a prayer is said or they are simply asked to leave.

Table I Helpful communication with someone after an apparition

1. Foster a client-centered approach by asking the client to describe the experience
2. Bracket your preconceived ideas about the client's experience
3. Regard the client's description with positive regard avoiding distortions or corrections to the individual's descriptions
4. Listen for visual, auditory, and/or kinesthetic descriptions
5. Normalize the experience
6. Assess the emotional impact
7. Encourage communication with the entity if still present
8. Provide support and resources

Table II Documentation of the apparition

1. The person's physical and mental condition at the time of the occurrence
2. Description of what occurred
3. Immediate emotional response to the occurrence
4. Obtain a visual depiction of the entity when possible

CHAPTER 8

DEATHBED COMMUNICATIONS

Keywords: deathbed communication, deathbed visions, terminal restlessness, veridical perception

"Hi, Mrs. Tavlock. I'm happy to meet you," I said. Mrs. Tavlock was in her early seventies. She had a twinkle in her eye most of us recognize in people who have a good sense of humor. A fleece throw of blues and greens covered her lap down to her feet as she sat on her couch. She was a hospice patient. Cindy, a hospice nurse, told me unusual events were happening to Mrs. Tavlock.

"Good morning," Mrs. Tavlock replied. "Pardon me if I don't get up. Won't you please have a seat?" she said pointing to the beige wingback chair opposite her. "I know you want to hear about how my former husband is contacting me. My daughters think I'm off my rocker but I know it's my husband," Mrs. Tavlock continued.

"Let's start with how your husband is contacting you. Is it all right with you if I record this conversation?"

"Record away. Frank died three years ago of cancer. We were married for 49 years." Mrs. Tavlock's eyes started to fill up with tears and her voice cracked a little. "We had our issues, but we were happy. Frank was a bit of a jokester. He loved playing tricks on people. You never knew when a whoopee cushion would show up or other silly things would happen."

Sadness overcame her for a moment as tears ran down her cheeks. "Take your time. It's fine with us if you cry." Cindy handed her a tissue.

"I'm OK. About a week ago, I was sitting here watching TV, when I felt this poke in my arm." Mrs. Tavlock rubbed the upper part of her left arm. "It was a definite poke. At first I ignored it, but then it happened again. Poke, poke. There was nothing near me to cause the poking. It stopped, so I forgot about it. The next day there was more poking, this time in my leg." She rubbed the upper part of her right leg on the anterior surface. "Pretty soon, I was getting poked about two or three times a day, just a few pokes at a time. I knew it was Frank." She smiled broadly.

"How did you know it was Frank?" I asked.

"I just knew it was something he would do to let me know he was around. I just felt it was him. It's so much better knowing he's around waiting for me."

"How is it better?" I asked.

"I don't feel alone anymore. I know when the day I die comes, Frank will be there. He's here already."

Poking is not the typical way dead friends and relatives let a dying person know they are present. Deathbed communications (DBCs), commonly known as deathbed visions, are one of the oldest documented transpersonal experiences associated with death and dying described in literature. The term deathbed communications, as opposed to deathbed visions, is used to reflect experiences that not only involve seeing but also hearing and feeling. Most people who experience a DBC see, hear, or sense the presence of the deceased who has come to be with them. DBCs are not limited to visions of the deceased or otherworldly persons or places. DBCs include hearing music, sensing a presence, or even as was the case with Mrs. Tavlock, being poked.

A major issue for practitioners and family members is distinguishing between true DBCs, drug-induced hallucinations, and confusion. Osis and Haraldsson (2012) in their research studies were also concerned with making this distinction. In some instances, dying persons see or otherwise experience individuals or events others near them cannot see but are not considered to be DBCs. In these cases, the person who is dying might be reliving memories from their past. Much like a person who cannot focus on present events but is back in time experiencing life as it once was. Osis and Haraldsson used a former naval officer's experience of piloting a battleship when death was imminent as an example (p. 58). In other cases, the person experiences the here and now but in a confused sense. They may believe what they are eating is something other than the food being served, for instance. They may lack orientation to time and place. Living in the past or being confused by current circumstances often become states of existence with moments of clarity. Some medications like morphine can also induce confusion, lethargy, and on rare occasions, hallucinations.

In the case of a DBC, the person is alert to time and place. They know where they are and who is in the room with them. In addition, they experience a vision, sound, or a touch usually not experienced by anyone else and not accounted for by someone or something objectively present. The dying person may or may not be aware others cannot see, hear, or otherwise experience their reality.

Another distinguishing characteristic is the length of DBCs. These are short events and not a continuous state of being. Osis and Haraldsson found approximately 50 percent of deathbed communications lasted five minutes or less. In addition 17 percent lasted from six to fifteen minutes with another 17 percent lasting more than an hour (p. 68). These time-limited events are consistent with other parapsychological phenomena.

The description of a DBC in this book only includes the events that occur before a person dies in that person's environment. This is done to distinguish deathbed communication from near-death experiences (NDEs) or out-of-body experiences not associated with an NDE which are perceived as occurring out of the environment of the person who is near death. DBCs are also distinctive from near-death visits (NDVs) which occur to individuals in their environment but when the person is not imminently dying although they have been close to death.

DBCs, as compared to hallucinations, generally have an emotionally positive effect on the dying person. He or she will typically feel calmer, less anxious, and even elated. Hallucinations often result in a person feeling frightened or more anxious.

Here is a classic example published in 1882 by Cobbe.

> I was watching one night beside a poor man dying of consumption...
> he was in full possession of his senses, able to talk with a strong voice
> and not in the least drowsy. He had slept through the day and was
> so wakeful that I had been conversing with him on ordinary subjects
> to while away the long hours. Suddenly, while we were thus talking
> quietly together, he became silent, and fixed his eyes on one particular
> spot in the room, which was entirely vacant, even of furniture. At the

same time, a look of the greatest delight changed the whole expression of his face, and after a moment of what seemed to be intense scrutiny of some object invisible to me, he said to me in a joyous tone, "There is Jim." Jim was a little son whom he had lost the year before, and who I had known well: but the dying man had a son still living, named John, for whom we had sent, and I concluded it was of John he was speaking and that he thought he heard him arriving. So I answered, "No. John has not been able to come."

"I do not mean John, I know he is not here; it is Jim, my little lame, Jim. Surely, you remember him?"

"Yes," I said, "I remember dear little Jim who died last year quite well."

"Don't you see him, then? There he is," said the man, pointing to the vacant space on which his eyes were fixed, and when I did not answer, he repeated almost fretfully, "Don't you see him standing there?"

I answered that I could not see him, though I felt perfectly convinced that something was visible to the sick man, which I could not perceive. When I gave him this answer, he seemed quite amazed, and turned round to look at me with a glance almost of indignation. As his eyes met mine, I saw that a film seemed to pass over them, the light of intelligence died away, he gave a gentle sigh and expired (p. 255-256).

When they occur

Deathbed communications generally occur within a few weeks of death. At one time it was believed deathbed communications or visions only occurred at the time of death. Recent research has shown these can occur up to three or four weeks before death but the most common times are from two days before and up to the moment of death (Lawrence & Repede, 2012; Callahan & Kelley, 1992).

It is commonly reported a person who is dying and already unconscious may suddenly sit up in bed, alert and oriented. They may report seeing dead friends or relatives and/or angelic figures. The report may include a description of warmth or a glow on their face. Death occurs shortly thereafter.

Here is a report of a case by Barrett (1926)

> A young boy, aged fourteen ... dying of consumption, had wasted away
> very rapidly in four or five months. During the whole of that period
> he was very bright, full of interest in all around (him), and did not
> seem to be aware of his rapidly failing strength. About a week before
> he died he slept in a room off his mother's, with no door between, he
> called her ... full of excitement about a door he could see at the corner
> of his room, which he said was "opening wider and wider and, when
> it is open wide, I shall be going through it, Mother."

> On the morning of the day he died, his mother ... found him sitting
> up in bed, looking towards the corner of the room. There is a nice old
> man coming for me; he is holding out his arms for me. I must go'...
> he fell back gently on his pillow and was gone, without any struggle
> for breath, and with a smile of joy on his face, which remained (p. 45).

What is seen, heard or felt

According to Horan and Lange (1997), the results of analysis of 49
accounts of deathbed communications from Barrett's 1926 descriptions,
included communications that were visual, auditory, and sensed presences. The visual, auditory, and kinesthetic results are consistent with
the Neurolinguistic programming learning styles approach.

Based on the writings of Cobbe (1882); Barrett (1926); Osis (1961);
Callahan & Kelley, 1992) the terminally ill client can perceive deceased
relatives, angelic beings; borders which can include water or heavenly gates. Angels are described without wings standing in the room or
near the bed. They can also sense the presence of others and possibly
be poked, like Mrs. Tavlock was in the description at the beginning of
this chapter. Also patients can hear music. In Chapter 5 of Barrett's
book (1926), he described several instances of not only the patient but
some family members hearing beautiful music.

Here is one example:

> Mrs. Z, became very ill and expected to die. She was, however, perfectly
> composed and in the full possession of her senses, and was anxious
> to arrange some business affairs. For this purpose her husband came
> to her bedside and talked over these matters with her. Suddenly she

changed the subject and said to her husband, "Do you hear those voices singing?" Col. Z, who narrates the incident, replied that he did not, and his wife continued, I have heard them several times today and I am sure they are the angels welcoming me to Heaven but," she added, "it is strange, there is one voice among them I am sure I know, but I cannot remember whose voice it is." Suddenly she stopped and said, pointing straight over her husband's head, "Why, there she is in the corner of the room. It is Julia X. She is coming on, she is leaning over you; she has her hands up, she is praying. Do look; she is going." Her husband turned round but could see nothing. His wife then said, "She has gone (p.78)."

Incidence of deathbed communications

In 1961, the Parapsychology Foundation, Inc. published *Deathbed Observations of Physicians and Nurses*, a monograph containing the results of a study by physician Karlis Osis. This was a retrospective, stratified random survey of 10,000 physicians and nurses of whom 640 responded. The doctors and nurses reported 39.2 percent of the deathbed patients experienced some type of vision (p. 29). The nurses reported 270 of these observations with physicians reporting 59 (p. 28). These visions occurred from under 10 minutes before the time of death to over a day (p. 31).

In a follow-up study, Osis, with Haraldsson (1977) received 1,708 usable questionnaires from their survey of 10,000 doctors and nurses in the US and India. The doctors and nurses reported 471 cases of apparitions in the survey (p. 217).

At the Hour of Death was first published in 1977, which meant the data was collected before that time and before the hospice movement took hold in the US and started in India. The first hospice unit in the US was opened in Branford, CT in 1974. The Hospice Medicare Benefit funding, which provides payment for the majority of hospice care, did not become available until 1982. India's first hospice, Shanti Avedna Ashram, opened in Bombay in 1986. At the time of the Osis surveys, physicians and nurses took care of the dying patients in addition to patients with other nonterminal illnesses. It was not until three decades later hospice nurses and oncologists focused exclusively on the care of the dying.

In the above two studies the doctors and nurses were asked, from all their experiences caring for terminally ill patients, about the number of these patients who visualized apparitions. The studies only asked about visual experiences and not experiences that involved hearing or touch. The responses by the doctors and nurses also involved their memory of these cases over years of professional practice. We know from these studies that deathbed communications occur, but the actual incidence was dependent on the accuracy of the long-term memory of these health professionals. From other studies (Jones & Anderson, 1987), we know long-term memory is not reliable to produce accurate detail.

Lawrence and Repede (2012) attempted to obtain a more specific incidence of deathbed communications in the study. The purpose of the study by Lawrence and Repede (2012) was to determine the incidence of deathbed communications, including vision, hearing, and feeling the presence of the deceased or otherworld beings and places during the 30 days before death and their impact on the dying process.

At first, 60 hospice charts were audited to find descriptions of deathbed communications during the 30 days before the death of the patient. These chart audits revealed five (8.33 percent) of the 60 charts included descriptions of DBCs. This low number was inconsistent with the number of DBCs nurses, social workers, and chaplains claimed to have occurred. There was no specific area in the charts where a description of DBCs was requested. During weekly meetings of current hospice patients approximately 10 percent of the patients were experiencing DBCs.

As part of the same study, 75 hospice nurses across the United States responded to a survey about the incidence of DBCs during the last 30 days caring for dying patients. The 75 hospice nurses identified 363 incidences of DBCs, with an average of 4.8 patient occurrences per nurse in the last 30 days. When nurses were asked to look over the past 30 days of their care of dying patients, they were able to identify a significant number of patients having these experiences, much higher than previously described.

Typical response of patients and family members

Patients generally are instant believers in the reality of the DBCs they are experiencing. Not only do they believe what they are seeing, hearing, or feeling is real, they also believe these experiences represent a glimpse of the afterlife. Family members, on the other hand, are often concerned their loved ones are experiencing mental health issues and hallucinating. They are less likely to view these experiences as positive events.

Mazzarino-Willett (2009) published a table (p. 129), which summarized the results of three articles describing the responses to deathbed communication. Patients who experienced deathbed communications had a calm, peaceful state, or elation which was spiritually transformative.

According to Lawrence and Repede (2012), 89 percent of the hospice nurses reported patients who experienced a DBC had a peaceful and calm death, with only 40.5 percent reporting a peaceful and calm death without the DBC.

According to a description by his sister, Mona Simpson, in her eulogy, it is probable Steve Jobs had a deathbed vision right at the time of his death. According to Mona these events occurred at his final moments.

> Before embarking, he'd looked at his sister Patty, then for a long time at his children, then at his life partner, Laurene, and then over their shoulders past them.

> Steve's final words were:

> Oh wow, oh wow, oh wow.

Terminal Restlessness

Lawrence and Repede (2012) define terminal restlessness as a condition during the last days of life that include agitation, restlessness, moaning, and physical irritability with a decrease of consciousness. When terminal restlessness is combined with pain and anxiety, dying becomes a state of almost intolerable suffering (Brajtman, 2005).

Estimates from the literature state this occurs in 25 to 85% of patients (Head & Faul, 2005). This state is distressing not only for the patient, but also family members and caregivers. The vision of such a disturbing death often brings feelings of remorse and guilt in those who are witnesses. While medications can be used to treat terminal restlessness, pain, and anxiety, usually it is at the expense of meaningful, last moment communication between the dying patient and loved ones.

All researchers who have studied DBCs or deathbed visions, as they may have called the phenomena, report a decrease in terminal restlessness and anxiety after a DBC (Cobbe, 1882; Barrett, 1926; Osis and Haraldson, Callahan & Kelley, 1992; Lawrence & Repede, 2012). Patients who experience a deathbed vision have lower incidence of terminal restlessness and require less sedation and anti-anxiety medication. In the Lawrence and Repede study, 89 percent of the 75 hospice nurses reported patients who experienced a DBC had a peaceful and calm death. If patients did not experience a DBC, the nurses reported only 40.5 percent reporting a peaceful and calm death (Lawrence & Repede, 2012).

Here is an example of the type of change that can occur

A woman in her seventies, suffering from pneumonia, was a semi-invalid who spent a painful, miserable existence. Her face became so serene, as if she had seen something beautiful. There was a transfixed illumination on her face—a smile beyond description. Her features were almost beautiful on so old a face. Also, her skin had a transparent, waxy quality—almost snow white—so different from the usual yellow discoloration which follows death (Osis and Haraldson, 2012, p. 128).

Veridical perception

We know deathbed communication can have a positive emotional effect on the dying patient. Clinically this effect is significant in reducing pain, restlessness, and anxiety regardless of the objective reality of these experiences.

What is additionally significant for most researchers, health professionals, and family members is the knowledge the dying person has of people and/or events unknown to them through normal sense experiences. Sometimes these individuals have knowledge of the death of a person, when they have not been told a person had died.

Barrett, in his book on deathbed visions (1926), described ten cases of deathbed visions where the dying person saw a dead friend or relative without being told of their deaths. In some of the cases the dying person was not told a close friend or relative had died because of the severity of their own illness. The family knew the person had died but withheld the information to not worsen the patient's condition. Here is one example;

In a neighboring city were two little girls, Jennie and Edith, one about eight years of age and the other but a little older. They were schoolmates and intimate friends. In June, 1889, both were ill of diphtheria. At noon on Wednesday, Jennie died. Then the parents of Edith, and her physician as well, took particular pains to keep from her the fact that her little playmate was gone. They feared the effect of the knowledge on her condition. To prove that they succeeded and that she did not know, it may be mentioned that on Saturday, June 8th, at noon, just before she became unconscious of all that was passing about her, she selected two of her photographs to be sent to Jennie, and also told her attendants to bid her goodbye. ... she appeared to see one and another of the friends she knew were dead. ... but now, suddenly, and with every appearance of surprise, she turned to her father and exclaimed, "Why, papa, I am going to take Jennie with me!" Then she added, "Why, papa! You did not tell me that Jennie was here!" And immediately she reached out her arms as if in welcome, and said, "Oh, Jennie, I'm so glad you are here (p. 27)!"

In the world of parapsychology research, a researcher may account for the knowledge of the death of the person by the dying individual through telepathic communication. The fact that the family knew someone close to the dying person had died could have been transmitted telepathically to the patient.

Lawrence (1997) conducted a research study in an electrophysiology laboratory (EPS) at a major hospital in Connecticut. From previous research it was known 30% of the EPS patients would become unconscious. Of those unconscious patients, 30% would have an out-of-body or near-death experience. An electronic message machine was placed high overhead making it only visible to someone at that height, anticipating one of the patients would be able to report on the message.

William G. Roll (1926 – 2012), noted psychologist and parapsychologist, warned to not share the content of the message with the EP staff. In parapsychological research, telepathic communication is one variable that is controlled. It might be possible a staff person in the EP lab who knew the message could transmit that knowledge to the patient telepathically. Any knowledge of the message could be ascribed to a telepathic communication as opposed to an out-of-body visualization of the sign.

Other researchers point out nonverbal cues by those knowledgeable of the significant person's death being withheld could have informed the dying person. Matsumoto, Frank, and Hwang (2012) define nonverbal communication as the transmission of messages without words. That transmission can be through body language which includes eye movements, facial expressions, body movements, as well as the clothes worn and general manner of dress. It is possible, thus, for someone to receive messages that someone has died from nonverbal communication.

If the dying person had asked about a sick friend or relative, the family could have avoided the topic, averted their eye gaze, lowered their voices, and avoided brightly colored clothes in mourning for that person. These nonverbal cues would have sent a message that not all was well with the person being discussed. From there, the dying person could have surmised the ill person had died.

More conclusive accounts of these deathbed communications are offered by Barrett, with descriptions of dying persons seeing someone in the family who had died but the information had not been sent to the family. No one in contact with the dying person knew the family member had died, thus unable to communicate the information telepathically or through nonverbal communication.

> Between forty and fifty years ago a young girl, a near connection of mine, was dying of consumption. She had lain for some days in a prostrate condition taking no notice of anything. When she opened her eyes, and looking upwards, she said slowly, "Susan, and Jane, and Ellen," as if recognizing the presence of her three sisters, who had previously died of the same disease. Then after a short pause she continued, "and Edward too!" naming a brother then supposed to be alive and well in India, as if surprised at seeing him in the company. She said no more, and sank shortly afterwards. In the course of the post, letters came from India announcing the death of Edward, from an accident a week or two previous to the death of his sister (p. 31).

Another explanation for these visions of the dead is the psychological need for the dying to obtain comfort and support. In one case I interviewed a hospice patient who described his wife's brother perfectly from his deathbed vision. He had never met his brother-in-law and had never seen a picture of him. The family had cut off connections with this relative and no one spoke of him. However, the dying man was able to give an accurate description of him and have a conversation with him. Since he had not ever met the brother-in-law and lacked any emotional ties, the reason for his appearance was unknown, but certainly not based on an emotional connection.

Deathbed communications seen by others

Occasionally family members and health professionals also are privy to the deathbed communication. Here is an example put forth by Barrett (1926).

> Mrs. Wilson (a professional nurse) was pretty well worn out with her long vigil, believing that Mrs. Rogers was dying, she was naturally very nervous and timid and, having heard Mrs. R. speak frequently of seeing her departed friends, etc., she had a feeling of expectancy and dread with regard to supernatural visitations. Between two and three a.m., while her daughter was asleep, and while she was resting on the settee but wide awake, she happened to look toward the door into the adjoining chamber and saw a man standing exactly in the doorway, the door being kept open all the time.

> His expression was grave, neither stern nor pleasant, and he seemed to look straight at Mrs. Wilson and then at Mrs. Rogers without moving.

> Mrs. Wilson had initially been frightened by the apparition thinking a live man had entered the house. The apparition left within a minute or two. In the morning she checked all the doors and windows which still were securely shut and locked. When Mrs. Wilson described this apparition to the patient's niece, she said it was the exact description of Mrs. Rogers' first husband (p.61-62).

Processing deathbed communications

Many families have accounts of deathbed communications occurring to family members or close friends when they were near death. These events are typically kept within the family system for discussion and transmission to younger family members. For members of these families, deathbed communications are at least familiar.

For some patients and family members, as well as health professionals, these deathbed communications are new and unnerving. As discussed in Chapter 2, we all carry a world view made up of facts, theories, and beliefs that help us interpret life experiences. This world view comes from information learned from family members, religions, schools, books, television, and so forth.

Deathbed communications can be interpreted in many ways, depending upon an individual's world view. Medical training will often lead a person to describe these communications as hallucinations consistent with psychopathology or at the least thought confusion. Family members will often feel the dying person is now "crazy." Well-meaning family members or visitors might make comments like, "He is confused," or "She's out of it now," or "She's losing it." There is no evidence that deathbed communications are associated with psychopathology. Interestingly, the dying person does not have that notion. They are generally convinced of the reality of the event as being a visit from someone who has died.

According to the studies carried out by Osis and Haraldsson and Lawrence and Repede, the individuals having these experiences have been and continue to be alert, oriented, and of sound mind.

When being close to a person who is dying, whether a family member, friend, or health professional, it is important to have positive regard for the dying person's experience. One of the first steps in processing the deathbed communication in a helpful way is to normalize it for all involved. There is no need to try to identify its cause. We, at this point in time, do not understand the cause. What we do know is millions of people, who are in good mental health, have these experiences. It is not only OK to have these experiences, it is a positive event.

Secondly, it is important to validate the person's experience. The person may be seeing deceased friends or relatives, having visions of angels or religious figures, or hearing beautiful music. It is important to acknowledge the dying person's experience even though we are not sharing that experience.

The third step is to allow the person who is having the experience to talk freely about what they see, hear, and feel. When someone is dying, they want to be connected emotionally with those who are close friends and family members before their transition. Encouraging the person to talk about the deathbed communication maintains that closeness. Telling the person to not talk about it or to dismiss it, creates distance.

Here is an example from the book, *Final Gifts* (1992), of a positive interaction with someone who is seeing someone not alive.

> Martha described several visitors unseen by others. She knew most
> of them - her parents and sisters, all of whom were dead, but couldn't
> identify a child who appeared with them. That didn't bother her.

"Don't worry," she told me. "I'll figure it out before I go, or I'll find out when I get there. Have you seen them?"

"No, I haven't," I said. "But I believe that you do." (validation)

"Are they here now?" (encouraging the conversation)

"They left a little while ago," Martha said. "They don't stay all the time. They just come and go."

"What is it like when they are here?" I asked. (emotional impact)

"Well, sometimes we talk, but usually I just know that they're here," Martha said. "I know that they love me, and that they'll be here with me when it's time."

"When it's time...?"

"When I die," Martha said matter-of-factly (p. 89).

Documentation of the events

It is valuable for family members and practitioners to keep track of transpersonal events as they occur. These events document the stages and transition the ill or dying person is experiencing that impact on his or her emotional well-being. As a person experiences less anxiety and discomfort, he or she requires less medication. Less medication enables an ill or dying person to be more present with loved ones.

Table I Characteristics of a deathbed communication

1. Can be visual, auditory, or kinesthetic
2. Can involve seeing deceased friends, relatives, places, or religious figures
3. The experience occurs in the dying person's environment
4. Occurs for a short, limited period of time
5. Dying person is generally otherwise oriented to time, place, and people
6. Impact is emotionally and spiritually positive

Table II Helpful communication with someone having a deathbed communication

1. Create a client-centered approach by asking the dying person or family members to describe who they encountered
2. Bracket all preconceived ideas, listening to the description of the experience
3. Listen for visual, auditory, and/or kinesthetic description, asking for details when appropriate
4. Validates the dying person's experience
5. Normalizes the experience
6. Assesses the emotional impact

Table III Documentation of the deathbed communication

1. The time and length of the occurrence
2. The type of experience, visual, auditory, or kinesthetic
3. Description of what occurred
4. Hours or days before death
5. Emotional impact including facial expressions
6. Need for less pain and anti-anxiety medication

CHAPTER 9

CHOOSING THE
TIME OF DEATH

Keywords: Cardiopulmonary resuscitation (CPR), broken-heart syndrome, Lazarus syndrome, morgue, pronouncement, resuscitation

A woman traveled to see her 90-year-old mother, Sophie, who had fallen at home and was now in a rehabilitation hospital. She needed physical therapy to improve her walking and was being treated for pneumonia. She was ill but was expected to recover. After spending almost a week with her mother, the woman decided to go back home. She had had long talks with her mother about her finances and therapy. Sophie was reluctant to participate in the therapy but understood it was necessary for her well-being. She kept saying, she had had a good run.

Other family members and friends visited with Sophie. She was alert and oriented for the next week but continued to refuse treatment. Then Sophie's granddaughter, the woman's daughter, came to be with her grandmother. She called her mother to say death was coming close. The woman called Sophie's doctor about hospice. The doctor said Sophie was sick but not terminal, was expected to recover, and did not need hospice care. That was a Monday. The woman drove the two-day trip to see her mother anyway, arriving on Thursday.

When she arrived, Sophie was unresponsive. The woman sat next to her mother rubbing her arm, telling her she was there. Sophie died 24 hours after her grandson arrived and 45 minutes after her daughter came back (Lawrence, 2014).

I n spite of a diagnosis that was medically treatable, Sophie chose her time to die. Even though unresponsive, she waited for her grandson and her daughter to arrive before she died. According to our biological paradigm, death occurs when specific bodily functions stop working. Those bodily functions are controlled by intricate physiological and physical relationships. However, in actual dying situations, other factors seem to influence the time of death. There appears to be an ability on the part of the dying person to choose the moment of death. Individuals may choose to wait until family members arrive or choose to die when everyone has left them alone in their room. The following is a report by a nurse working in long-term care of a patient who waited until everyone left her room.

> One patient and her family stand out. The husband would not leave her side for a couple of days. His children, grandchildren, and I, all pleaded with him to go with them to their house (literally 2 minutes away) if to do nothing else but to shower, change, and brush his teeth.

> Thankfully, he agreed to do just that. He came back and she was still with us, which made him realize that his leaving would not cause or stop her from going. The family all gathered around again and then later left. The husband stayed behind. He told me he was running to the vending machine downstairs and that he'd be right back while the CNA's tended to the patient. It was no sooner than the elevator doors closed that the CNA came to me and said the patient had passed. I know she was waiting for him to leave (Allnurses, 2013).

Some subjects near death will report being pulled back by prayers or pleadings from family members. Some patients who experience sudden near death, or an episode of unconsciousness, report going through the tunnel toward a light and hearing family members calling to them to come back. Moody describes the report of an elderly aunt who complained to relatives their prayers were keeping her from staying in the afterlife. She told them to stop praying and, when they did, she was able to leave her body permanently (Moody, 2011).

However, some patients do not seem to be influenced by the presence or lack of presence of friends and relatives. To date, there is no systematic research on the number of patients who wait for friends and/or relatives to arrive or leave before dying to know even an estimated incidence of these occurrences.

During near-death experiences (NDEs) there are reports also of patients who chose to come back to their lives and those who are told to come back by a higher power. The following is a report by Lawrence (1997) of the decision by one woman to come back from her NDE.

> I heard them talking about the baby's heart rate being low. The next thing I knew I was above everyone. I watched them scurrying frantically, checking my blood pressure, giving me oxygen. I soon noticed a dark area and started walking toward it. I saw my mother who had recently died and was so happy to see her. She called me to her. As I started walking away, I looked back at my husband. I knew he would feel bad about me not being with him but I thought he would get over it. I assumed the baby had died. I started walking toward my mother again. I felt wonderful, totally at peace. Then I remembered my son, Todd, who was four at the time. I knew I couldn't leave him. I had to go back to take care of him. The next thing I remember was being back in my body, feeling the labor pains. Soon my daughter was born. She was fine (p.122).

Characteristically, the person close to death does not consider if his or her body is functioning well enough to support life while making the choice to come back. The deliberation to stay in the perceived afterlife or to come back into their body often involves a purpose or responsibility needing to be met in their life. To date, there are no reports of someone considering if they could not go back because their body was too ill or damaged to support life. It may be the level of consciousness they are experiencing indicates adequate bodily function. One of Moody's (2001) subjects believed once he got back into his body, he was able to repair his body by stopping the bleeding, enabling it to support his life.

During an NDE a person can be told they must go back, that it is not their time yet. This message can be given by a deceased relative, friend, or an angel, or God-like figure. In our biological paradigm, the message could theoretically include something that says their body is still functioning so they could return.

During near-death visits or apparitions of angels, grim reapers, and shadow people, a person also seems to be able to choose to not die by sending these entities away. We know during episodes when these entities appear, the individual is or has been near death. Health professionals are supporting biological life during this time. The exact relationship between the choice to not die at a certain time or be sent back to live and the condition of the body is unclear. We do not know if the body must be able to sustain life in order for the person to return to fulfill their purpose. It is unknown if during an NDE, when a person chooses to return or is told he or she most return, there is a physiological change in the body enabling that return. In other words, a person may have been pronounced dead. In their perception of the afterlife, they choose to return to their body or are told they must return, what happens to the non functioning body that makes it function again? In most cases we have assumed, there was an error in the diagnosis of death. Another possibility is there was no error in the diagnosis. The choice or the directive to return somehow enabled the body to regain its ability to function.

Providing support and guidance

If a person is told they must come back, that it is not their time to die, that person may be upset or angry when awakened. This is not unusual but can be difficult for loved ones to experience. The loved ones have been anxiously hovering over the person close to death, worried about their survival. The critically ill person may have had an NDE and felt wonderful. Both parties need to become aware of the others' experiences.

Sometimes it is difficult to encourage a loved one to die when the loss will be great. It is important that all who are present be supportive of the dying person. It is a great gift to a dying person knowing family and friends and even caregivers are able to release him or her. Saying good-byes and holding the person's hand or providing other physical contact can be helpful. It is important to check for unfinished business and to assure the person whatever needs to be done, will be done. Assessment of whether the person wants to be alone or with others during that time and respecting those wishes provides comfort and support.

Table I Helpful communication with the dying choosing his or her time of death

1. Encourage communication about choices being made
2. Assess who the person wants to be present if death is to occur
3. Determine if there is any unfinished business
4. Respect the person's desire to be alone or have others present

Table II Documentation of the experience

1. The person's physical and mental condition at the time of near death
2. Description of what occurred
3. Immediate emotional response by loved ones to the death

Spouses who die soon after each other

There are many reports of couples who have lived together for years and have loving, caring marriages. In some cases, the connection seems so strong, they die within hours or days of each other, even without medical cause.

Donald Dix, 85, collapsed at home in Cardiff in the UK. His wife, Rosemary, to whom he had been married for 56 years, called for an ambulance. Mrs. Dix, 76, stayed home to call her daughters when the ambulance took her husband to the hospital. She then collapsed at home and died about the same time her husband died in the ambulance. The daughters described the couple as inseparable although physically doing well. Their deaths were unexpected. Mr. Dix was recovering well from the flu and Mrs. Dix had been planting heather in the front garden and chatting with the neighbors (Salkeld, 2011).

Ruth (89) and Harold Knapke (91) were married for 65 years. They lived in Fort Recovery, Ohio, when Ruth became ill. Their children told Mr. Knapke that Mrs. Knapke was not expected to recover from her illness. He became upset and agitated for a few days and then calm. Their family said they were a very close couple. Harold Knapke died on August 11 at 7:30 a.m. and Ruth Knapke died the same day at 6:30 p.m. (Kindela, 2013).

Younger couples

Olga Whitfield, 61, of West Boldon, South Tyneside, died at home on October 18, 2009. When her husband Stewart, 56, called for an ambulance, he was instructed on how to perform CPR. When the ambulance arrived they found both Olga and her husband, Stewart, dead at their home. The postmortem examinations showed Mrs. Whitfield to have kidney infections and an abscess, although the conditions were not said to be serious enough to cause immediate death. Mr. Whitfield had an enlarged, scarred, and diseased heart. It was believed the stress of his wife's death and the CPR lead to heart failure. The family described the couple as completely devoted to each other (Sims, 2009).

There are some cases where a death occurred to one spouse who did not know their husband or wife had recently died.

Frank (87) and Eleanor Turner (87) were married for nearly 65 years before they died six hours apart on November 29, 2013 near Charlotte, NC. Eleanor had died in the morning in hospice care and nine hours later Frank died of respiratory failure. He had not been told his wife had died (Arriero, 2013).

Les (94) and Helen (94) Brown were married for 75 years and reported to have a lifetime of love. Les was suffering from Parkinson's disease and had recently gone into a coma state, unaware of his external environment. He was only expected to live a few more days. Helen had stomach cancer but was not imminently dying and expected to live for several months. Helen died on July 16 and Les the next day (Ruiz, 2013).

Explanation

Some experts believe close deaths of spouses can be due to a variety of causes ranging from the spiritual intertwining of souls to severe grief response. Many doctors and scientists attribute these deaths to the physical stress of losing a loved one. This phenomenon is often referred to as the broken-heart syndrome, or Takotsubo cardiomyopathy. This syndrome results in the left ventricle of the heart taking on a balloon-like appearance. It is believed to be triggered by severe emotional stress appearing primarily in postmenopausal women. It is also a reversible occurrence (Nykamp & Titak, 2010). Studies have shown widows and widowers are at least 30% more likely to die with the six months following a spouse's death.

Dr. David Casarett of the University of Pennsylvania Health Care System has seen spouses die within days or weeks of each other at their hospice care center. Why it happens is still under investigation (Carroll, 2013).

Providing support and guidance

Since it is known 30% of surviving spouses die within six months of each other, it is crucial to determine the impact of the first spouse's death on the other. Grief can be overwhelming, both psychologically and physiologically. However, the severity of grief is generally limited. There also might be survivor guilt. It is important the living spouse be provided with support and comfort and understands of the limits of grief. It is also important all concerned realize the surviving spouse, especially the elderly, is at risk for an early death and may need medical assistance during this time. If a person does have a choice about the time of death, that choice should be made seeing the realistic alternatives.

Table III Helpful communication

1. Encourage discussion about the limits of grief with surviving spouse
2. Assess physical responses as well as psychological ones
3. Provide information about what is known to happen in other cases
4. Provide assistance about living or dying being an informed choice for surviving spouses.

Table IV Documentation of the death and reactions

1. The person's physical and mental condition at the time of the occurrence
2. Description of what occurred
3. Immediate emotional response to the occurrence

Pronounced dead but still alive

> Louise was a 56-year-old woman who had come to the emergency room in a large metropolitan hospital in Connecticut because of an asthma attack. She progressed to severe respiratory distress and ultimately to an electromechanical dissociation (EMD) cardiac arrest. A code was announced and for over 20 minutes the code team attempted to resuscitate her. While there was some electrical activity on the monitor, the heart was not responding. For more than 20 minutes she had no pulse and no blood pressure. Her breathing was supported by a ventilator. All the monitoring equipment indicated Louise was not responding to any of the resuscitation attempts, so the code was stopped and all the equipment shut off. The doctor called the family and began filling out the death certificate. Ten minutes later, as the nurse prepared Louise to be seen by the family, she started breathing on her own. In a flurry of excitement, the equipment was reapplied and efforts to support her life continued (Lawrence, 1997, p. 148).

Louise agreed to an interview after this event. In spite of a lack of pulse and blood pressure for an extended period of time and being pronounced dead, she was alert and oriented to her surroundings. During this episode Grace could hear people calling her but was not sure to whom the voices belonged. She remembered being in a dark place, maybe a room that contained a coffin she knew was hers. She saw a friend of her son who had died three or four years earlier and a friend of hers who had died during the past year. She was told by both of them it wasn't her time and she had to go back.

Louise said this was the second time this type of experience had happened to her. Her main concern after being brought back was a lack of clarity about her purpose. The first time she came back she knew she needed to take care of her children. This time she was not sure what her purpose would be.

Babies who come back after being pronounced dead

Australian mom, Kate Ogg, gave birth to premature twins, a boy named Jamie, and his twin sister, Emily. Ogg was told her son had died even though resuscitation efforts had been made. The nurses gave baby Jamie to Ogg to hold across her bare chest. This skin-to-skin contact, also known as "kangaroo care," is widely practiced throughout the world.

The Oggs wanted him to know how much his parents loved him. Jamie made some startled movements after five minutes. The Oggs were told by the doctor those were reflex movements. The movements became stronger but again the doctor confirmed the child was dead and the movements were nothing more than reflexes.

The Oggs held the baby for two hours when suddenly the baby opened his eyes. Kate put a drop of breast milk on her finger and Jamie sucked on it happily. At this time, the hospital personnel continued to refuse to contact the doctor, reinforcing his position the baby was dead. While the Oggs urged hospital personnel to summon him, they were repeatedly told what they were seeing was still just reflex from a baby already declared dead. Finally the doctor returned, checked Jamie's heart rate with his stethoscope and agreed he was alive, as unbelievable as that was (Inbar, 2014).

Robin Cyr delivered her fourth child at a Halifax Hospital March, 2014. The baby girl weighed 9 pounds, 14 ounces. Because of difficulties with the baby being wedged in the birth canal, she showed no signs of life. She was pronounced dead at birth. About 25 minutes later, the baby started breathing on her own. The doctors have no explanation other than to call the incident a miracle (Walsh, 2014).

Adults who came back after being pronounced dead

Anthony Yahle, 37, had been having some difficulty breathing. His wife, a nurse, called for the ambulance to come to their home when she found he had no pulse. He was pronounced dead at Kettering Medical Center in Ohio after a 45-minute attempt to resuscitate him. When his son heard what had happened, he ran to his father's beside and said, "Dad, you're not going to die today." Soon there were electrical movements on the cardiac monitor. Five days later, Anthony Yahle was back home with his family (Lupkin, 2014).

Val Thomas (59) suffered two heart attacks, had no pulse, and had no brain waves for 17 hours. Rigor mortis had set in. She was placed on a ventilator while the possibility of organ transplant was discussed. To everyone's shock and amazement Val woke up and started talking. She was transferred from this West Virginia hospital to the Cleveland Clinic for further evaluation. The doctors there said they could find nothing wrong. Val was concerned about her purpose. "I know God has something in store for me, another purpose," Val Thomas said. "I don't know what it is, but I'm sure he'll tell me (FoxNews, 2008)."

Walter Williams, 78, was pronounced dead by the local coroner at his home in Lexington, Mississippi. He was put in a body bag and taken to the funeral home. When they were getting ready to embalm him, he started kicking inside the body bag. The coroner said in his 12 years of service, he had never seen anything like that. Williams was rushed to the hospital where it was surmised his pacemaker may have shut down and then started working again. Williams did die two weeks later (Moisse, 2014).

Definition of death

In 1978, the Uniform Brain Death Act was passed to institute criteria for determining biological death. It was established that irreversible cessation of all functioning of the brain, including the brain stem, is death. In addition, irreversible cessation of circulatory and respiratory functions may be used as an alternative standard for determining death (Uniform Law Commission, 2014).

In earlier times, equipment to monitor heart rate, cardiac output, blood oxygen levels, and electric heart activity was severely lacking. However, for more than a few decades equipment has been available to measure cardiac function and blood oxygen level in great detail. A doppler can be used during resuscitation to measure cardiac output. EEG equipment can be also used to detect brain functioning.

In spite of more sophisticated cardiac and brain activity monitoring equipment, individuals who were pronounced dead have come back to life. This happens with enough frequency to be referred to as the Lazarus phenomenon or Lazarus syndrome. According to Adhiyaman, Adhiyaman & Sundaram (2007), the Lazarus phenomenon is the delayed return of spontaneous circulation (ROSC) after cessation of cardiopulmonary resuscitation (CPR) (p. 552). The authors, from an analysis of 38 cases in the literature, found 82% of the 28 patients with recorded time intervals, exhibited spontaneous circulation within 10 minutes of cessation of resuscitation. While it is possible the delay of 10 minutes or longer could be due to dynamic hyperinflation, current explanations for the phenomena are considered inadequate (Maleck, Piper, Triem, Boldt & Zittel (1998).

These cases are seen as separate from NDEs, although some individuals who were pronounced dead will report having an NDE. Not all individuals who have NDEs are pronounced dead – some in fact are not close to dying. Most have momentary cessation of cardiac or respiratory functions which are restored quickly and not leading to a death pronouncement.

In his book, *Proof of Heaven*, Eban Alexander describes the primitive parts of his brain that controlled breathing/heart rate as fully functioning during his seven-day coma. As a neurosurgeon he could tell by the brain scans, lab numbers, and neurological exams he reviewed after his recovery, the functions of his brain that enabled thought and awareness had not been operating. During that time, he had an NDE during which he could see, hear, and think. He concludes the following:

> The part of my brain that years of medical school had taught me was responsible for creating the world I lived and moved in and for taking the raw data that came in through my senses and fashioning it into a meaningful universe: that part of my brain was down, and out. And yet despite all of this, I had been alive, and aware, truly aware, in a universe characterized above all by love, consciousness, and reality.... What I'd experienced was more real than the house I sat in, more real than the logs burning in the fireplace. Yet there was no room for that reality in the medically trained scientific worldview that I'd spent years acquiring (p. 129-130).

Dr. Alexander fully recovered from his illness.

Summary

The determination of the time of death described in this chapter shows the influences of our biological, psychological, and transpersonal natures. The physical health of the individual can lead to death but the descriptions seem to indicate psychological influences, like being called to by family members, waiting to see loved ones can influence the time of death. Coming back after being pronounced dead, currently assessed by known physiological indicators, can be due to transpersonal phenomena yet to be understood. How all these factors interact with each other is a mystery yet to be solved.

Table 5
Providing support

In many cases, these individuals will want to explore the purpose of their survival. It is natural to want to know why they were saved and what path to take at this juncture point. We know little of the emotional aftereffects of awakening in a body bag at the morgue. Some of these individuals may have fear reactions that could be assisted with counseling.

Table VI Helpful communication

1. Encourage communication about any aspect of the experience
2. Assist with communication about life purposes
3. Assess the emotional impact, particularly fears associated being in the morgue if that occurred
4. Provide resources, including references about life purposes

Table VII Documentation of the apparition

1. The person's physical and mental condition at the time of the occurrence
2. Description of what occurred
3. Immediate emotional response to the occurrence

CHAPTER 10

MISCELLANEOUS OCCURRENCES AT THE TIME OF DEATH

Keyword: Cutis anserine (goose bumps), hands reaching down, glowing faces, mist, music, shared death experience, ultraviolet light, veridical perception

A hospice patient, ill with cancer, was finishing dressing in preparation for a check-up with his oncologist. His daughter was with him in his room as he gathered up his things, including his transition (photochromatic) glasses. As they walked to the door of the bedroom, the man collapsed falling to the floor against his daughter. She held him in her arms as he lay dying. At the moment of death, his transition glasses turned from clear to dark as if in the presence of ultraviolet (UV) light (Lawrence, 2010).

Photochromatic lenses contain substances such as silver chloride or silver halide, invisible to the naked eye when UV light is absent. The energy from the sun includes visible light that we can see easily. The sun's energy also includes light with longer wavelengths (infrared light) and light with shorter wavelengths (ultraviolet light) that are not visible to the naked eye. Inside a house or car, out of UV light, these photochromatic glasses remain clear. In the presence of UV light, like direct sunlight, a chemical reaction occurs that absorbs portions of the light, leading to the darkening of the lenses.

When the photochromatic lenses changed indoors as this father was dying, ultraviolet light was present. It is theoretically possible this ultraviolet light came from something leaving the body. Another explanation offered is something brought ultraviolet light into the room.

Miscellaneous occurrences

The presence of ultraviolet light is only one of the occurrences happening near death or at the time of death as yet thoroughly investigated. Some family members see a radiant glow on the dying person's face at the time of death. Other family members and patients see the presence of light in the rooms of dying patients. Some dying individuals experience a sudden awakening and burst of energy right before the moment of death. Family, friends, and healthcare professionals have reported what appears to be mist or smoke leaving the body when the person dies. Others report the dying person sees hands coming down to reach out toward them. Yet others hear music. As of yet the incidence, relevance, and impact of these experiences are not well documented but they do occur to many individuals.

Radiant faces and the presence of light

There are reports of some hospice patients having a golden glow on their face at the time of death. Previous to this event, the individual usually looked gaunt or ill. This glow creates a dramatic change in the dying person's appearance, with family members reporting how much younger the person looks. What percentages of individuals have this experience at the time of death is unknown. It seems to be an underreported phenomenon. Here is one woman's description of her mother:

> "They put in her teeth. She looked as if forty years had been taken off her. She hadn't a line on her face. She looked beautiful. I have to say absolutely beautiful" (Donnelly & Battley, (2010).

Fenwick and Fenwick (1996) describe a light present in the dying person's room, not just radiating on the person's face. This light is often described as comforting but also sad to be left behind.

Suddenly there was the most brilliant light shining from my husband's chest, and as this light lifted upwards, there was the most beautiful music and singing voices, my own chest seemed filled with infinite joy and my heart felt as if it was lifting to join this light and music. Suddenly, there was a hand on my shoulder and a nurse said "I'm sorry love. He has just gone." I lost sight of the light and music, I felt so bereft at being left behind (p. 266).

What this light is, is unknown. Many family members are deeply moved by the change in appearance of the dying person. They interpret the glow as changes occurring as the soul departs the body. Some family members who see the presence of light believe they are in the presents of spirits, angels, or spirit guides. Some are moved to a change in belief about life after death.

Bursts of energy just before death

Another phenomenon that occurs at the time of death is a remarkable burst of energy in the dying person. That type of occurrence is reported frequently but with no exact percentage of incidences. Sometimes, one or two days before death, or right before dying, the dying person will be more alert and talkative. They may have been unconscious before this occurred and now are actively engaged with individuals in their environment. Family members often become hopeful their loved one is improving. This is a temporary condition with just enough time for family and friends to have more conversation.

Sir William Barrett documented this occurrence to a sergeant during the American Civil War in 1862.

The man was dying and all the afternoon he could only speak in whispers; his father was sent for, and at 11 pm Sergeant Adams to all appearance died. ... Dr. Ormsby ... returned to the bedside, intending to close the eyes of Adams, who he thought had expired. Dr. Ormsby then states: "As I reached towards the bedside the supposed dead man looked suddenly up in my face, and said, 'Doctor, what day is it?' I told him the day of the month, and he answered, 'That is the day I died.' His father had sprung to the bedside, and Adams turning his eyes on him said, 'Father, our boys have taken Fort Henry, and Charlie (his brother) isn't hurt. I've seen mother and the children, and they are well.' He then gave comprehensive directions regarding his funeral, speaking of the corpse as 'my body' and occupying, I should think, as much as five minutes. He then turned towards me and again said, 'Doctor, what day is it?' and I answered him as before. He again repeated, 'That's the day I died,' and instantly was dead. His tones were quite full and distinct, and so loud as to be readily heard in the adjoining room, and were so heard by Mrs. Ormsby" (pp. 72-73).

Burst of energy and glowing

In some cases there are reports of an increase in alertness and the radiance occurring together right before the time of death. This event was reported by Frances Power Cobbe (1822-1904) in 1882. Ms. Cobbe was an Irish writer and leading women's suffragist. She was an activist and ahead of her times formed a marriage with another woman. She was a member of a prominent family descended from Archbishop Charles Cobbe, Primate of Ireland. Her essay, *The Peak in Darien: The Riddle of Death*, includes various experiences individuals have at the moment of death. She preceded Barrett in describing deathbed visions, veridical perceptions, and this energy and radiant occurrences before death. This is an account of her brother's dying moments.

As the tardy dawn of the winter morning revealed the rigid features of the countenance from which life and intelligence seemed to have quite departed, those who watched him felt uncertain whether he still lived; but suddenly, while they went over him to ascertain the truth, he opened his eyes wide, and gazed eagerly upward with such an unmistakable expression of wonder and joy that a thrill of awe passed through all who witnessed it. His whole face grew bright with a strange gladness, while the eloquent eyes seemed literally to shine, as if reflecting some light on which they gazed. He remained in this attitude of delighted surprise for some minutes, then in a moment the eyelids fell, the head drooped forward, and with one long breath the spirit departed (pp. 258-259).

Explanations

Researchers at George Washington University Hospital in Washington, D.C. reported a spike in brain activity moments before death.

Seven patients who were conscious and made the decision to withdraw care because of extensive illness were monitored with bispectral index (BIS) monitors or patient state index (PSI) to measure levels of consciousness. These values are derived from the EEG to measure levels of consciousness. There was loss of blood pressure and a decline in BIS/PSI activity initially. As the researchers monitored the changes associated with removing treatments and the patients drew closer to death, they noticed a spike in BIS/PSI activity typically associated with consciousness (Chawla, Akst, Junker, Jacobs, & Seneff, 2009).

The researchers believe the loss of oxygen to the brain neurons causes this spiking. The researchers believe this spiking may account for near-death or out-of-body experiences. Near-death experiences are not always associated with imminent death. It may be that this spiking may explain the increase in activity in the terminally ill and possibly the radiant effect. However, PSI and BIS values have not been found in some research studies to be adequate to detect awareness in individual patients (Schneider, Gelb, Schmeller, Tschakert & Kochs, 2003). Much more investigation needs to be carried out in this area before conclusions can be drawn with certainty.

Hearing music

Hearing music is a common experience during a transpersonal experience associated with near death or dying. Individuals who have deathbed communications and near-death experiences often report hearing beautiful music, described as indescribably beautiful. Also interesting is the incidence of veridical perceptions associated with this music and the incidence of shared death experience. In the shared death experience, not only does the person near death have the experience, in this case hearing music, but those around them do also.

Hearing music and veridical perception

Several years later, Mrs. Z. became very ill and expected to die; she was, however, perfectly composed and in the full possession of her senses, and was anxious to arrange some business affairs. For this purpose her husband came to her bedside and talked over these matters with her. Suddenly she changed the subject and said to her husband, "Do you hear those voices singing?" Col. Z., who narrates the incident, replied that he did not, and his wife continued, "I have heard them several times today and I am sure they are the angels welcoming me to Heaven, but,' she added, "it is strange, there is one voice among them I am sure I know, but I cannot remember whose voice it is." Suddenly she stopped and said, pointing straight over her husband's head, "Why, there she is in the corner of the room; it is Julia X. She is coming on; she is leaning over you; she has her hands up; she is praying. Do look; she is going." Her husband turned round but could see nothing. His wife then said, "She has gone" (Barrett, p 780).

Hearing music during a deathbed communication was at first believed by her husband to be just a hallucination of a dying person. Two days after his wife heard this music, Colonel Z. read in the newspaper that Julia, of whom Mrs. Z had spoken, had died. He later learned she had been singing on and on until her death.

Music during a near-death experience

Fenwick & Fenwick (2008) report 20% of the people who contacted them about their NDEs, said they heard music. Most will report the music as beautiful and/or heavenly, but historically there is lack of clarification about what that means. Some have said the heavenly music may be associated with traditional church music. Also, sometimes the experiencers will report hearing just music but not voices, or the reverse, or a combination of voices with music. Here is an example of a woman hearing music during her NDE:

I too felt this lovely feeling after an operation. I remember going into a tunnel. At the end of it was a very bright light. I heard beautiful music, something I'd never heard before: saw people standing around, all being happy with one another. Someone turned to me and said, 'She's not ready to come to us yet.' I remember coming around in a side ward and asking a nurse where the music came from. She looked at me with a funny look. But there was no music near the room (pp. 86-87).

Music with a shared death experience

One of the more interesting cases of shared death experience was described by Barrett (2011).

> More than one person attending the dying person heard the music but some did not. Just after dear Mrs. L's death between 2 and 3 am, I heard a most sweet and singular strain of singing outside the windows; it died away after passing the house. All in the room (except Mr. L.) heard it, and the medical attendant who was still with us, went to the window, as I did and looked out, but there was nobody. It was a bright and beautiful night. It was as if several voices were singing in perfect unison a most sweet melody which died away in the distance. Two persons had gone from the room to fetch something and were coming upstairs at the back of the house and could hear the singing and stopped, saying, 'What is that singing?' They could not naturally, have heard any sound from outside the windows in the front of the house from where they were at the back (p. 76).

The investigation of music in parapsychology is called paramusicology. There are a number of books and articles on the use of music as targets in parapsychological research studies. Also there are multiple descriptions of paranormal manifestations of music published in the *Journal of the Society for Psychical Research* (Willin, 1996; 1997; 1999).

Fenwick and Fenwick (2008) believe the right temporal lobe is involved in hearing beautiful music. If the right temporal lobe is damaged, there should be an inability to hear music at the time of death. In 1962, Milner reported a decrease in the ability of patients after a right temporal lobectomy on scores of loudness, time, timbre, and tonal memory on the Seashore Measure of Musical Talents. One of the criticisms of explanations for transpersonal occurrences being due to physiological or physical changes has been the fact that all individuals with these changes do not have these events. Only approximately 15% of individuals who are close to death, for example, will have an NDE. Presenting a physical disability, like a right temporal lobe disruption, can help explain why transpersonal phenomena only occur to a certain percentage of individuals. In the case of hearing music, others have found the right temporal lobe may not be as significant as previously thought to be in our ability to hear music.

In a more recent study (1996) by Atsushi Koike, et al., no difference on scores of the Seashore Measures of Musical Talents was found between patients undergoing right temporal lobectomy versus patients undergoing left temporal lobectomy for severe seizure disorders. The times of onset of the seizures and their severity were more significant influences on hearing music.

We know family and friends who have no known terminal illness, present at the time of death of a loved one, also hear music. The biological explanations do not explain the incidence of hearing music not objectively present by the dying person and those present at the time of death.

Raising hands

Lawrence (2010) describes the events of a dying patient as told to her by the patient's wife. The hospice patient had had a near-death experience years before being stricken with cancer. He was not afraid of death, in fact anticipated he would experience the same joy again. The wife said during the time of his death he lifted up his arms toward the ceiling. He told his wife he was raising his hands toward those he saw coming down. He died within a few moments. His wife also said she saw mist leave his body as he took his final breath.

In a research study of hospice patients at the time of death, Lawrence & Repede (2013) analyzed 60 hospice charts and surveyed 75 hospice nurses about events within 30 days of data collection. The analysis of the 60 hospice charts retrieved three (5%) descriptions of patients who had raised their hands at the time of death. In one case the following notation was found: "Twenty-three minutes before death patient opened eyes and raised his arms up - arms fell and then patient expired" (p. 634).

In the survey of the 75 hospice nurses, 65 said they had seen or heard from family members the patients had lifted up their hands before dying. In all, there were 241 reports of patients raising their hands before death during the previous 30 days. In a month's time, the average hospice nurse surveyed, saw, or was told, about at least 3 patients who raised their hands at the time of death.

Deathbed mist/smoke

As he died, something which is very hard to describe since it was so unexpected and because I had seen nothing like it, left up through his body and out of his head. It resembled distinct delicate waves/lines of smoke (Smoke is not the right word but I have not got a comparison) then disappeared (Fenwick and Fenwick, 2008, p. 161).

It is not unusual for friends and/or relatives and even healthcare professionals to report mist or a smoky form leave the body of a person as they die. An estimate of how often this occurs is unknown. The descriptions are remarkable since they are not only witnessed by those with close emotional ties to the dying person but also healthcare professionals whose first encounter may have been only at the time of death.

Fenwick and Fenwick (2008) report the account by a physician who went over to help a person who had a heart attack on a golf course. While there, the physician saw a "white form rise and separate from the body" (p. 160).

The vision of a mist leaving the body of a dying person is not infrequently a shared death experience. Barrett describes an experience of a dignitary of the church in New South Wales as he and his wife were present at the death of their son.

> ... just as his breathing ceased they both saw "something rise as it were from his face like a delicate veil or mist, and slowly pass away." He adds, "We were deeply impressed and remarked, 'How wonderful! Surely that must be the departure of his spirit.' We were not at all distracted so as to be mistaken in what we saw" (Barrett, 2011, p. 83).

While reports of this mist or smoky form leaving the body at the time of sustained death are frequent, reports of these occurrences of individuals later describing a near-death experience are rare, if not unreported. For many years, investigators have attempted to photograph paranormal experiences including this mist leaving the body.

In 1939, Kirlian photography was developed. Photographic film placed on top of a conducting plate with another conductor on the object, initially plant life, when energized by high-voltage power produced images with light around the object. Since that time scientists have used this photography in research studies and have elaborated on this technique.

More recently, a Russian scientist, Konstantin Korotkov (2002), developed an advanced technique of Kirlian photography. He calls it an energy imaging technique used to monitor the progress of patients treated for diseases. Energy healers, using techniques like Reiki, and therapeutic touch, have long described the use of life force energy to heal and balance subtle energies within our bodies. Korotkov's techniques are said to measure this life force energy. More recently reports include Korotkov's approaches being used to photograph a person at the moment of his death with a bioelectrographic camera.

In their book, *The Dark Side of the Brain*, Drs. Harry Oldfield and Roger Coghill have joined the ranks of scientists who study bioelectric life fields. This area of study involves the exploration of electromagnetic waves that influence brain mechanisms.

Measurement of weight loss immediately after death

In 1907, Dr. Duncan MacDougall of Haverhill, Massachusetts, believed at the time of death the departed soul would cause a loss of body weight. It was his hypothesis that the soul was made up of matter that had mass and weight. He weighed six patients who were terminally ill immediately before and after death. He weighed these patients using a platform beam scale. Results from two patients were discarded. The average weight loss of the remaining four was from one-half ounce to nearly an ounce and a quarter (MacDougall, 1907). Around the same time MacDougall measured the weight loss of 15 dogs in a similar fashion. He found there was no weight loss amongst the animals. Fundamental to the discussion is the makeup of the soul or spirit, if one does exist. Most of the current research is based on the assumption the soul, spirit or life force is energy, thus not having weight, rather than matter.

Goose bumps, cutis anserine

On occasion, a person near death, or a relative caring for a dying person will report having goose bumps. We know from human physiology that goose bumps are caused by the contraction of tiny muscles at the base of each hair follicle called arrector pili muscles. The release of adrenaline in our bodies during a flight-or-fight experience will cause the contraction of these tiny muscles. As these muscles contract, the hairs usually on the arm or the back of the neck, stand erect. These goose bumps occur when we feel cold, threatened, excited, scared, or deep emotions. This phenomenon is particularly evident in cats that can raise their fur to a great extent during times when they feel threatened.

In the world of psychics, parapsychologists, and new-age practitioners, goose bumps can indicate the closeness of a spirit. Doreen Virtue, author of *Angel Dreams: Healing and Guidance from Your Dreams*, believes chills or goose bumps down one side of your body indicates the presence of angels. Others say the chills or goose bumps indicate a connection with spirit energy and truth. This is also referred to as the quickening of the flesh. It is not an unusual experience for those who witness a death. Individuals who witness the Grim Reaper might feel coldness. That coldness, in conjunction with feeling threatened by the apparition can result in goose bumps being present even when the room is warm.

Helpful communications

All of the above events will lead to questions, concerns, and even transformations when they occur. These miscellaneous experiences are generally not well researched or explained. However, for some experiencers and family members these experiences are quite profound and change their beliefs about life after death. The reports of these events should be received with an openness and validation. The individual having these experiences should be encouraged to discuss the components therein and their meaning ascribed to them. These experiences occur to a number of individuals without indication of any psychopathology. That should be made clear.

In some cases, experiencers can be validated by participating in legitimate research on those experiences. Sharing those research sites may be helpful.

On occasion, a person may wonder why they do not hear music or see a light or see a mist leaving the body when others are able to do so. We do not understand how these events are experienced to some but not others. We do know it is not an indication of rejection by the dying or deceased friend or relative. Some individuals, because of their makeup, are more receptive to these experiences than others.

It is also important to recognize the spiritual aspect of these experiences. It is important to integrate this spiritual or transpersonal aspect into the physical and psychological care of the dying person and their family members.

Table I Helpful communications

1. Establish client-centered communication by encouraging an open description of any event
2. Bracket any preconceived ideas about end-of-life phenomena
3. Listen for visual, auditory, and/or kinesthetic descriptions
4. Normalize the experience
5. Assess the emotional impact
6. Encourage communication with legitimate researchers
7. Provide resources

Table II Documentation of the event

1. The time and place of the event
2. Description of what occurred
3. Immediate emotional response to the occurrence
4. Obtain a visual depiction of the entity when possible

CHAPTER 11

AFTER-DEATH COMMUNICATION

Charlene, a hospice nurse, made her daily visit to Sam to monitor his pain level and his emotional status. He seemed comfortable. Since she had known him, he had been in a hospital bed downstairs in the dining room of his house, his converted bedroom. His wife told Charlene he had finished telling her how to manage the finances in the house, which he had so deftly done all of their 43 years of marriage.

That evening, Charlene was reading in bed before sleep. The phone rang. The evening hospice nurse called to tell her Sam had died. A feeling of sadness covered Charlene. She reached over to turn out the lights, when Sam appeared at the foot of her bed. He had forgotten to tell his wife about insurance papers he had left in an upstairs bureau. Charlene had not been upstairs in the house but Sam gave her specific instructions about the location of the bureau and the papers. Charlene assured him she would visit his wife and find the papers. Sam then left as quickly as he had arrived (Lawrence, 2010).

After the funeral, Charlene followed up with a bereavement visit to Sam's wife. She informed her of the visit she had had from Sam. Curious, they both went upstairs to the bedroom Sam and his wife had shared. Charlene recognized the bureau from Sam's description and found the insurance papers tucked in a book in the middle drawer.

While Charlene had heard of other incidences of after-death communications (ADCs) from family members who had had them, this was her first experience. Because she could verify what was told her by Sam when she found the insurance papers, she was amazed, delighted, and confused at the same time. As a nurse, she had been instructed on the anatomy and physiology of the human body and the pathophysiology of diseases. She had not been instructed on the possibility of being contacted by a person after he had died. And yet, after-death communications (ADCs) are probably the most common of all transpersonal experiences associated with near death and dying and well documented in the literature.

The early researchers often referred to these experiences as hallucinations. Because of the association of the word hallucinations with mental illness, researchers in the 1980s advocated for a different name. Other terms like anomalous, extraordinary experiences were used until after-death communication (ADCs) became the preferred nomenclature.

Early descriptions

In 1889, Henry Sidgwick started a five-year project designed to obtain evidence of telepath during waking hallucinations. With his team and a host of volunteers, 17,000 replies were obtained. Approximately 10% of them answered yes to the question of hearing, seeing, or being touched by something not due to any external cause. These investigators examined the veridicality of the instances when someone reported they knew a person had died before that information was shared with them through objective means (Sidgwick, Johnson, Myers, Podmore, Sidgwick, 1894).

Recent studies

There are many studies of ADCs. The ones described are just a sample of those available. A more complete list of studies is enumerated in Appendix B.

A study of widows and widowers living in Wales in 1971 resulted in a report of more than 50% of all interviewed describing contact with deceased spouses (Rees, 1971).

Grimby (1993; 1998) studied ADCs occurring to the elderly. She found 80% of these elderly subjects reported having contact with the deceased.

Haraldsson (1988) interviewed 100 individuals in Iceland. They reported visual contact with the deceased as being the most common, 59%. The next more common way of contact they reported was sensing a presence (16%).

Their seven-year experience of interviewing 2,000 people who had an ADC, led Bill and Judy Guggenheim (1995) to estimate 50 million people in the US have had this experience. That is compared to the estimated 10 to 15 million who have had an NDE. The Guggenheims approximate 67% of bereaved individuals experience ADCs. ADCs are common in most cultures, but some have a greater openness to communicate these types of experiences.

Arcangel and Schwartz (2005) studied the aftereffects of ADCs on their perceivers. They found 98% of respondents found these experiences comforting.

In 2011, Streit-Horn conducted a systematic review of research on ADCs. She analyzed 35 research studies. From the integrated review we know ADCs occur to approximately 80 to 85% of the recently bereaved. The research to date has focused primarily on the incidence of ADCs and the times of their occurrences.

Description of ADCs

After-death communications are often defined as a direct contact between a bereaved individual (not a dying person) and a deceased person. The word spontaneous is often included in the definition to distinguish between unassisted ADCs and contact made through psychics,, mediums, or even therapists. Spontaneous ADCs frequently occur during the first 24 hours after a loved one's death. Sometimes these ADCs only occur once to a person, but they can occur more frequently, tapering off as time advances.

The Guggenheims describe twelve common types of ADCs: sensing a presence, hearing a voice, feeling a touch, smelling a fragrance, partial appearances, full appearances, ADC visions, twilight ADCs, sleep-state ADCs, telephone ADCs, ADCs of physical phenomena, and symbolic ADCs.

ADCs can be visual, auditory, or kinesthetic. They also have a range of clarity regarding the contact. There can be direct observation of the deceased person with details of the person's appearance to a symbolic representation. The contact can occur during a waking or a dream state. In addition, the purpose of the contact can include reassurance of the state of the deceased person, sharing information, a warning to the bereaved, and even an intervention. ADCs are common in small children who will often report playing a game with the deceased. In 79% of the cases reported by Bill Guggenheim, ADCs occur to a family member with a close emotional connection but this is not always the case. In some cases, the ADC occurs to a person who has had an antagonistic relationship or little emotional connection. In Charlene's case, for example, Sam appeared to her instead of to his wife, to whom he had the closest emotional connection. The information was most significant to her. Yet, he appeared to his hospice nurse to share the information.

Kelly (2002) studied 90 emergency service workers to determine if ADCs occurred from victims of fatal injuries. He found 28% had sensed, felt, or seen the victims after their deaths.

Visual ADCs

In a visual ADC, the bereaved person will see the person who has died. Here is an example of a clear visual experience while the bereaved daughter was awake. The purpose of this interaction by the father was to provide comfort.

> I was lying in my bed, on my side, crying. This was the evening of my father's death - around 7 pm. I was heart-broken. I suddenly saw my father's face. He was also on his side - looking me straight in the eyes. He was surrounded by light - I could only see his face - and he had a radiant smile on his face. I had never seen him look so happy. I didn't hear anything, but I felt him say "Don't be sad - this is wonderful." I sat up in bed and he was gone (Diane, 2002).

This next description is an example of a primary visual ADC that occurred in a dream. What is interesting in this experience is the telepathic communication between the grandson and grandmother. This is a typical type of communication during these transpersonal experiences usually not known to be typical by the first time experiencer. This experience also includes some kinesthetic components as the grandson held his grandmother's hand and felt this radiating vibration.

The next thing I know, my grandmother (who passed at 74) appeared to me, young, vibrant, happy and whole, in the driver's seat. She took her hands off of the steering wheel and turned around to see her family members in the back. I was the only one who noticed her, and her face lit up when she realized I could actually see her. We spoke through telepathy I believe, and as I held her hand during the conversation, I felt the most stimulating radiating vibration coming from her, a vibration and peace I still felt when I woke up, and I still feel today (Jeff, 2002).

Shared after-death communication

By far the majority of ADCs occur to only one person at a time. Sometimes two individuals will see the same deceased person at the same time, a shared after-death communication experience. It was not unusual for a nurse, she reported, to see her grandmother, who also on occasion appeared to the nurse's mother. In one instance the grandmother was seen by both the mother and daughter at separate times on the same day with the grandmother appearing on a distinct street corner. As the nurse drove by the street corner, she saw her grandmother, fully dressed. The nurse's mother, later in the day, passed the same street corner where she also saw the nurse's grandmother. Both saw the deceased not only on the same street corner but in the identical clothes (Lawrence, 2010).

Here is another example of a shared after-death communication that was primarily visual. In this case the deceased had always had a disability that caused him to walk with a limp. He no longer had the limp during the ADC, which occurred to his sister. In this case the sister no longer needed to grieve which is common after an ADC.

During his memorial service, I looked out the window and saw Donald walking towards the church! His body was not solid, and I could see the trees behind him. He looked a bit younger and seemed to be whole – and he didn't have his limp anymore!

He was wearing a plaid shirt that he liked and a pair of trousers. He looked very peaceful and happy, like he was out for a stroll. Donald walked up to the window as if to beckon me to come with him. Then he just disappeared.

143

After the service, my sister-in-law, Joyce, said, "Did you see Donald?"
I was quite surprised and said, "Yes!" She said, "I saw him too!"
(Guggenheim, 1995, pp. 289-290).

The sister believed this was her brother's way of saying good-bye.
She also said it brought an end to her grief.

Prophetic visual ADC

The following happened to a woman when she was 11 years old. She
didn't know when this ADC occurred that her grandmother had died.

> I was only a child of 11 years old when she died but during the
> night of her death I became awake (I don't know what made me
> wake up) and saw my Nan at the end of my bed ... I can remember
> feeling very sleepy and wondering why I was awake during the night
> and why Nan was by my bed and asking her what was the matter.
> Nan began to tell me that she was going away and that meant
> that I wouldn't be able to see her for a long, long time, but that I
> wasn't to worry because she would be alright where she was going
> because it was a lovely place. I asked if I could come and visit her
> there but she said that wouldn't be possible but she would still be
> able to see me ... would watch over me, and would always be there
> for me if I ever needed her. I said something like "ok nanny, that's
> nice" she said "I love you" and I said "I love you too" and with that
> she told me to lie down and go back to sleep ... so I did (Fenwick
> & Fenwick, pp. 263-264).

The next morning this woman was told by her parents her grandmother had died. The woman told her parents she already knew that
because she had seen her.

Auditory ADCs

Hearing the voice of a deceased person is also a frequent occurrence.
Individuals can hear the voice externally, like people normally do, or
internally. Internal auditory communication is hearing inside their
mind. It is referred to as telepathic communication, communicating

thoughts without using sound. In both cases, the person is able to recognize the thoughts as coming from a distinct person.

External auditory ADCs

> She had told one of her friends from Sunday school that if she should die, she would like everyone to have a party for her and not to mourn. Her friend reminded us of this statement.

> So the night of Tina's funeral, we had a very large gathering at our home with 200 to 300 kids, some with their parents. It was wall-to-wall people!

> I was passing through the hallway downstairs when I heard Tina say, "I love you, Daddy!" I wheeled around because this was an audible, external voice.

> ... however, this experience took a good bit of the sting out of the loss because you know you really haven't lost them (Guggenheim & Guggenheim, 1995, pp. 32-33).

This occurrence was written by Tina's father, a psychiatrist. Tina was 15 years old when she died in a car accident. He described himself as the scientific type who had not expected to hear from his daughter. His feeling of comfortable and diminished grief is evident in this case.

Internal auditory ADC with veridical hearing

> I was at Duke at a conference and was alone in my hotel room. I was resting after a lecture. The TV was not on. It was quiet. I had NOT taken any medications, drugs or alcohol. All at once, an indescribable sense of inner peace and love enveloped me. This was NOT subtle. I heard "it's OK" over and over but not with my ears. I was able to ask questions and receive answers - what is OK? The answer was "everything is OK." The whole of human history is like a grain of sand on an infinite beach. About 30-60 min into the experience I received the

call that my grandmother had died. I believe the experience occurred at the exact time that she died (Larry, 2012).

This grandson's description of not hearing with his ears is a common way individuals will describe telepathic communication. Others might say something about hearing the information in their mind. In this case also, the grandson was not aware of his grandmother's death. He knew of it through this contact with his grandmother before being told she had died. This description is also interesting because of the implication of receiving knowledge. This occurs also in deep NDE experiences.

Kinesthetic

After her funeral, I found myself in the living room curled up in a ball, really mourning my loss of her. All of a sudden, I sensed my mother hovering in the room, on my right side. At first I thought I was hallucinating, but then I felt her putting her arms around me, comforting me. She wrapped herself around me like a big, cushiony, warm cloud, rocking me as if I was a scared little girl. I had been really crying a long time, and she calmed me down. There was a feel about her hugs, a nurturing energy, and it seemed it lasted about fifteen minutes.

I knew it was my mother. I just knew it! And I'm very grateful she was there to help me through my pain (Guggenheim & Guggenheim, 1995, pp. 50-51.)

Sensing the presence of a deceased loved one is common. As in the above description these experiences provide comfort and reduce the pain of grief. Generally experiencers have more difficulty validating these experiences to both themselves and others. In this case, the woman is certain of her mother's presence. There are some shared kinesthetic experiences where more than one person will sense the presence of the deceased at the same time.

Symbolic experiences

Sometimes the experiences are indirect communications from the deceased. One woman, for example, after her husband died was informed by a neighbor her tax bill was due. Her husband managed all the finances, so she had no knowledge of where to even look for this tax bill. As she stood in her husband's office, frustrated by her inability to find this bill she spoke out loud to her deceased husband about her frustration. All of a sudden her husband's thick appointment book, that had been closed, opened to the page that contained the tax bill (Guggenheim & Guggenheim, 1995).

Another woman flying home for Christmas after her husband's death, was frustrated by the plane boarding experience. She was wishing her husband was there to help with this boarding process. As she had this wish, his name was paged over the loudspeaker system (Daggett, 2005).

Others will see animals or other symbolic representations of the individuals. Some have reported the phone ringing with the deceased person's phone number showing on the caller identification system. When answered, there is no one the other end of the phone. Sometimes there is a certain smell like perfume, chocolate, or roses that reminds family members of the deceased person.

These symbolic ADCs are more likely to be experienced by more than one person than any other type of ADC. The other types are more likely to be verified by others after the experience, as in the cases of knowing someone has died before being told.

Messages

As seen in the previous cases, deceased persons often send messages of love to the bereaved as well as telling the bereaved they are fine and happy. In some cases, the deceased have sent messages that are warnings.

About two years after his friend died, Jeff was driving home late at night. He was tired and had fallen asleep at the wheel. He heard a scream, "Wake up!" At that point he saw his dead friend sitting in the passenger seat, aglow with light. Jeff looked to see he was heading straight at a house going 45 miles an hour. He decelerated in time to avoid the accident (Guggenheim & Guggenheim, 1995).

Some of the messages may also include advice. One person reported being told by her deceased brother to tell his son to go to a certain school. At first the sister did not understand the message but spoke to her nephew. He had been accepted to three medical schools and did not know which one to pick. The sister did not know her nephew had even applied to medical school. He followed his deceased father's advice and did well.

Some individuals also report deceased family members and/or friends appearing asking for forgiveness. This occurs to people whose family members have committed suicide, been alcoholics, or otherwise caused pain to the family members.

Negative ADCs

The majority of ADCs are positive with messages of survival, love, and peace. Some elicit negative emotions in the experiencer or describe unpleasant situations occurring to the deceased.

In some cases, the deceased is trying to present a positive message to a loved one. However, the loved one becomes frightened and anxious from seeing the person. The Guggenheims (1995) describe a young woman helping with her wedding reception at her family house. Alone in her room taking a rest, she was thinking about her recently deceased grandmother. She regretted she could not be there to see this time in her life. Suddenly her grandmother's face and shoulders appeared. She looked "solid" to the woman as she told her not to worry; she would see her getting married. Having seen and heard this, the young woman became terrified and ran out of her room.

In some cases, it is the deceased that is not in a place that is the best for them. They may report being in a "holding place" or a place that is neither positive nor negative but not where they want to be. Some describe these places as temporary and ask for prayers so they may move on.

Explanations

There are not many scientific explanations for ADCs. The individuals who have them are not ill, so explanations about low oxygen levels, temporal lobe abnormalities, spikes in EEG readings are not applicable as explanations. Many do believe these experiences are "proof" of life after death. What is believed and what can be proven are two distinct aspects of understanding ADCs. The veridical perceptions that occur are the distinctly most convincing evidence of the existence of an afterlife. So far, though, verification by researchers of what someone has learned only through an ADC has not been done in a large scale study.

What is known through the collection of ADC experiences is that millions of individuals who are not ill, but often are grieving, have these experiences. Clinically these experiences are positive for the friends and family members, bringing joy and happiness, while at the same time decreasing the pain of the grief process.

Induced ADCs

ADCs do not occur to everyone, but when they do, they are significant to the experiencer in many ways. They are spontaneous occurrences with little understanding by the scientific community of how or why they occur to some bereaved individuals but not to others. Their clinical significance has been the driving force for centuries for individuals to contact mediums to reach out to deceased loved ones. Unfortunately, it has been difficult for the average person to discriminate between valid mediums and fraudulent ones. The early psychical researchers spent decades attempting to do just that (Tymn, 2011).

New approaches are being tried to assist people to establish contact with the deceased, that experience an induced ADC (IADC). Therapists and others are using techniques involving a psychomanteum, a modified version of eye movement desensitization and reprocessing (EMDR) and automatic handwriting to help the bereaved receive messages from those who have died.

Automatic writing

In 1920, L.M. Bazett authored a book entitled *After-Death Communication*. Using automatic writing she was able to be in contact with a soldier, a relative, who had died during the war. She asked about another soldier whom she was told her relative knew. That soldier, Chris, who was reported missing was seen by Ms. Bazett at the foot of her bed. He informed her he had been killed in action. Ms. Bazett states in her book she was in contact with 50 to 60 deceased individuals using automatic writing.

Mirror gazing

The ancient technique of involving a psychomanteum was reinitiated in the 1990s by Dr. Raymond Moody. This technique includes gazing into a large mirror in an environment relatively free from distractions. Moody directs individuals to bring photographs or some artifact that reminds the person of the deceased to whom they wish to be in touch. They are encouraged to not drink or eat any foods that are considered stimulants. Watches, cell phones, and other such items need to be taken off and put where they would not cause a distraction. Artwork, or soothing music was encouraged.

Moody had created space in his Grist Mill in Alabama that included an apparition chamber. This chamber included a four-foot by three-and-a-half foot mirror and a comfortable chair. Sometimes individuals would have visions in this chamber. Some did not. On occasion, some would have visions at home after the experience of being in this chamber.

Here is an example of a woman who connected with her deceased grandfather.

> I was so happy to see him, I began to cry. Through the tears, I could still see him in the mirror. Then he seemed to get closer and he must have come out of the mirror because the next thing I knew he was holding me and hugging me. It felt like he said something like, "It's ok. Don't cry." Before I knew it he was gone. I can still feel his touch. I also feel warm, like someone has been hugging me (Moody, 1993).

IADCs using modified EMDR

Induced after-death communication using modified EMDR approach was first described by Dr. Allan L. Botkin (2014). He accidentally stumbled on how using EMDR could induce an ADC with a client. Sam was a soldier in Vietnam who was formed a beautiful friendship with a ten-year-old orphaned girl named Le. They became so close Sam decided to adopt her. Before the adoption became official, one day an order came down to send all the orphaned children on base to a Catholic orphanage in a distant village. Devastated by the news, he reluctantly helped put all the children on a truck. Shots rang out and the soldiers quickly removed the children from the truck to safety. Sam later found out his future daughter had died from a bullet wound on the truck. Sam was devastated and fraught with grief. The grief was so intense when he came back to the US and fathered a daughter; he could not form a close connection with her.

During his EMDR session with Dr. Botkin, he saw Le.

> When I closed my eyes, I saw Le as a beautiful woman with long black hair in a white gown surrounded by a radiant light. She seemed genuinely happier and more content than anyone I have ever known. Sam's tear-reddened face glowed. She thanked me for taking care of her before she died. I said, "I love you, Le," and she said "I love you too, Sam," and she put her arms around me and embraced me. Then she faded away (p. 13).

Dr. Botkin did not anticipate this IADC would have a lasting effect. He checked the impact on Sam three months later. He still felt the re-connection with Le and was able to relate in a much more caring way to his daughter. Eight years later that same was true. He now has a much improved relationship with his own daughter.

Dr. Botkin offers training on his technique to bring about an IADC (Botkin, 2000).

Providing support

ADCs, as has been documented, are common occurrences. Generally this contact helps relieve the grief of the loss. Most survivors report feeling relieved and comforted by the contact. Individuals who have recently lost a love one should be prepared that some contact with the deceased may occur. Knowing this might happen may prevent someone from being frightened by them. Also knowledge of symbolic communication may help the bereaved be more alert for these messages. They are easy to overlook or doubt but their presence, if noticed, may provide consolation.

There may be some feelings of rejection on the part of the bereaved who have not received a communication from the deceased. No one knows why a bereaved person choses to communicate to one person versus another. It is possible some individuals are naturally more open to these types of communications than others. It does not seem to be a matter of favoritism on the part of the deceased.

Bereaved individuals who have heard of ADCs but have not had the experience may be interested in contacting mediums and others who claim to be able to contact the deceased. The field of mediumship is generally not well regulated and has historically been the subject of fraudulent investigation (Randi, 1997; McMahon & Lascurain, 1997). Some have taken advantage of grieving individuals, charging large fees for fake contacts with deceased loved ones.

In 1951, the Fraudulent Mediums Act was passed in England and Wales. It was designed to protect the public from making money from deceptive claims. This act was repealed and then replaced by a new consumer protection regulation in 2008. In the US, individual towns and states may require criminal background checks or licensing.

IADCs are more likely to be carried out by credentialed individuals. They also involve the grieving person receiving any communication rather than an intermediary.

Table I Helpful communication

1. Encourage a client-centered approach by asking the individual to describe his or her experience
2. Be open to all descriptions, bracketing any preconceived ideas
3. Give attention to visual, auditory and/or kinesthetic descriptions of the event
4. Encourage communication about any aspect of an experience
5. Assess the emotional impact from the occurrence
6. Normalize the experience
7. Provide resources about ADCs and IADCs

Table II Documentation of the contact by the deceased

1. Description of what occurred
2. Description of length of time from the death of the person
3. Immediate emotional response to the occurrence
4. Information provided

CHAPTER 12

LEVELS OF EVIDENCE

Keywords: convenience samples, levels of evidence, near-death visits, near-death experiences, out-of-body experiences, meta-analysis, prospective studies, qualitative research, quantitative research, retrospective studies, systematic reviews

This chapter and the next include analyses of what constitutes evidence or proof, if you will, about the existence and veracity of the transpersonal experiences described in this book. Because of the abundance of research, particularly of near-death experiences (NDEs), two chapters, 12 and 13, are devoted to this discourse. Chapter 12 will contain discussions about the research strides made regarding near-death visits (NDVs), out-of-body experiences (OBEs) not associated with NDEs, OBEs associated with NDEs and NDE occurrences. Chapter 13 will include research strides on the aftereffects of NDEs, deathbed communications, and after-death communications.

What constitutes proof or evidence?

In everyday life we determine evidence or proof from the following ways: what we experience through our senses, what makes logical sense to us, what we have been told to be true by authority figures, and, what is traditionally established as truth. So if we see, hear, or feel something, we believe that something exists. If we hear about an accident on a road, it makes sense to us to avoid that road to arrive at a certain destination. If our parents, teachers, or religious authorities have told us we need to behave in a certain way to achieve eternal salvation, we believe that is true. If our culture defines the roles of men and women in certain ways, we accept those ways as correct. All of these ways of knowing are important to our daily lives and our ultimate development as adults. Our experiences and beliefs provide information, motivation, and a sense of purpose to our lives.

Scientific evidence requires different standards for proof or evidence. Here is John Palmer's (2001) distinction between knowing from experience and proving scientifically a phenomenon exists or there is truth in what is inferred about it.

As you may know, some people who have a close brush with death report having had a vivid internal experience that convinces them survival is real and that they have gained direct knowledge of the hereafter. To a parapsychologist, this inference is not justified, because it is based on an experience that was subjective. This does not mean that the inference is necessarily wrong, just that we cannot claim to know it is right (p. 31).

As Palmer says, these transpersonal experiences of individuals may or may not be correct but definitely give the scientific communities direction for research which defines evidence or proof differently from personal growth and impact.

Evidence is weighed in terms of the strength of accurately describing the truth about a phenomenon. Evidence is described in levels of validity, with some levels being stronger than others. The levels vary generally from four to seven depending upon the discipline and types of phenomena being investigated. The higher the level of evidence, the more confidence we have that what is said about a phenomenon in the research, is valid.

Generally in most disciplines the levels of evidence are structured in the following manner with Level VI being the lowest and Level I being the highest level:

Level VI. Opinions of authorities and/or reports of expert; individual case reports.

Level V. Evidence from descriptive or qualitative studies.

Level IV. Evidence from systematic reviews of descriptive and qualitative studies.

Level III. Quasi-experimental, prospective studies lacking control, or randomization or both.

Level II. Evidence from one prospective randomized study with appropriate controls.

Level I. Evidence from prospective (started before the intervention or manipulation occurs), randomized (each subject has an equal opportunity to be selected) studies with appropriate controls (a control group is used and outside influences are reduced) or systematic review of these studies.

Explanations of the levels

Level VI. Opinions of authorities and/or reports of expert; individual case reports.

There are individuals in every field who have been studying a phenomenon for many years. They often understand subjects well and have insights into the truth of a situation. We consider their opinions valuable, and these opinions are often used to indicate a direction for future research. Kubler-Ross is an excellent example of an expert who first described stages of dying. These stages subsequently were studied in a number of different ways to determine the process experienced by grieving and dying individuals.

Level V. Evidence from descriptive or qualitative studies

Qualitative studies are often carried out when a phenomenon is new or under researched. Researchers use unstructured interviews with open-ended questions, and/or observations of subjects, and/or collection of artifacts or analysis of written documentation to obtain their results. Qualitative studies describe the major concepts, components, and/or themes that are at the heart of a phenomenon. They are crucial to future researchers in identifying aspects of a phenomenon that can be studied. In this type of research, scientists often ask people who have an experience to describe that experience in their own words and reactions, i.e. describe what happened when you were out of your body.

Qualitative research is not used to describe the who, what, where, how, or when of a phenomenon. That is done in descriptive studies. Descriptive studies are often carried out through large surveys but sometimes also by large numbers of structured interviews. If we know, for example, through a qualitative study, that individuals report having out-of-body experiences, researchers would want to know how many people have them, are there certain characteristics of individuals who report these experiences more often than others, when these experiences are most likely to occur, and what might precipitate them.

Even though qualitative and quantitative studies are seen as being at a Level V, they are essential building blocks to the more sophisticated research levels that involve experiments. If through a descriptive study researchers know that out-of-body experiences happen with some frequency to near-death experiencers who have increased psychic abilities, that knowledge legitimizes the study of OBEs of near-death experiencers.

Level IV. Evidence from systematic reviews of descriptive and qualitative studies.

Systemic reviews of qualitative and quantitative research means someone has looked at the results of a number of similar studies and synthesized the research results. If there are five studies on the frequency of OBEs in NDErs, the reviewer of these studies will analyze the results and state with more certainty the actual incidence based on five studies versus just one. There are databases, like the Cochrane Collaboration, that let us know what systematic reviews are available.

Levels III, II, and I

Levels I, II, and III involve experimental studies of some type. The strongest experimental studies include randomization, control, and manipulation. Randomization means all subjects have an equal opportunity to be included in the experimental group. Control means external influences have been modified or able to be measured using a control group or controlling situations that could influence the outcome. Manipulation is the intervention, or what is done to the subject. By definition, all experimental studies involve some manipulation. In human subjects it is not always possible to have randomization and/ or control. When either or both are missing, they are referred to as quasi-experimental studies. They are by far the most common in human subject research.

Experimental studies are generally done prospectively, meaning the researcher is able to collect data before the manipulation, event, or intervention. Retrospective studies involve data collection after the event or manipulation. Retrospective studies include information collected for other reasons besides the research. In the case of NDEs, blood pressure levels, oxygen levels, and brain scans are done for the clinical assessment of the underlying trauma or illness. The event, like the NDE, has already happened when the study starts. Retrospective studies look back after the event has occurred; prospective studies look forward and collect data and control the environment before the event has occurred (Peat, 2002).

If a researcher, for example, wanted to know if certain medications decreased the incidence of an OBE during sleep, in a prospective study they would collect data on the subject before giving the medication and then after giving the medication. In that type of study the researcher could make sure no other medication was taken, as well as vital signs, for example, before and after the occurrence. In a retrospective study, the researcher would not be able to obtain firsthand information of what happened before the OBE.

Systematic reviews and meta-analysis

If there were five studies done prospectively using experimental designs, a systematic review of these studies could be done. Further analysis, called a meta-analysis, would increase the precision of the results by statistically combing results of similar studies. A systematic review is different from a literature review, the latter of which is common in the literature. The literature review is used more to give the history of study of an experience and then synthesis the literature to present the next needed research in the area. A systematic review is an unbiased approach to appraise, synthesis, and present the results of the totality of the studies.

Strength of current research on transpersonal experiences associated with near death and dying

Generally speaking, most research studies done on transpersonal experiences associated with near death and dying are at the Levels VI and V. Very few systematic reviews, Level IV, have been done. Many of the early studies involve the use of convenience samples. Convenience sampling involves the use of subjects that are accessible and proximate to the researcher. Subjects can be obtained from ads in newspapers and other media and referrals.

This type of sampling is non random. As an example, a researcher might want to study elementary teachers' attitudes about their salaries and work conditions. If the researcher lived in Rhode Island, he or she might give a questionnaire to teachers who work in local schools. That would be a convenience sample of teachers. In that case, the researcher cannot say those teachers' attitudes represent all the teachers in the country. It is a good thing because Rhode Island, at this writing, is one of the states with the highest teacher wages in the country. What a researcher can do to obtain a representative sample from the US is randomly select five states from five demographic areas in the country. Then from those states, randomly select counties and then from those counties randomly select elementary schools and then the teachers. In that approach all teachers have an equal chance of being selected to participate in the study, thus representing the attitudes of teachers across the US. Being able to sample from a list of all the teachers in the country would be more ideal but, given the large numbers, impractical.

A number of researchers studying NDEs particularly improved on the convenience sampling approach by studying subjects immediately after an experience occurred in a healthcare setting. Their subjects were from a specific group with similar medical conditions within a limited period of time.

The emphasis in this book has been on the clinical importance of validating and supporting the individuals who have had transpersonal experiences associated with near death and dying. It seems worthwhile to look at the levels of scientific research of these various experiences to provide validation for those who experience them. An attempt was made to include all major studies for each area of discussion. It is possible to have missed significant studies because of the volume of research that has been carried out and continues to be reported in the literature.

Research on the existence of NDVs

Lawrence (1997), in her study of 111 patients who had experienced an unconscious episode documented in a hospital record, described several transpersonal experiences, including NDVs. Before being interviewed, all the research subjects were screened for a history of mental illness. No one who had a history of mental illness, drug, or alcohol abuse was admitted into the study. Out of the 111 subjects who had been interviewed, six described being "visited" by someone who had died. Two of the "visits" involved auditory communication. One involved olfactory communication. Four involved visual communication

– one person had an experience that was both auditory and visual. Unlike the near-death experience, these subjects saw the person in their homes or hospital rooms and not in some other dimension perceived to be beyond this world. Unlike patients experiencing deathbed visions, these patients had been critically ill but had recovered and were not imminently dying.

Lawrence's study would qualify as a qualitative descriptive study, at a Level V in research terms. There were 111 subjects, all of whom were interviewed in one hospital with nearly all patients recovering from an unconscious episode being included. This would be generally judged as a valid study. There are no known additional studies of near-death visits. From this study, it could be said 5% of patients who are unconscious may experience an NDV. In order to raise the validity of the incidence of near-death visits, more descriptive studies need to be done. Also more studies would need to be done to determine how many of the events involve visual, auditory, or kinesthetic experiences.

Impact of the near-death visit (NDV)

The purpose of the NDV was to provide comfort and support for the ill patient and/or help with the transition to another place. Of the six patients, two said the deceased persons were there to support them in difficult critical events. Two said the deceased individuals were beckoning them to come with them. Two were not sure why the deceased were standing at the foot of their hospital beds. More subjects who had this experience would need to be interviewed to determine the impact of this experience. Also in the Lawrence study, only descriptions of the immediate impact were obtained. Descriptions of long-term impact would also be useful.

Veridical perception during an NDV

One patient saw his dead sister along with his deceased mother at the foot of his hospital bed. He had not been told his sister, who had been ill, had died. His wife requested no one tell him his sister had died. That information was verified with the nursing staff. The patient said he knew his sister had died because she was with his mother. He denied being told of her death. Because this was a descriptive study without controls, it was not possible to control the conversations of all who spoke to the man or near the man who saw his deceased mother and sister. Someone could have mentioned his sister had died, even though that was unlikely. More subjects would need to be interviewed to determine the incidence and validity of perceptions not possible through our objective senses.

Out-of-body experiences (OBEs) surrounding death

We know OBEs are common occurrences in the general populations with estimates of 10% to 20% of people having such experiences at least once (Alvarado, 1984; Monroe, 1977; Blackmore, 1984). There are two types of OBEs that can occur to a person while close to death: spontaneous OBEs and those occurring in conjunction with an NDE.

Spontaneous OBEs while close to death

Olson (1988) interviewed 200 hospitalized subjects. Six reported having an OBE during the current hospitalization. That is an incidence of 3% of hospitalized patients having OBEs not associated with NDEs.

Lawrence, in her study of 111 unconscious patients states seven subjects reported an OBE not associated with an NDE. Most of the subjects reported seeing themselves from above. This is an incidence of 6% of previously unconscious patients experiencing an OBE.

Satori carried out a study of 243 patients admitted to an Intensive Therapy Unit (ITU) in Wales, UK. She placed brightly colored symbols on top of the cardiac monitors of each patient. There were 10 patients who had an OBE, none of which saw the colored symbols. Two OBEs occurred without being associated with an NDE (Satori, 2006). This is an incidence of about 1% of patients admitted to an ITU reporting an OBE not associated with an NDE.

Veridical perception of OBEs not associated with NDEs

In Lawrence's (1997) study, one patient said he saw the nurses popping popcorn in another room. Another patient had an OBE during labor. A doctor she had never seen before, nor seen after the delivery, came in to consult on her case while she was unconscious. Interestingly, she was able to describe this doctor, including the bald spot on the top of his head. After consulting the patient's medical record, Lawrence found the name of the consulting doctor. She was able to confirm he was taller and thinner than the patient's regular doctor, with less hair, just as the patient described.

In OBEs not associated with a progression to an NDE, the individual does not experience the wonderful feeling of love and peace characteristically connected with NDEs. They also have more concern about being out of body and how to return to their physical body. In addition, individuals with a spontaneous OBE remain in their worldly environment, while those with an NDE will travel to what is perceived as life after death.

These three studies by Olson, Lawrence, and Satori have systematically studied the incidence of OBEs not associated with NDEs in hospitalized patients. These would be considered to be at a Level V on the evidence scale. We know from these three studies between 1% and 6% of patients who are hospitalized will have an OBE. More descriptive studies need to be carried out to validate the incidence of these occurrences and their veridical perceptions. Once a few more studies have been completed, an integrated review and/or meta-analysis could be done. That would raise the level of research to a Level IV. Also, there needs to be more investigation into the predisposing factors of these occurrences.

OBEs associated with near-death experiences

In 1975, Moody published what would become the present day impetus for future research on NDEs. This study would be termed a qualitative study on NDEs – a Level V on the evidence scale. He interviewed a number of subjects who reported having NDEs, many of whom reported out-of-body experiences.

Moody's study was followed by a study by Kenneth Ring, a psychology professor at the University of Connecticut. He interviewed 102 subjects who had had an NDE. Of those 102 subjects, 37% experienced a body separation (Ring, 1980).

In 2001, van Lommel studied 344 patients who had undergone 509 successful resuscitations. 62 of these patients experienced an NDE. Of the 62, 15 (24%) reported an OBE associated with an NDE.

In Satori's study of 243 patients admitted to an Intensive Therapy Unit (ITU) in Wales, UK, eight patients reported an OBE associated with an NDE.

Veridical perception during OBEs associated with NDEs

Many researchers reported individual cases involving veridical perceptions during NDEs (Clark, 1984; Ring & Lawrence, 1993). Here are a few of the more exceptional examples that have been verified.

Maria's shoe

Sharp (1995) reported a patient who claimed to have seen a worn, dark blue tennis shoe on the ledge outside of her hospital room during an OBE. Sharp was able to verify a shoe was there. The patient had also seen the part of the shoe facing outward, only visible external to the hospital room.

The red shoe

Ring and Lawrence (1993) described a case where a patient during a cardiac arrest reported seeing a red shoe in the northwest corner of the roof of a hospital. The nurse passed on the report to a resident who was able to have the door to the roof of the hospital opened. He came down carrying the red shoe.

The missing dentures

A patient during an OBE watched a nurse place his dentures in a drawer in the crash cart used during his resuscitation. After he was alert, he recognized the nurse and told her where she had put his dentures (van Lommel, 2001).

These individual cases would be classified as a Level VI. They are considered retrospective case studies.

Systematic studies

Michael Sabom, an Atlanta cardiologist, compared the knowledge of the resuscitation of 32 patients who claimed to have OBEs with 25 patients who had been resuscitated but not out of their bodies. None of the individuals who claimed to have been out of their bodies made major errors in describing the resuscitation process. Twenty-three of the 25 individuals who did not have an OBE made major errors (Sabom, 1982). This study would be classified as a retrospective, comparative descriptive study at a Level V.

In a study by Lawrence (1997), an electronic message was placed high on a cabinet in an electrophysiology laboratory (EPS). Milne (1995) found in a convenience sample of 86 patients undergoing EPS studies, 6 of those who lost consciousness reported an NDE

Lawrence interviewed patients before the EPS study administrating a personality inventory and a dissociative experience scale. The electronic message in the EPS lab was changed by an outside person and not divulged to anyone else, including Lawrence. The sign was not visible to healthcare personnel. A person needed to be out of their body or on a high ladder (not present in the lab) to see the message. It was a nonsense message that would not be normally spoken. The first message, for example, said "the popsicles are in bloom." Unfortunately, this research was terminated because of downsizing before any persons were able to see the message. A few individuals reported the experience of starting to leave their body but none did so enough to see the sign (Lawrence, 1997). This study would be considered a prospective, quasi-experimental study with controls. It would be at a Level III.

NDE research

To date, thousands of articles and books have been written about NDEs. Many of these are individual experiences of lay individuals and/or opinions of experts in the healthcare, psychology, physics, and parapsychology fields. In the Ovid Medline database alone, there are 127 articles related to NDEs listed since 1977. What are discussed in this section are only the major research studies, frequently cited in the literature.

Measurement

There are two tools most frequently used to determine if an NDE has occurred: the Weighted Core Experience Index (WCEI) developed by Ring (1982), and the Near-Death Experience Scale (NDE Scale) developed by Greyson (1983). The WCEI is a 10-item scale designed to measure the depth of an experience. The NDE Scale is a 16-item Likert multiple choice tool with two questions asked about each item. In order to qualify for an NDE occurrence, the subject needs to score at least a 7 out of 32 possible points.

Both these tools have been used in determining the incidence of an NDE, with the NDE Scale used more frequently. The NDE Scale has been tested for reliability and validity. However, these tools are now both over 30 years old. There is confusion about the use of these tools as more components of the NDE have been reported. The items on the scales may need to be changed to assure the validity of the tools.

Occurrence of NDEs

The initial researchers attempted to validate the occurrence of NDEs. There was the need to identify the existence of NDEs. The subjects in these studies were obtained through solicitations in newspapers, referrals from physicians, personal contact. These reports were generally self-reports, many of which occurred years after the NDE occurrence.

Here is a list of the earlier research studies:

Raymond Moody (1975) published his description of 150 cases of NDEs.

Kenneth Ring (1982) described 102 incidences of NDEs and documented the common components of the occurrence.

A Gallup Poll in 1982 reported that 4% of the population had experienced an NDE (Gallup and Proctor, 1982).

Grey (1985) reported 38 subjects, mostly British, with NDEs, establishing the NDE as a cross-cultural phenomenon.

Fenwick and Fenwick (1995) documented 500 subjects who had experienced an NDE who wrote in after they saw or heard a TV program, radio broadcast, or newspaper article in the UK.

Long and Perry (2006) captured case studies of 613 individuals with NDEs on their website.

Perera, et al. (2005) in an Australian telephone survey of 673 individuals, identified 9% who had experienced an NDE.

Distressing NDEs

Greyson and Bush (1996) analyzed 50 accounts of distressing NDEs. These individuals were also obtained through a convenience sample. They were able to identify the four types of distressing NDEs through the interviews.

In the studies done by Sabom (1982), Parnia (2001), and van Lommel (2001), none of the individuals reported distressing NDEs. Lawrence, in her study of 111 previously unconscious patients, reported one individual with a distressing NDE. It is unclear if distressing NDEs are rare or if they are also underreported because of the negative connotation of having a distressing NDE.

From the above research, it was clearly established that millions of individuals had what became called a near-death experience. This is not a random occurrence of just a few individuals, but a significant event associated with being close to death. The early researchers used convenience samples, appropriate to establish the occurrences and components of NDEs. The later researchers selected discrete samples from which they could describe the incidence of NDEs.

Demographics of experiencers

In the studies carried out by Ring (1980) and Sabom (1982), age, gender, marital status, religious affiliation, and types of medical emergency had no effect on the incidence of NDEs. Ring noted that knowledge of the existence of NDEs was inversely related. Those that had less information about NDEs had more occurrences. Other researchers have reported similar findings but to date there are no integrated reviews or meta-analyses of similar studies to confirm these findings using multiple studies.

Incidence of NDEs in discrete samples

Later researchers attempted to document the incidence of NDEs within a certain population soon after the occurrence in a hospitalized setting. Many of these researchers referred to these studies as prospective studies because they were interviewed soon after the occurrence. While these studies were more valid than previous studies because of data collection close to the occurrence of the NDE, by most scientific definitions they would not be called prospective studies. In order to be a prospective study, the researchers would need to have been in contact with the subjects before the NDE and collected data beforehand. Many NDErs, for example, claim to lose their fear of death after the experience. In a prospective study, documentation of the fear of death level before the NDE would have been carried out and compared with the subject's fear of death level after the NDE.

Here are some research studies of discrete populations interviewed shortly after a near-death event:

Milne (1995) interviewed 86 patients undergoing electrophysiology studies (EPS) over a year's time. Six of the 20 patients who lost consciousness during the study described an NDE occurrence.

Greyson (1991) studied the incidence of NDEs in 61 suicide attempters. He found 16 subjects had positive NDEs. Suicide attempters who experienced an NDE were less likely to make another suicide attempt when compared with those who did not experience an NDE.

Lawrence (1997) found in her study of 111 previously unconscious patients, 11 (10%) experienced an NDE. Patients with a history of mental illness or drug or alcohol abuse were not included in the research.

Van Lommel, et al. (2001) studied 344 patients in Dutch hospitals after a cardiac arrest. In that study 62 (18%) reported an NDE.

Parnia, Waller, Yeates, and Fenwick (2001) interviewed 63 survivors of cardiac arrests within a week of their arrest. They found 7 (11.1%) subjects reported memories, with the majority having NDE features.

Schwaninger, Eisenberg, Schechtman, and Weiss (2002) followed 174 patients immediately post cardiac arrest. Thirty patients from the 174 were able to be interviewed with 7 (4%) reporting an NDE.

Satori (2006) studied 243 patients admitted to an Intensive Therapy Unit (ITU) in Wales, UK. She found 15 (6%) of those studied experienced and NDE.

Greyson (2003) studied over 1,500 patients in a cardiac ICU and cardiac step-down unit. His results indicated 27 (2%) of these patients scored 7 or higher on the NDE scale.

Lai, et al. (2007) in a study of 710 patients receiving dialysis treatment found 10% of the patients reported an NDE. According to these authors, "The high occurrence of life-threatening events, availability of medical records, and accessibility and cooperativeness of patients make the dialysis population very suitable for NDE research" (p. 130).

From these studies, it was shown between 2% to 18% of subjects who had experienced life-threatening events will have an NDE.

Veridical perception within the NDE

During an OBE associated with the NDE, the individual often sees medical interventions or individuals that are in the earthly plane. Veridical perceptions have also been documented through research as occurring in the ethereal world, as described by the subjects. Often these perceptions involve seeing or learning about relatives whose existence they were not aware, often siblings who had died early in life. Some subjects also saw individuals in this ethereal world whose death had been not reported to them. Individuals who were either blind from birth or had blindness affect them later in life also reported seeing during their NDE.

Seeing siblings unknown before the NDE

Vi Horton described a brother she met in the afterlife. He told her he was her baby brother. She never knew she had a brother who had died (Turning Point, 1995).

Callanan and Kelley (1997) report a woman who saw her sister during an NDE. That was the first she knew she had had a sister who had died.

Dr. Eben Alexander saw a lovely young girl during his NDE. He later was shown a photo of his sister who had died and recognized her as the same young girl (Alexander, 2012).

Visual Perception in the Blind

Dr. Kenneth Ring (1993) described 21 cases of visual perception in the blind during their near-death experiences.

Summary

The question is often asked if these transpersonal experiences are real. This question has two primary aspects: Do they occur to normal individuals who are not influenced by drugs or mental illness, and do what the individuals see or otherwise experience prove the existence of an afterlife?

As described above, there is considerable, if not overwhelming, evidence that these experiences occur to individuals not influenced by drugs or mental illness. Millions of individuals all over the world report similar transpersonal experiences in well-designed qualitative and quantitative studies. The reality of these occurrences has been established as occurring to individuals who come close to death. What is unknown is why some individuals have these transpersonal experiences when acutely ill and others in the same circumstances do not.

Is there scientific evidence to support the existence of an afterlife? So far the research that has been done provides some evidence that some part of us is able to exist outside the body. There are abundant examples of veridical perceptions during which individuals are able to see, hear, or feel events outside the scope of our normal senses.

Veridical perceptions are phenomena historically unique to parapsychology. In parapsychology, studies of remote viewing, for example, report the abilities of individuals to perceive an object or scene at a distance unable to be seen with normal eyesight. While this research has shown inconclusive results except with exceptional individuals, the researchers used approaches to demonstrate ability beyond the normal senses (Persinger, Roll, Tiller, Koren & Cook, 2002).

With remote viewing testing, a researcher can have someone photograph a scene, or be present at the scene before the testing of remote viewing for verification. To date, verification of what is seen during a transpersonal episode is done mostly retrospectively with some attempts to place signs that could be visible during the occurrence.

In order to demonstrate clear proof or evidence of the existence of nonlocal consciousness, prospective studies need to be carried out where data can be collected beforehand as well as after the NDE with sufficient controls in place. Strong evidence for nonlocal consciousness is the first step in demonstrating life after death.

CHAPTER 13

EVIDENCE OF AFTEREFFECTS OF NDES, DEATHBED VISIONS, AND AFTER-DEATH COMMUNICATIONS

Keywords: after-death communication, aftereffects, deathbed visions, evidence, integrated review, materialism, near-death experiences, psychic phenomena, religiosity, research.

Research on the aftereffects of near-death experiences

Numerous aftereffects of near-death experiences have been reported in the literature (Sutherland, 1990; Greyson, 1983, 1992; Ring, 1984). Some aftereffects have been well researched with others just described in occasional studies. The most significant aftereffects include an increase in spirituality, an increased sense of purpose, decreased participation in organized religion, decreased interest in materialism, increased difficulties with close personal relationships, increased self-improvement through learning and healthier life choices, a loss of fear of death, electromagnetic aftereffects, and an increase in psychic sensitivity.

In 1984, Ring developed an instrument to quantify some of the life changes following an NDE. This tool was named the Life Changes Inventory (LCI). It was revised in 2004 by Greyson and Ring with a name change to the Life Changes Inventory-Revised (LCI-R). This revised tool was developed from research carried out by Greyson, Ring, and Flynn. These researchers added items to this 50-item tool based on interviews with NDErs. The tool includes nine clusters of elements designed to measure life changes, particularly those reflecting values and beliefs following an NDE.

1. Appreciation of life
2. Self-acceptance
3. Concern for others
4. Concern with worldly achievement
5. Concern with social/planetary values
6. Quest for meaning/sense of purpose
7. Spirituality
8. Religiousness
9. Appreciation of death
   (p. 46-47)

Each of the nine clusters has a number of sub items that make up that cluster. For example, appreciation of death includes the following sub items: fear of death, conviction that there is life after death, and interest in issues related to death and dying.

Four additional items were added that were not part of these nine clusters: interest in psychic phenomena, desire for solitude, involvement in family life, and openness to the idea of reincarnation.

NDErs are asked to indicate whether each of these 50 values strongly increased, somewhat increased, not changed, somewhat decreased, or strongly decreased after their NDE. Typically post NDE, individuals have less concern with worldly achievement. Even though individuals post NDE do not value materialism, they would score high on concern with worldly achievement as decreasing and being a life change.

Instrument development

Greyson and Ring state the LCI and the LCI-R are the most frequently used tools to measure aftereffects of NDEs. Both authors acknowledge the face validity of the tools due to the decades of research in the area, but recommend the necessary psychometric testing that needs to be done (Greyson & Ring, 2004). Neither the LCI nor the LCI-R have had published psychometric testing completed.

Instruments, including mechanical and paper and pencil versions, are tested for reliability and validity. Thorough psychometric testing may take five to ten years or longer. The tests for reliability involve showing the consistency of the results of an instrument. Individuals, for example, frequently test the reliability of a bathroom scale. The second reading moments after stepping on the scale the first time should read the same weight (often to our dismay). A scale that reads 140 lbs the first time and 125 lbs the second would be deemed unreliable, however desirable.

Cook and Beckman (2006) describe concepts of reliability and validity useful in the development of instruments useful in healthcare research. Reliability of paper and pencil tools can be tested using tests of internal consistency or test-retest reliability. In the case of the LCI-R, a researcher could administer the tool to a group of individuals who had an NDE a first time and then a second time a few weeks later. The statistical analysis of the comparison of the two administrations should show a high correlation; the scores between the two measurements should be similar, meaning the tool is consistent.

Validity tests are carried out to determine if an instrument measures what it is designed to measure. Tests for validity involve different levels, including but not limited to face validity, criterion-related validity, and construct validity. Face validity involves the input from experts in the field who offer their opinion on the degree to which an item on a tool measures what the instrument is intended to measure. The LCI-R could improve its face validity by asking other NDE researchers to agree or not agree on the items as measuring a concept.

Criterion-related validity is often tested by comparing a developing tool with one that has already been tested for validity. Also, some other measure that is objective can be used as a comparison. For example, individuals who say they are less religious but more spiritual on the LCI-R can be asked the number of times they attend church now compared with before the NDE.

Construct validity is frequently determined by statistical analysis and factor analysis of large numbers of subjects answering the questions on an instrument. The rule of thumb is there should be five to ten subjects per item tested. In a 50-item instrument like the LCI-R, between 250 and 500 NDErs would need to take the test. The computer would cluster the similar answers into factors. The LCI-R now has nine clusters. With a large number of subjects there may be more or less factors. Some may "cluster" differently and some items may not correlate at all with other items. It is the individuals who take the instrument who determine the clusters as opposed to the researchers.

Using tools or instruments with sufficient psychometric testing increases the strength of a research study. A tool that has only face validity would be at the Level VI in the levels of evidence.

The LCI-R is designed to measure life changes related to values and beliefs. Additional changes have been described by other researchers such as difficulties with close personal relationships, increased psychic tendencies, and electromagnetic aftereffects.

In a follow-up of patients two years after an NDE, van Lommel (2001) was able to use the LCI to determine life changes. The results of the scores on the LCI of those who had an NDE were compared with individuals in a control group without an NDE. There was a statistically significant difference between the two groups on social attitude (more caring and empathetic), religious attitude (more spiritual), attitude toward death (less fearful), and interest in the meaning of life.

van Lommel also conducted an eight-year follow-up. Both the NDErs and the non NDErs increased their scores in social attitude with the NDE group still scoring higher. The non NDE group scored higher than the NDEs in some religious attitude categories, such as the understanding of the purpose of life. The NDErs significantly increased their score on interest in spirituality with the non NDErs dramatically decreasing their score. Both groups decreased their fear of death. Using the non NDErs as a comparison group demonstrated the changes that occur in attitude toward interpersonal relationships, spirituality, and fear of death that due to aging as well as events such as the NDE.

Difficulties with close personal relationships

In 1991 Insinger conducted a qualitative study with 11 NDErs conducted through the International Association for Near-Death Studies (IANDS). Her objective was to identify aftereffects, particularly those that influenced family relationships. The NDErs found the NDE to have a positive impact on them personally but, in some instances, created difficulties with family members. Some family members were accepting and supportive of the event, others did not want to discuss the NDE, and others accepted the description of the experience and its impact as time went on. Insinger cited the need for more research with larger numbers in the future. This would have been a Level V research study.

Christian (2005), studied 26 NDErs using the Locke-Wallace Marital Adjustment Test (Locke & Wallace, 1959), the Weiss-Ceretto Marital

Status Inventory (Gottman, 1999), and a modification of Gottman's Shared Meanings Questionnaire (Gottman,1999) to determine marital status. All three of the tools used had been tested for reliability and validity. The NDErs were compared with 26 non NDErs who had other life changing events (LCEs). Sixty five percent of the marriages in which the NDErs were involved at the time of their NDEs ended in divorce. In the LCE group, only 19% had marriages which ended in divorce. Besides the increased divorce rate, NDErs compared with the LCE participants, were less satisfied in their marriages, their marriages were less stable, and there was not a high level of shared meaning in the marriages.

Christian also used a retrospective design with a convenience sample. Strengths of this study included the use of valid and reliable tools and a comparison group. Much more research is needed in this area. A study of a larger group immediately after an NDE and then with follow up at different times would help identify the process of adjustment or lack thereof with family members after an NDE.

Loss of fear of death

In Sabom's study (1982) of 45 NDErs and an equal number of non NDErs, belief in an afterlife increased dramatically among NDEs. There was no change in that belief among non NDErs during the same time frame. Almost all the NDEs said they had no fear of death.

Greyson (1992) studied fear of death of 135 NDErs, 43 individuals close to death but without an NDE, and 112 never close to death. He found the NDErs scored the lowest on the Threat Index instrument, a valid and reliable tool.

van Lommel's study (2001) described previously showed a difference in the fear of death between the NDErs and non NDErs in the two-year and eight-year follow-up. The non NDErs decreased their fear of death significantly also at the eight-year interval.

Lawrence (1997) carried out a pilot study of hospice patients who had had an NDE previous to the terminal illness. The purpose of the study was to determine if, at the time of death, NDErs still had no fear. All three individuals showed no fear of dying. One said he could not wait to feel the same way he had felt during the NDE.

One aspect of this research has focused on fear of death before an NDE and after an NDE. For more accuracy, this type of research needs to be done before an NDE and then after the experience with individuals who are at risk for a cardiac arrest. Also the fear of death seems to change over time. More longitudinal research, using reliable and valid instruments, like the Threat Index, would be important to carry out. It would also be important to know if hospice patients who have had an NDE still have no fear of death. This would change the approaches used to care for these patients and their families.

Electromagnetic after effects

There are two tools available to measure electromagnetic effects after an NDE: the Electromagnetic Effect Questionnaire (EMEQ) developed by Nouri (2008) and rhe Electromagnetic Phenomena Questionnaire (EPQ) developed by Greyson and Liester (2011).

The EMEQ is a five-point Likert scale, consisting of 16 questions. It has been tested for validity and reliability. The EPQ is a qualitative/quantitative tool with 59 questions.

Knittwies (1997) used a thermistor and electroscope to measure heat and electron flow comparing the hands of seven NDErs with ten non NDErs. This was the only laboratory type study that was found. There was no difference between the two groups in measures of heat or electron flow.

Ring (1992) compared 74 individuals with 54 controls on possible aftereffects of NDEs. These subjects were part of a convenience sample. In this study 24% of the NDEs and only 7% of the controls reported an increase in electric or electronic malfunctioning. Subjects in the interviews could describe various experiences such as difficulty with watches, computers, televisions, streetlights, cell phones, and other electronic equipment.

Other studies involving self-reports by the subjects of problems with electronic or electric equipment were carried out by Nouri (2008), Morse and Perry (1992), and Fracasso & Friedman, (2012). All found NDErs reported an increase in difficulties with electronic or electric devices from 24% to 70% of NDErs making these assertions. To date, these studies have been conducted using convenience samples, some with or without control groups. What we know is many NDErs notice malfunctioning in electric or electronic devices. Testing NDErs who report these difficulties by placing electronic devices near them to determine the actual objective frequency of these occurrences would strengthen this area of NDE research. This might also increase our understanding of what happens to the energy of individuals after an NDE.

In van Lommel's study at the eight-year follow-up, 11 of the 37 individuals who had had an NDE, died. Twenty of the 37 non NDErs at that eight-year marker died. van Lommel does comment that the NDErs were younger than the non NDErs, however, the question of NDErs living longer after a cardiac arrest has not been addressed.

Increase in psychic phenomena and abilities

Several researchers have studied the incidence of paranormal experiences after an NDE. The Community Mail Survey of Psychic Experiences (CMSPE) developed by John Palmer (1979) was used by Kohr (1982) and Greyson (1983) to determine the incidence of psychic phenomena post NDE. To date, no reports of reliability and validity testing have been done on the CMSPE.

Other researchers, Ring (1980), Grey (1985), and Sutherland (1989) interviewed subjects. All were convenience samples. Sutherland published the results of the more common psychic phenomena and compared the results with the general population, before the NDE and after the NDE. The subjects all reported higher scores on psychic abilities after their NDE. Here are some of the results:

	General population	Before NDE	After NDE
Clairvoyance	38%	43%	73%
Telepathy	36% - 58%	46%	87%
Precognition	-	57%	89%
Déjà vu		76%	84%
OBE	12%-14%	18%	51%
Spirits	26%	24%	68%

According to Sutherland, the differences between pre-NDEs and post-NDEs were all statistically significant.

Because this was a retrospective, descriptive study, with self-reporting pre and post experiences, it would be classified as a Level V research study. No attempt was made to verify the psychic claims. Self-selection and self-reports are often an issue in research studies. In this case, it was unclear if individuals who have psychic experiences after an NDE were more likely to volunteer for the study than those who had no such experiences. Historically, issues of honesty, comprehension of the questions, memory, and introspective ability, to name a few, can interfere with the validity of answers.

Deathbed Communications (DBCs)

Cobbe in 1882 and Barrett in 1926 published the first contemporary descriptions of deathbed communications. Cobbe called these events visions of the dying. Barrett in his book, referred to them as deathbed visions. These researchers were instrumental in describing this phenomena qualitatively with details about the events. These events were often told directly by relatives to Barrett or written to him. In some cases, Barrett was present at the time these deathbed communications occurred. From Horan and Lange's analysis (1997), of the 49 accounts we know, deathbed communications include not only visions but auditory and kinesthetic communications.

Veridical perceptions (actual, genuine experiences) were also noted in Barrett's book. There were ten cases of deathbed visions where the dying person saw a dead friend or relative without being told of their deaths.

In 1961, Karlis Osis surveyed 10,000 physicians and nurses of whom 640 responded on observations of deathbed visions of dying individuals. This was an important study because of the number of credible participants who verified the existence of deathbed communications. The doctors and nurses reported 39.2% of the deathbed patients experienced some type of vision (p. 29). The nurses reported 270 of these observations, with physicians reporting 59 (p. 28).

These visions occurred from under ten minutes before the time of death to over a day (p. 31). Osis and Haraldsson (1977) surveyed doctors and nurses in the US and India, demonstrating the occurrences of deathbed communication in other cultures.

These researchers also reported a decrease in terminal restlessness and anxiety after a DBC (Cobbe, 1882; Barrett, 1926; Osis and Haraldsson, 1977). These were descriptive studies with the use of convenience samples. In addition, the deathbed communications that doctors and nurses reported on often occurred many years previous to the survey. This would be considered a Level V research study.

With the advent of the hospice movement in the US in 1974 and in India in 1986, dying patients received more attention. The experiences they had were more a focus of concern and research.

Lawrence and Repede (2013) attempted to obtain a more exact incidence of deathbed communications in their study and to include, not only visions, but also auditory and kinesthetic communications near death. The staff of a community-based hospice with home care and an inpatient unit reported experiences with deathbed communications. It was reasoned that chart audits during the 30-day period before death would include descriptions of DBCs.

These chart audits of 60 patients revealed five (8.33%) included descriptions of DBCs. This low number was inconsistent with the number of DBCs nurses, social workers, and chaplains in the organization claimed to have occurred. During weekly meetings of current hospice patients, approximately 10% of the patients were experiencing DBCs. Medical records were not currently devised to include a specific area in the charts where a description of DBCs was requested.

As part of the same study, 75 hospice nurses across the United States responded to an online survey about the incidence of DBCs during the last 30 days only when caring for dying patients. The 75 hospice nurses identified 363 incidences of DBCs, with an average of 4.8 patient occurrences per nurse in the last 30 days. They also reported a significant reduction of terminal restlessness, agitation, moaning, pain, and anxiety after the DBC. Deathbed communications generally occur within a few weeks of death. At one time it was believed deathbed communications or visions only occurred at the time of death. Also the results showed DBCs can occur up to three or four weeks before death, but the most common times are from two days before and up to the moment of death (Lawrence & Repede, 2012; Callahan & Kelley, 1992). This study also would be a descriptive study using a convenience sample.

The steps forward included the use of a 30-day time limit to recall the event, the inclusion of auditory and kinesthetic communication, as well as visions and a quantitative description of the impact of the DBCs to produce a calm and peaceful death. It would be considered a Level V study.

After-death communications (ADCs)

In 1889, Henry Sidgwick, with his research team and volunteers, carried out a survey of 17,000 individuals asking if they had seen, heard, or been touched by something or someone not objectively present. This was a convenience sample. He also checked the veridical perception of those who had seen someone after death, not being informed through objective means (Sidgwick, Sidgwick & Johnson, 1894). This would be classified as a Level V research study.

More qualitative interviews were conducted by Rees (1971) and Haraldsson (1988) about contact with deceased spouses. Up to 50% of those interviewed described some contact with the deceased. These qualitative studies would be classified as Level V research studies.

In 1995, the Guggenheims interviewed 2,000 people who had experienced an ADC. These were qualitative interviews of individuals who had experienced an ADC, a Level V study. The Guggenheims were able to delineate the twelve common types of ADCs, providing valuable information for future research.

In 2011, Streit-Horn conducted a systematic review of research on ADCs. She analyzed 35 research studies with the following elements included in her evaluation rubric: clarity and completeness of explanation of the purpose of the study; clarity and completeness of the description of the method; validity of the instrument; representativeness of the sample surveyed; sampling method, sample size, bias and response to bias, response rate, attempt to explain difference between respondents and non-respondents and results, conclusions, and discussion (p. 33).

The following studies were judged to be the strongest studies listed in descending order with the strongest first: Grimby (1993; 1998); Parkes (1970); Silverman and Nickman (1996);

Barbato, et al. (1999); Yamamoto, et al. (1969); Lindstrom (1995); and Parkes (1965). The participants in these studies were from the United States, Sweden, England, Australia, Japan, and Norway. Silverman and Nickman's study was with bereaved children. This integrated review was at a Level IV.

From the integrated review we know the incidence of ADCs is between 80 to 85% of the recently bereaved. The research to date has focused primarily on the incidence of ADCs and the times of their occurrences. Qualitatively individuals report a positive impact from the ADCs. More systematic research with objective evidence on the impact of the grieving process of ADCs on bereaved individuals would extend research in this area. Streit-Horn also describes the need for the development of valid and reliable tools to measure ADCs.

Summary

Most of the research on transpersonal experiences associated with near death and dying is at the qualitative and descriptive level. Because of the volume of research in some areas, integrated reviews and meta-analyses could be conducted to strengthen the level of research. The documentation of the millions of individuals who have had these experiences establishes the need for the integration of descriptions of these events into handouts for experiencers, families and friends, and into courses for health professionals. This field has been woefully lacking in funding sources for research. Most researchers obtain monies from their employing institutions or carry out research without funding.

CHAPTER 14

VIEWING THE TRANSPERSONAL EXPERIENCES IN TOTALITY

A ll the experiences described in the previous chapters include events that occur before, during, and after death. Limiting a discussion to only one of these experiences in some ways is like the proverbial elephant being viewed from different perspectives by blind men. The stories of the blind men vary a little depending upon the source but, in essence, the men just touch one part of the elephant. When they get together, they argue that the part they have touched provides the true description of the elephant. A sighted man who sees the entire elephant is able to show them how to put their assessments together to obtain the true picture of the elephant.

Even though individual subjective experiences, as with the elephant, are true, they are limited. It is necessary to view all these transpersonal phenomena in total to obtain a truer and more holistic description of the nature of these experiences. It is also important to attend to all the descriptions of each type of experience without judgment. As in Phenomenological analysis, it is important to look at the data from the perspective of the experiencers and the impact and meanings of the events for them. By bracketing preconceived ideas and explanations about these experiences, we are able to comprehend their nature from the perspective of those to whom they have occurred. This discussion is based on the description by the participants of their experiences viewed holistically.

Where the experience occurs

The transpersonal experiences surrounding death can occur among three commonly described regions: the earthly plane, the intercosmic region (Baker, 1954) and the ethereal region. The earthly plane is the one individuals experience through the five senses, also referred to as the physical plane. The intercosmic region is the area in between the earthly plane and the ethereal plane experienced beyond the body. The ethereal plane, or spiritual plane, is beyond the body into what would be commonly referred to as an afterlife.

Near-death visits (NDVs)

Who they communicate with and the senses that are used

In the case of near-death visits (NDVs) individuals who are in the earthly plane are able to see, experience auditory communication, detect a smell associated with the deceased, or feel the presence of someone from either the perceived intercosmic or ethereal region. A man was able to see his deceased mother and sister at the foot of his bed. Another person was able to detect the presence of his deceased father by the smell of chemicals his father worked with when alive. A woman could see and hear her deceased son and even feel him hold her hand when she was on a stretcher in the hospital. In the cases of known NDVs, the deceased did not alter any objects in the earthly plane.

Presently, the only reports are between the ill person and a deceased relative or friend. However, individuals who experience the same degree of illness can also report a visit from the Grim Reaper.

Physiological state

All the individuals had been seriously ill before the NDV occurred. One woman, for example, had had a respiratory arrest but was out of the intensive care unit. Another had had a myocardial infarction but was recovering. Generally, they are progressing toward recovery and not typically in pain or receiving pain medication.

Veridical perception

The man who saw his mother and sister had not been told the sister had died. The family had requested no one tell him for fear that news would be detrimental to his health (Lawrence, 1997).

Shared experience

There are no reports of shared experiences with more than one person being able to see a deceased individual.

Length of time of the death of the deceased seen during the NDV

In most cases of NDVs, the deceased had been dead for a number of years. Only the sister described above was a recent death.

Length of time of the event

NDVs tend to be short events, less than five minutes, but the person may appear more than once. The descriptions of individuals having these experiences indicate the deceased is there to provide comfort or to encourage them to come with them through bodily death. Once comfort is provided or the experiencer makes it clear he or she is not ready to die, the visits end.

Transforming event

Reports of NDVs being a transforming event have not been described. It is unknown if NDVs continue after the hospitalization. No alteration in the person's physical condition has been described.

Incidence

Lawrence reported approximately 5% of seriously ill individuals who had once been unconscious stated they had had an NDV.

Deathbed Communication (DBCs)

Who they communicate with and the senses that are used

In the case of deathbed communications (DBCs), individuals who are imminently dying are in the earthly plane but ready to transition away from there. They experience communication with not only deceased friends and relatives, but also ethereal beings like angels. They also see borders or gates to a perceived afterlife. The communication is most commonly visual although auditory and kinesthetic contact has been described. Some individuals are also able to hear music that is ethereal in nature. The communication with the deceased loved one does not generally involve the deceased altering any objects in the earthly plane.

These DBCs can occur within a month of dying, although most commonly within a few days of dying. The DBCs that occur within weeks of dying are usually communications with dead friends and/or relatives. They can also include communications with the deceased unknown to them to have died. The communications with ethereal beings generally occurs closer to the time of death.

Physiological state

DBCs occur to individuals who are imminently dying. Often they have a terminal diagnosis of cancer or are in the last stages of an incurable illness. They are often receiving medication for pain and anxiety.

Veridical perception

Many instances of veridical perceptions have been reported. For many decades individuals have reported seeing a person whom they have not been told was deceased. In earlier days, when communication was less timely, no one in the room with the dying person might be aware of a death that occurred. Here is the example from Barrett's (2011) book. A woman was very ill and expected to die. Her husband was present. The woman reported hearing music and a voice singing that belonged to someone known to the family. No one knew the woman singing had died.

Suddenly she changed the subject and said to her husband, "Do you hear those voices singing?" Col. Z, who narrates the incident, replied that he did not, and his wife continued. "I have heard them several times today and I am sure they are the angels welcoming me to Heaven, but," she added, "it is strange, there is one voice among them I am sure I know, but I cannot remember whose voice it is." Suddenly she stopped and said, pointing straight over her husband's head, "Why, there she is in the corner of the room. It is Julia X. She is coming on; she is leaning over you; she has her hands up; she is praying. Do look; she is going." Her husband turned round but could see nothing. His wife then said, "She has gone (p.78)."

Shared experience

There are reports of others seeing or hearing the deceased person, although it is not common. Health professionals being in the room with the dying individuals have reported seeing the apparition or music being described by the person.

Length of time of the death of the deceased seen during the DBC

The deceased person being seen could have died recently or years before. The length of time does not seem to be as significant as the emotional connection between the dying person and the deceased. That is described as the constant influence of the appearance.

Length of time of the event

The DBC is generally occurring in short time frames of five minutes or less with a range of up to an hour. Often the deceased person will be in communication more than one time.

Transforming event

The DBC markedly reduces the fear of death and pain. Hospice nurses frequently report a decrease in restlessness and the need for pain medication (Lawrence & Repede, 2013). Some patients also experience a radiant glow at the time of death. It is unclear if this is more common with individuals experiencing a DBC. At the time of death, those present have reported seeing mist or smoke leaving the body.

Incidence

The incidences of DBCs have been reported to be 10% to 20% of dying patients. These occurrences are not generally recorded in hospice records. Lawrence & Repede (2013) report the average hospice nurse will see five patients a month with a DBC.

The communication with these deceased friends or relatives can occur to others in the room with the dying individual. DBCs have been reported to reduce the anxiety, terminal restlessness, and pain associated with the dying process.

After-death communications (ADCs)

Who they communicate with and the senses that are used

In the case of after-death communications (ADCs), the person again is in the earthly plane and able to see, hear, or feel the presence of a recently deceased individual connected to them. Sometimes the auditory communication is telepathic. Occasionally a person will smell a fragrance, a perfume, a flower associated with a deceased individual. On occasion, the communication is symbolic. The bereaved may see an animal or object that reminds them of the deceased person. Manipulation of physical objects can occur. In some cases phones ring, televisions start, and/or music comes on spontaneously. As reported in Chapter 11, a book was opened to a page that contained an important bill for a grieving widow by her deceased husband. Purposes of the contact can include reassurance the deceased person is in a good place, sharing information, a warning to the bereaved, and even an intervention. The person having the ADC is typically grieving the loss of the deceased individual. Most often it is a family member, but it can also be a health professional involved in the care of the deceased when alive.

Physiological state

Grief has been known to alter cortisol levels, change sleep patterns, decrease the immune response, and alter heart rate and blood pressure (Buckley, Sunari, Marshall, Bartrop, McKinley & Tofler, 2010). Family members and health professionals involved in the care of the deceased experience varying degrees of grief. In the case of a prolonged death, a person can experience anticipatory grief and start the grieving process before the person actually dies.

Veridical perception

Veridical perceptions include being warned of a dangerous situation. In many cases, the bereaved was able to respond and avoid harm. There are reported incidences of individuals seeing the deceased before they were told of the person's death. A bereavement counselor was getting ready to go see a hospice patient after being called by the family. As she walked into her closet, she felt the patient's presence. She felt his joy and freedom and appreciation for being there for him. She noted this experience happened at 4:23. When she arrived at the patient's house, his family told him he had died at 4:23 (Guggenheim, 1995, p. 24).

Shared experience

In some cases, there is a shared experience with more than one individual being able to experience the communication with the deceased. This is often the case when physical objects are altered. More than one person can see or hear what has changed. ` Carolina right before she went to sleep saw her deceased uncle. The family was concerned about his afterlife experience because of his alcoholism and general lifestyle. The uncle told the woman to tell her mother, aunt, and his two sisters, not to worry about him. He was fine. When she went to meet up with her mother and aunt, she found the aunt had had the same experience (Guggenheim, 1995, pp. 232-233).

Length of time after the death of the deceased seen during the ADC

The incidence of ADCs is more common within the month after a person's death gradually diminishing by the sixth month. However, some ADCs occur years after a person's death.

Length of time of the event

Usually the ADCs are short, less than five minutes. Most ADCs are singular events. The memories of these events tend to fade over time and lack vividness as they fade.

Transforming event

ADCs have been reported to significantly alter the grieving process. This alteration is described as occurring spontaneously at an emotional or ethereal level and not at a cognitive understanding level. Most experiencers report a decrease in the feelings of grief and an increase in feelings of comfort, love, and security.

Incidence

Streit-Horn (2011) in her systematic review of research on ADCs describes the incidence of ADCs to grieving family members during the year after death to be between 73% and 85%. Kelly (2002) who studied 90 emergency service workers, found 28% had sensed, felt, or seen the victims of tragic accidents after their deaths.

Out-of-body experiences (OBEs) operating in the nonphysical plane

Who they communicate with and the senses that are used

A person perceiving their self to be out of their body spontaneously or during an NDE, can experience sight and hearing. Hearing may be normal or telepathic. Reports include difficulties when attempting to move objects, and experiencing "going through" objects or individuals. Reports of taste have not been recorded. While a person having the OBE can hear and see people in the environment, those people generally cannot see or hear them, although rare cases have been reported.

The individual is able to move from an "on high" vantage point within and outside the room. Persons experiencing OBEs not associated with an NDE feel concern about getting back to their body.

Physiological state

Spontaneous OBEs in the hospital setting not associated with an NDE often occur when a person is experiencing severe pain. Other traumatic experiences, like having tubes put in a throat can precede an OBE. Some individuals find when pain returns, they may be able to put themselves out of their bodies again.

Veridical perception

They are able to see or otherwise notice events or people, the experience of which would not be possible if in their body. One man while out of his body in a hospital did describe being able to see nurses making popcorn but did not report being able to smell the popcorn.

Shared experience

No shared experiences were reported in the study of OBEs occurring to hospitalized patients.

Length of time of the event

From the case studies and estimate of the length of time out of body would be five to ten minutes.

Transforming event

The feeling of severe pain can be eliminated during an OBE. There are no reports of OBEs producing major transformations that go on after the hospital experience. There are no reports of mist or smoke leaving the body during the OBE.

Incidence

Olson (1988) in her study of 200 hospitalized subjects found 3% experience an OBE not associated with an NDE. Lawrence found 6% of the 111 previously unconscious patients had an OBE. Of the 243 intensive care patients Satori (2006) interviewed, 1% reported an OBE.

Near-death experiences (NDEs) going from the earthly plane to the intercosmic to the ethereal

Who they communicate with and the senses that are used

Persons experiencing OBEs who move on to an NDE can also experience sight and hearing from the earthly plane. In addition, they have a wonderful feeling of peace and love. Most individuals who report being out of their bodies will describe themselves as being themselves even though their bodies are seen as elsewhere. During this time they can see and hear about resuscitation events not able to occur given the condition of their physical body. They are unable to move objects even though they attempt to do so. However, there have been reports of NDErs during the OBE component entering someone else's body in order to communicate with that person. Greyson and Bush (1996) describe the experience of a man who attempted suicide by hanging himself. He changed his mind and sought out his wife while out of his body. She could not hear him so he went inside her body. Apparently this way he was able to communicate clearly since she went to the kitchen for a knife and then to her husband to cut him down.

The individuals with an NDE move from the earthly plane to the intercosmic realm, then into the ethereal realm. In the ethereal realm they communicate telepathically almost exclusively and have enhanced vision and hearing. Smell and taste are absent in most reports. McVea (2013) described God as a brightness she would feel, taste, touch, hear, and smell. Mostly NDErs report passing through solid objects but on occasion report feeling a resistance (Gabbard and Twemlow, 1984, p. 158). They can see deceased friends and relatives and spiritual beings, (God, Jesus, angels, for example).

Physiological state

Often NDEs occur during a cardiac arrest or a sudden life-threatening event. Lawrence (1997) reported NDEs occurring to patients who were unconscious for a number of reasons, including coma, surgery and childbirth.

Veridical perception

There are numerous accounts of veridical perception by individuals who experienced an NDE. During the OBE phase, the subjects can accurately recall resuscitation efforts, descriptions of physicians, articles of clothing, and out-of-place objects in hospitals that only appear during resuscitation. Even individuals born blind are able to see objects. As the individual moves on to the ethereal realm, they often report seeing deceased individuals not previously known to them to have died. Many of these experiences have been verified.

Individuals will also report seeing beautiful flowers, heavenly music, barriers, radiant light, and religious figures

To date, it is not possible to verify these perceptions except that the same type of experience is reported by millions of individuals. The interpretation of the communication varies according to cultural and religious beliefs.

Shared experience

There are instances of shared NDEs when individuals come close to death at the same time from the same accident or dangerous situation. Gibson (1996) interviewed a firefighter who, with other firefighters, was trapped during a wilderness fire in 1989. Jake remembered thinking he was going to die and then found himself above his body and seeing other members of his crew also out of their bodies. One firefighter was born with a defective foot. Jake called out for him to notice his foot was straight. Jake saw a brilliant light and his great grandfather who guided him further into the NDE. He and his grandfather communicated telepathically. Jake did not want to leave where it was so beautiful and peaceful to go back to a burned body. The grandfather said he and any of his crew who went back would not suffer ill effects from the fire.

When Jake returned to his body, he noticed the shovel near him had nearly melted from the intense heat. He and his crew were able to walk up the hill to safety with only some singed hair from the fire. For weeks afterwards they compared their shared NDE stories.

Length of time of the event

There is no definitive description of the time of an NDE. A cardiac arrest can take up to 15 to 20 minutes. A way to determine when an NDE occurs during a resuscitation effort has not been discovered. NDErs say time does not apply in the ethereal world.

Incidence

Estimates of the prevalence of NDEs is between 4% and 18% of any given population.

Transforming event

Both positive and distressing NDEs are transformative. NDEs are transformative in a number of ways: commonly individuals become more spiritual, less materialistic, can have increased psychic abilities, difficulties with electronic equipment, and lose their fear of death. The memory of NDEs is vivid even years later.

During the time of an actual death with no return, individuals have reported seeing a mist or smoke leaving the body of the deceased. To date, there have been no reports of that occurring during an NDE. Also, those observing individuals at the time of death on occasion report radiant faces which cause the dying person to look years younger. To date, there are no reports of this radiance occurring to those who have an NDE.

Table I

Comparisons of the characteristics of the five main transpersonal experiences

	NDVs	OBEs	NDEs	DBCs	ADCs
Plane	earthly	intercosmic	intercosmic	earthly	earthly and ethereal
visual	yes	yes	yes	yes	yes
auditory	yes	yes	telepathic	yes	yes
touch	yes	no	no	no	yes
smell	yes	no	no	no	yes
taste	no	no	no	no	no
Physiological state	serious illness	pain	near-death	dying	grieving
Veridical perceptions	yes	yes	yes	yes	yes
Shared experience	not reported	not reported	yes	yes	yes
Incidence	5%	1%-6%	4%-18%	10%-20%	73%-85%

Trans-formative	somewhat	no	highly	yes	yes
mist or smoke	not reported	not reported	not reported	yes	NA
leaving body					
radiant faces	not reported	not reported	not reported	yes	not reported

Summary

Taste is not a sense reported in the transpersonal experiences that involve being in the intercosmic or ethereal plane. The other four senses have been reported as part of the communication process during these experiences. As the person in the transpersonal experience moves away from earthly situations, auditory communication is more likely to be telepathic. Vision is enhanced during the ethereal part of the NDE, including the ability of blind individuals to see. Also as a person 'moves' out of the earthly plane, they lose the ability to move material objects.

These descriptions provide a consistency of movement between the earthly to the intercosmic and then the ethereal plane as the use of senses and abilities change. A spirit form would not need a sense of taste or be able to move dense objects. These reports are consistent from thousands of subjects at this time across cultures.

In all five transpersonal experiences, individuals have reported evidence of veridical communications. In these experiences, knowledge of events or people who have died was acquired during the experience and not through normal means. Again, the types of reports are consistent across subjects.

These veridical communications can be seen as similar to circumstantial evidence used in a court of law. In the case of circumstantial evidence, a series of facts can be used to infer a crucial point for which there is no direct evidence. Contrary to popular depictions in books, movies, and television shows, circumstantial evidence, like DNA found at a crime scene, is used successfully in obtaining a conviction (Heller, 2006).

The overwhelming number of reports of veridical experiences during all five experiences should provide enough "circumstantial evidence" to enable us to say individuals can have transpersonal experiences where they obtain information from nonphysical means.

In all these experiences, an altered physiological state was present in varying degrees from less severe to imminently dying. Of all the states, the grief state resulted in the greatest number of transpersonal communications in an ADC. The grief state produces the largest number of descriptions of transpersonal events. While individuals experience grief more frequently than near-death, it is unknown what it is about the grief state that leads to this ability to connect with a deceased individual. In most of the transpersonal experiences physical objects cannot be moved. The major exception is the ADC. Either the recently deceased have more ability to communicate with individuals in the earthly plane, or grieving facilitates the communication, or a combination of both occurs.

There are many reports of individuals who at the time of death have an altered appearance. They may have a radiant face and look much younger. If this is occurring because of contact with ethereal beings, it would be expected that individuals who have an NDE and are exposed to the Being of Light would have a radiant face. None such have been reported. A woman who saw the image of the Virgin Mary at Medjugorje said others told her how radiant and youthful the woman looked after the experience. In her case, this radiance was not present all the time but would come and go (Lawrence, 2014)).

Also at the time of death, individuals have reported seeing mist or smoke leave the body of the deceased. That has not been reported in the research and cases of OBEs and NDEs. Again, it is unknown if those phenomena do not happen in other circumstances, or if no specific observations of those phenomena were carried out.

It is hoped the integration of the study of all transpersonal experiences associated with near death and dying leads us to a richer and more complete understanding of these phenomena.

APPENDIX A

Post NDE psychic and electromagnetic after effects

William Howell

In 2009 I had a heart attack and cardiac arrest at the age of 44. There were many times before and when I was in hospital that I'd feel sick or dizzy and have chest pain. Once in work it happened and I woke up in the cold store with a cut on my head and bad chest pain. When I was in the hospital ward my aunt was visiting me, the next thing I knew I woke up in CCU. Another time, I was talking to the doctor and she said 'are you ok?' I said yes but there were colors in front of my eyes. I must have been out for a while because I came to with the doctor standing over me asking if I was still there. I have no idea what happened in between me losing consciousness and waking up. I have an ICD (Implantable Cardioverter Defibrillator) pacemaker now.

The day I had the cardiac arrest, I was lying in the hospital bed and my wife was visiting then the nurses said to my wife I think you'd better go outside for a few minutes.

All of a sudden I was in a long dark tunnel with voices all around and people calling me. I was just floating down and I could hear voices around me. There was a man at the end of the tunnel calling me. He was a dark figure but I knew he was friendly – it may have been my grandfather. He was calling me towards him.

Next thing I could see the doctor in front of me – I could just see his eyes and teeth and he said to the nurses, 'It's ok, he's back'.

After Effects

Since then some really weird things have been happening to me. I thought I was losing it and I was traumatized after the heart attack so I went to counselling. The more I talked about it the more these things were happening, but my counsellor seemed to understand and helped me a lot.

About two or three months after I got home the dog started looking at something behind me, it just had a fixed stare and was wagging its tail while looking at something behind me. I turned and saw a white shadow just disappear.

Then I started having out of body experiences – any time of day. I feel as if I'm drifting away and I can see myself below then find myself in my grandmother's house. I can see everything that's going on. I went back to when I was ten or eleven years old. It's like I'm reliving something that's already happened.

When I have these experiences and go to my grandmother's house I can smell the smoke from her cigarette. She always used to have a cigarette in one hand and a rolling pin in the other hand. It's all so plain and real, I'm actually there again.

When these things happen, I can't respond to anyone in the room with me. My wife said I just look ahead with a fixed stare, I don't blink. My body is down there but my spirit is up there and they can't interact with each other.

I hear voices and people calling me, then people touching me on the shoulder. I was talking about a dead friend to someone else then heard a whistling noise, there was no one else around so I don't know where that whistling came from.

When I'm in a relaxed state things happen more. I was sitting at home with just the two dogs in the room with me. The dogs seem to notice if something happens. All of a sudden there were two pieces of paper and one started to flicker and the other one turned over completely right before my eyes. There were no windows open so how do you explain that?

I also get a lot of flashbacks of looking down that tunnel. I've had a lot of counselling to help me get over all of this but these experiences just keep happening, I don't know how to explain them.

Some really strange things I've also noticed is that I can't wear a watch, they just stop or the second hand will stop. My computer always crashes on me, I have to turn it off and reboot it nearly every time I use it. It works fine for my wife and the children; it only plays up with me. The last computer I had was quite new but didn't last long, the man who came to repair it found that the fan inside had completely melted and he didn't know why as there was no reason for it to have melted. I've also noticed that my hearing has become much more acute since my heart attack.

I'm not afraid of dying either, my time just wasn't up. I now live every day for the day and don't worry about going. I feel as if I've got something to do in my life but I don't know what it is.

When I'm in public places I can see spirits around people. This sounds mad I know, but I can see different auras around people, some have white, some have dark the different auras mean different things. The dark auras mean keep away. If I'm watching something like 'Most Haunted' on TV I can see something that others who are with me can't see. On one show there was a mist on the camera but I could see an actual man, I could see him but no one else could.

A friend of the family has been having strange things happening in her house like things moving for no reason. I went to visit one day and could see an old lady at the top of the stairs just looking at me. I said hello and she just disappeared. My friend made me a cup of coffee and I put it down on the side and it fell onto the hearth, it just moved off a stable, solid surface without anyone touching it. I've been back to the house twice since then and I haven't seen that woman again but my friend still senses her presence.

In our house an old man had passed away there before we moved in. I always hear a bang upstairs and it's always at a certain time. It comes from the room that he died in, I feel as if I am hearing him hit the floor and die.

I don't know why all of this is happening to me, I can't explain it. I didn't ask for it, it just started happening after my heart attack. I've had lots of counselling but no one can explain exactly why this has started to happen to me. I just have to learn to accept it and that my life is very different now.

* Reproduced with permission from http://drpennysartori.wordpress.com/nde-case-studies/

APPENDIX B

Resources*

After Death Communication Research Foundation (ADCRF)
P.O. Box 20238
Houma, LA 70360
http://www.adcrf.org/

American Society for Psychical Research, Inc.
5 West 73rd Street
New York, New York 10023 USA
Phone: 212-799-5050
Fax: 212-496-2497
email aspr@aspr.com
http://www.aspr.com/

Association for Death Education and Counseling (ADEC) Headquarters
111 Deer Lake Road, Suite 100
Deerfield, IL 60015 USA
Phone: 847-509-0403
Fax: 847-480-9282
http://www.adec.org//AM/Template.cfm?Section=Home#

Australian Centre for Grief and Bereavement
253 Wellington Road
Mulgrave Vic 3170 Australia

Phone: +61 3 9265 2100
Toll free: (Australia wide) 1800 642 066
Fax: +61 3 9265 2150
http://www.grief.org.au/

Canadian Hospice Palliative Care Association
Annex D, Saint-Vincent Hospital
60 Cambridge Street North, Ottawa, ON K1R 7A5
Phone: 613-241-3663
Toll Free: 800-668-2785
Fax: 613-241-3986
http://www.chpca.net/Home

Center for Consciousness Studies
University of Arizona
P.O. Box 245114
Tucson, AZ USA 85724-5114
Cell/Text: 520.247.5785
Phone: 520.621.9317
Fax: 520-626-6416
email: center@u.arizona.edu
consciousness.arizona.edu

Centre for Consciousness
School of Philosophy, Research School of Social Sciences
College of Arts & Social Sciences
Room 2211A
HC Coombs Building (Building 9)
Fellows Road
The Australian National University
Canberra
Phone: +61 2 6125 7529
Fax: +61 2 6125 7528
Email: consciousness@anu.edu.au

Center for Grief and Traumatic Loss, LLC
Dr. Allan L. Botkin, PhD
250 Parkway Drive, Suite 150, Lincolnshire, IL 60069
Phone: 847-680-0279
http://www.induced-adc.com/resources/

Compassionate Friends
PO Box 3696
Oak Brook, IL 60522
(or) 1000 Jorie Blvd.
 Suite 140
Oak Brook, IL 60523
Phone: 630-990-0010
Toll free: 877-969-0010
Fax: 630-990-0246
http://www.compassionatefriends.org/about_us.aspx

Hospice Foundation of America (HFA)
1710 Rhode Island Ave NW
Suite 400
Washington, DC 20036
Phone: 202-457-5811
Toll free: 800-854-3402
http://hospicefoundation.org/

International Association for Hospice & Palliative Care
5535 Memorial Dr.
Suite F - PMB 509
Houston TX 77007 USA
Phone: 936-321-9846
Toll Free: 866- 374-2472
Fax: 713-589-3657
http://hospicecare.com/home/

International Association for Near-Death Studies, Inc. (IANDS)
2741 Campus Walk Avenue,
Building 500
Durham, NC 27705-8878, USA
Phone: 919-383-7940
http://iands.org/home.html

National Hospice and Palliative Care Organization
1731 King Street
Alexandria, Virginia 22314
Phone: 703-837-1500 | Fax: 703-837-1233
http://www.nhpco.org/

Near Death Experience Research Foundation
P.O. Box 20238
Houma, LA 70360.
http://nderf.org/

The Monroe Institute
365 Roberts Mountain Road
Faber Virginia, 22938
Email: info@monroeinstitute.org
Phone: 434-361-1500
Toll Free: 866-881-3440
Fax: 434-361-1237
http://www.monroeinstitute.org/resources/out-of-body-experience-obe

Parapsychology Foundation, Inc.
P. O. Box 1562
New York, NY 10021-0043
Phone: 212-628-1550
Fax: 212-628-1559
office@parapsychology.org
http://www.parapsychology.org/

Rhine Research Center
2741 Campus Walk Avenue
Building 500
Durham, NC 27705
Phone: 919-309-4600
http://www.rhine.org/

Society Of Psychical Research
49 Marloes Road
London W8 6LA
http://www.spr.ac.uk

Sophia University
Graduate School of Transpersonal Studies
1069 East Meadow Circle
Palo Alto CA 94303
Phone: 650-493-4430 | Fax: 650-493-6835
http://www.sofia.edu/graduate-school-of-transpersonal-studies

St Christopher's Hospice
51-59 Lawrie Park Road
London SE26 6DZ
Phone: 020 8768 4500
email: info@stchristophers.org.uk
http://www.stchristophers.org.uk/

* This is not a complete list of available resources but rather an attempt to provide a starting place of resources with major and/or well known institutions. Also this list does not constitute a recommendation. Not all organizations list phone numbers or other contact information. Some only list digital communication on their websites.

REFERENCES

CHAPTER 1

Bushanan, L. (2003) *The Seventh Sense: The Secrets of Remote Viewing as Told by a "Psychic Spy" for the U.S. Military*, New York: Paraview Pocket Books.

Bartlett, J. (2002). *Bartlett's Familiar Quotations*. Boston: Little, Brown and Company.

Beloff, J. (1993). *Parapsychology: A Concise History*. London: The Athlone Press.

Carter, K.C. & Carter, B. (2005). *Childbed Fever: A Scientific Biography of Ignaz Semmelweis*. New Jersey: Transaction Publishers.

Clegg, B. (2013). *Extra Sensory: The Science and Pseudoscience of Telepathy and Other Powers of the Mind*. New York: St. Martin's Press.

de Kruif, P. (2002). *Microbe Hunters*. New York: Mariner Books.

Fisher, I. (2007). Miracles and the fast track to sainthood, *The New York Times*. http://www.nytimes.com/2007/04/08/weekinreview/08basics.html?_r=0. Retrieved 12/13/2013

Gauld, A. (1968). *The Founders of Psychical Research*. London: Routledge & Kegan Paul.

Grattan-Guinness, I. (1982). *Psychical Research: A Guide to its History, Principles & Practices - in celebration of 100 years of the Society for Psychical Research*. Aquarian Press

Haynes, Renée (1982). *The Society for Psychical Research 1882-1982: A History.* London: MacDonald & Co.

History of the Parapsychological Association. *The Parapsychological Association.* http://archived.parapsych.org/history_of_pa.html Retrieved 2013-12-11.

Irwin, H. & Watt, C. (2007). *An Introduction to Parapsychology.* Jefferson, NC: McFarland.

James, W. (1896). Address by the President. *Proceedings of the Society for Psychical Research.* 12, 5-6.

Kuhn, T. S. (1970). *The Structure of Scientific Revolutions.* Chicago: University of Chicago Press.

Lawrence, M. (2014). Unpublished interview with visionary at Medjugorje.

McMahon, J. & Lascurain, A. (1997). *Shopping for Miracles.* Los Angeles: Roxbury Park Books.

Medical Bureau of the Sanctuary http://en.lourdes-france.org/deepen/cures-and-miracles/the-international-medical-committee retrieved 12/13/1013

Moody, R. (2001). *Life after Life.* New York: HarperOne.

Pandarakalam, J. P. (2001). Are the apparitions of Medjugorje real? *Journal of Scientific Exploration,* 15(2) 229–239.

Playfair, G. L. (2012). *Twin Telepathy.* Guilford England: White Crow Books.

Rhine, J. B. (1934). *Extra-Sensory Perception.* Branden Publishing Company.

Ring, K. & Lawrence, M. (1993). Further evidence for veridical perception during near-death experiences. *Journal of Near-Death Studies,* 4, (11) 223-229.

Rogo, S. (1975). *Parapsychology: A Century of Inquiry.* New York: Taplinger Publishing Company.

Sabom, M. (1982). *Recollections of Death: A Medical Investigation.* New York, NY: Harper and Row.

Sidgwick, H., Johnson, A., Myers, F.W.H., Podmore, F., Sidgwick, E. (1894). *Report on the census of hallucinations. In: Proceedings of the Society for Psychical Research. Volume XXVI. Part X.* London: Kegan Paul, Trench, Trübner & Co.

Sullivan, R. (2004). *The Miracle Detective.* New York: Atlantic Monthly Press.

Thouless, R. H. (1972). *From anecdote to experiment in psychical research.* London: Routledge and K. Paul.

Tien, A.Y. (1991). Distributions of hallucinations in the population. *Social Psychiatry and Psychiatric Epidemiology,* 26, 287-292.

van Lommel, P., van Wees, R., Meyers, V., Elfferich, I. (2001). Near-death experience in survivors of cardiac arrest: a prospective study in the Netherlands. *Lancet,* (358) 2039-45.

Walters Art Museum, Baltimore, MD. Retrieved 12/17/2003. http://art.thewalters.org/detail/15244

CHAPTER 2

Allman, L. S., De La Roche, O., Elkins, D. N., & Weathers, R. S. (1992). Psychotherapists's attitudes towards clients reporting mystical experiences. Psychotherapy, 29, 564-569.

American Psychiatric Association. (1994). *Diagnostic and Statistical Manual, Fourth Edition.* Washington, D.C.: American Psychiatric.

Boeree, C. G. (2006). Carl Rogers: 1902-1987. Retrieved from http://webspace.ship.edu/cgboer/rogers.html, December 29, 2013.

Blackmore, S. (1993). *Dying to Live.* New York: Prometheus Books.

Christensen M. & Hewitt-Taylor J. (2006). Empowerment in nursing: paternalism or maternalism? *Br J Nurs.* 15(13) 695-9.

Davis, J. (2003). An Overview of Transpersonal Psychology. *The Humanistic Psychologist,* 31, 2-3, 6-21.

Fiske, S.T., & Taylor, S.E. (1991). *Social Cognition (2nd ed.).* New York: McGraw-Hill.

Forsterling, F. (2001). *Attribution: An Introduction to Theories, Research and Applications.* New York, NY, US: Psychology Press

Fracasso, C., Friedman, H., & Young, M.S. (2010). Psychologists' knowledge of and attitudes about near-death experiences: Changes over time and relationship to transpersonal self-concept. *Journal of Near-Death Studies.* 29(1), 273-281.

Greyson, B. (1993). The Physio-Kundalini Syndrome and Mental Illness. *Journal of Transpersonal Psychology*, 25 (1), 43-58

Greyson, B. (2000). Some Neuropsychological Correlates of the Physio-Kundalini Syndrome. *Journal of Transpersonal Psychology*, 32 (2), 123-134

Harvey, J.H. & Weary, G. (1985). *Attribution: Basic Issues and Applications.* New York: Academic Press.

Heckler R: (1998). *Crossings: Everyday People, Unexpected Events, and Life-Affirming Change.* New York: Harcourt Brace.

Hoobyar, R., Dotz, T. & Sanders, S. (2013). *NLP: The Essential Guide to Neuro-Linguistic Programming.* New York: William Morrow and Company.

Hood, R.W. (1974). Psychological Strength and the Report of Intense Religious Experience. *Journal for the Scientific Study of Religion.* 13, 65–71.

Jones, E. E. & Davis, K. E. (1965). From acts to dispositions: the attribution process in social psychology, in L. Berkowitz (ed.), *Advances in Experimental Social Psychology* (Volume 2, pp. 219-266), New York: Academic Press.

Jones, E.E., Kannouse, D.E., Kelley, H.H., Nisbett, R.E., Valins, S. & Weiner, B. (1972). *Attribution: Perceiving the Causes of Behavior.* Morristown, NJ: General Learning Press.

Kasprow, M.C. & Scotton, B.W. (1999). A Review of Transpersonal Theory and its Application to the Practice of Psychotherapy. *J Psychother Pract* Res. 8(1) 12–23.

Kelley, H. H. (1967). Attribution theory in social psychology. In D. Levine (ed.), *Nebraska*

Symposium on Motivation (Volume 15, pp. 192-238). Lincoln: University of Nebraska Press.

Kelley, H.H. & Michela, J.L. (1980). Atribution theory and research. *Ann. Rev. Psychol.* 3, 457-501.

Lajoie, D. H. & Shapiro, S. I. (1992). Definitions of transpersonal psychology: The first twenty-three years. *Journal of Transpersonal Psychology*, 24, (1), 79—98.

Lawrence, M., (1997). *In a World of Their Own; Experiencing Unconsciousness, Westport,* CT.: Greenwood Publishing Group.

Lawrence, M., (1995). The Unconscious Experience. *American Journal of Critical Care*, 4 (3) 227-232.

Lukoff, D. (1985). The diagnosis of mystical experiences with psychotic features. *Journal of Transpersonal Psychology*, 17, 155–181.

Maslow, A. (1976). *Religions, Values, and Peak-Experiences*. New York: Viking Penguin.

McLeod, S. A. (2007). Carl Rogers. Retrieved from http://www.simplypsychology.org/carl-rogers.html , December 29, 1013

McLeod, S. A. (2010). Attribution Theory. Retrieved from http://www.simplypsychology.org/attribution-theory.html, retrieved December 29, 2013.

Moody, R. (2001). *Life after Life*. San Francisco: Harper.

Ofri, D. (2012). "When the Patient Is 'Noncompliant'". *The New York Times*, published online November 15, 2012. Retrieved January 3, 2014.

Otterman, Sharon. "Merging Spirituality and Clinical Psychology at Columbia". *The New York Times*, published online August 9, 2012. Retrieved December 27, 2013.

Oudshoorn A. (2005). Power and empowerment: critical concepts in the nurse-client relationship. *Contemp Nurse*. 20 (1)57-66.

Rogers, C. (1951). *Client-centered psychotherapy*. Boston: Houghton-Mifflin.

Schneider, K. & Langle, A. (2012).The renewal of humanism in psychotherapy: Summary and conclusion. *Psychotherapy*, 49(4) 480-481.

Scotton, B.W., Chinen, A.B., Battista, J.R. (eds)(1996). *Textbook of Transpersonal Psychiatry and Psychology*. New York, Basic Books.

Taylor, E. (1996). William James and transpersonal psychiatry. In Scotton, B.W., Chinen, A.B.; Battista, J.R. *Textbook of Transpersonal Psychiatry and Psychology* (1 ed.). New York: Basic Books. p. 26 Vich, M.A. (1988). Some historical sources for the term "transpersonal." *Journal of Transpersonal Psychology*, 20,107–110.

Walsh, R. & Vaughan, F. (1993). On transpersonal definitions. *Journal of Transpersonal Psychology*, 25 (2) 125-182

Wilkins, P. (2000). Unconditional positive regard reconsidered. *British Journal of Guidance & Counselling*, 28, (1)23-36.

CHAPTER 3

Asaad, G. & Shapiro, B. (1986). Hallucinations: theoretical and clinical overview. *Am J Psychiatry.* 143, 1088–1097.

Beyerstein, B.L. (1996). Visions and hallucinations, in Stein G (ed): *Encyclopedia of the Paranormal.* Amherst, NY, Prometheus Books, pp 789-797.

Beyerstein, B. L. (1996). Believing is seeing: Organic and psychological reasons for hallucinations and other anomalous psychiatric symptoms. *Psychiatry & Mental Health eJournal.* 1(6).

Gersten, D. (1997). *Are You Getting Enlightened or Losing Your Mind?* New York: Harmony.

Greenberg, J. (2010). *Dreams, Hallucinations and Metaphors.* Keynote Address International Association of Society for Psychological and Social Approaches to Psychosis. Stockbridge, Mass.

Lawrence, M. (1997). *In a World of Their Own, Experiencing Unconsciousness.* Westport, CT: Praeger Publishers.

Lawrence, M. (2014). Unpublished interview about seeing a vision of Mary at Medjugorje.

Marks, D.F. (1998). The psychology of paranormal beliefs. *Experientia* 44, 332-337.

Martin, S. (2005). *Every Pilgrim's Guide to Lourdes.* Norwich, UK: Canterbury Press.

Moody, R. (2001). *Life after Life.* San Francisco: Harpers.

Place, C., Foxcroft, R. & Shaw, J. (2011). Telling stories and hearing voices: narrative work with voice hearers in acute care. J Psychiatr Ment Health Nurs. 18(9):837-42. Ryan, R.C., Caplan, J.P. & Stern, T.A. (2009) Visual Hallucinations: Differential Diagnosis and Treatment. J Clin Psychiatry. 11(1) 26–32.

Sacks, O. (2012). Seeing things? Hearing things? Many of us do. *The New York Times,* published November 3. http://www.nytimes.com/2012/11/04/opinion/sunday/seeing-things-hearing-things-many-of-us-do.html?_r=0 retrieved February 2, 2014.

Sacks, O. (2013). *Hallucinations.* London: Vintage.

Small, I.J., Small, J.G. & Andersen, H.J.(1966). Clinical characteristics of hallucinations of schizophrenia. Dis Nerv Syst. 27, 349–353.

Webster, R. & Holroyd, S. (2000). Prevalence of psychotic symptoms in delirium. *Psychosomatics*.41,519–522.

CHAPTER 4

Alvarado, C.S. (1984). Research on spontaneous out-of-body experiences: A review of modern developments, 1960-1985. *Proceeding of an International Conference held in New Orleans, Louisiana*, 140-174.

Blackmore, S. J. (1982). *Beyond the Body: an Investigation of Out-of-Body Experiences*. London: Heinemann.

Blackmore, S. J. (1984). A postal survey of OBEs and other experiences. *Journal of the Society for Psychical Research*, 52, 227-244.

Blanke, O. (2004). Out-of-body experiences and their neural basis. *BMJ*, 329, 1414-5.

Chadwick, H. (1984). *Early Christian thought and the classical tradition: Studies in Justin, Clement, and Origen*. USA: Oxford University Press.

Clark, K. (1984). Clinical interventions with near-death experiencers. In B. Greyson and C.P. Flynn (eds.). *The Near-Death Experiences: Problems, Prospects, Perspectives*. Springfield, IL: Charles C. Thomas, 242-255.

Fenwick, P. & Fenwick, E. (1996). *The truth in the light*. Guilford, UK: White Crow Books.

Gleyzes, S.,http://www.nature.com/nature/journal/v446/n7133/full/nature05589. html - a1 Kuhr, S., Guerlin, C., Bernu, J.http://www.nature.com/nature/ journal/v446/n7133/full/nature05589.html - a1, Deléglise, S.http://www. nature.com/nature/journal/v446/n7133/full/nature05589.html - a1, Hoff, U.B. et al. (2007). http://www.nature.com/nature/journal/v446/n7133/full/ nature05589.html - a1 Quantum jumps of light recording the birth and death of a photon in a cavity. Nature 446, 297-300.

Green, C. (1975). *Out-of-Body Experiences*. New York: Ballantine Books.

Greyson, B. (1983). Increase in psychic phenomena following near-death experiences. *Theta*, 11, 26-29.

Lawrence, M. (1997). *In a World of Their Own, Experiencing Unconsciousness*. Westport, CT: Praeger.

Lorenz, H. (2008). Plato on the soul, in *The Oxford Handbook of Plato*, G. Fine (ed.), Oxford: Oxford University Press.

Monroe, R. A. (1985). *Far Journeys*. New York: Broadway Books.

Moody, R. (2001). *Life after Life*. San Francisco: Harper.

Murray, C.D. & Fox, J. (2005). Dissociational body experiences: differences between respondents with and without prior out-of-body experiences. *Journal of Psychology*, 96(4), 441-56.

Myers, S. A., Austin, J. T., Grisson, J. T. & Nickeson, R. C. (1983). Personality characteristics as related to the out-of-body experience. *Journal of Parapsychology*, 47, 131-144.

Nicholls, G. (2012). *Navigating the Out-of-Body Experience: Radical New Techniques*. Woodbury, MN: Llewellyn Publications.

Olson, M. (1988). The incidence of out-of-body experiences in hospitalized patients. *Journal of Near-Death Studies*, 62(3), 169-174.

Palmer, J. (1978). The Out-of-Body Experience: A Psychological Theory. *Parapsychology Review*, 9, 19-22.

Palmer, J. (1979). A Community Mail Survey of Psychic Experiences. *Journal of the American Society for Psychical Research*, 73,221-252.

Palmer, J. and Dennis, M. (1974). A Community Mail Survey of Psychic Experiences. *Research in Parapsychology*, 1974, Morris, J. D., Roll, W. G. and Morris, R. L. eds. Metuchen, N. J.: Scarecrow Press, 130-133.

Persinger, M. A. & Makarec, K. (1992). The feeling of a presence and verbal meaningfulness in context of temporal lobe function: Factor analytic verification of the muses? *Brain and Cognition*, 20, 217-226.

Plato, & Grube, G.M. (2002). *Plato: Five Dialogues*. Cambridge, Mass: Hackett Pub Co.

Ring, K. (1980). *Life at Death*. New York: William Morrow & Co.

Ring, K, & Cooper, S. (1997).Near-Death and Out-of-Body Experiences in the Blind: A Study of Apparent Eyeless Vision. *Journal of Near-Death Studies*, 16(12) 101-147.

Ring, K. & Lawrence, M. (1993). Further evidence for veridical perception during near-death experience. *Journal of Near-Death Studies*, 8(4), 211-239.

Rogo, D.S. (2008). *Leaving the body.* New York: Simon and Schuster.

Sheils, D. (1978). A Cross-Cultural Study of Beliefs in Out-of-the-Body Experiences. *Journal of the Society for Psychical Research,* 49, 697-741.

Tart, C. T. (1971). *On Being Stoned: A Psychological Study of Marijuana Intoxication.* Palo Alto, CA: Science and Behavior Books.

Taylor, J. H. (2001). *Death and the Afterlife in Ancient Egypt.* University of Chicago Press.

Taylor, R. (2000). *Death and the Afterlife: A Cultural Encyclopedia.* Westport, CT: Praeger/ ABC-CLIO.

CHAPTER 5

Alighieri, D (2011). *The Divine Comedy* (Complete and Illustrated by Gustove Dore). ICU Publishing.

Burpo, T. (2010). *Heaven is for Real.* Nashville, TN: Thomas Nelson.

Bush, N. E. (2012). *Dancing Past the Dark: Distressing Near-Death Experiences.* Oak Island, NC: Nancy Evans Bush.

Clark, K. (1984). Visual perception during the naturalistic near-death out-of-body experience. *Journal of Near-Death Studies,* 7, 107-120.

De Morgan, S. E.(1863) *Matter to Spirit,* https://openlibrary.org/books/OL13499069M/From_matter_to_spirit. Retrieved April 14, 2014.

Fenwick, P. & Fenwick, E. (2001). *The Truth in the Light.* Guilford, UK: White Crow Books.

Gallup, G. (1982). *Adventures in Immortality: A Look Beyond the Threshold of Death.* New York: McGraw Hill.

Greyson, B. (1983). The near-death experience scale: Construction, reliability, and validity. *Journal of Nervous and Mental Disease.* 171(6), 369-375.

Greyson, B. & Bush, N.E. (1992). Distressing near-death experiences. *Psychiatry.* 55(1), 95-110.

IANDS, Blocked by a Golden Being. http://www.iands.org/experiences/nde-accounts/860-blocked-by-a-golden-being.html. Retrieved April 14, 2013.

IANDS (2002 -2004). Confirmation of Eternity. http://iands.org/experiences/nde-accounts/733-confirmation-of-eternity.html. Retrieved April 14, 2013.

Lawrence, M. (2012). *Dancing Past the Dark: Distressing Near-Death Experiences* by N. E. Bush. (book review) *Journal of Near-Death Studies*, 30(3) 178-186.

Lawrence, M. (1997). *In a World of Their Own, Experiencing Unconsciousness.* Westport: Praeger.

Moody, R. (1975). *Life after Life*. New York: Bantam.

Ring, K. (1982). *Life at Death: A Scientific Investigation of the Near-Death Experience.* New York: William Morrow & Co.

Ring, K (1984). *Heading Toward Omega: In Search of the Meaning of the Near-Death Experience.* New York, NY: Morrow.

Ring, K., Lawrence, M. (1993). Veridical Perceptions During Near-Death Experiences, *Journal of Near-Death Studies*, 7, 107-120.

Ring, K. & Cooper, S. (1997).Near-Death and Out-of-Body Experiences in the Blind: A Study of Apparent Eyeless Vision. *Journal of Near-Death Studies*, 16(12), 101-147.

Rommer, B. (2000). *Blessing in Disguise: Another Side of the Near-Death Experience.* St. Paul, MN: Llewellyn.

Sabom, M.B. (1982). *Recollections of Death: Medical Investigation.* New York, NY: Harper and Row.

Williams, K. Jayne Smith's Near-Death Experience. http://www.near-death.com/smith.html Retrieved June 14, 2014.

Whitfield, B. H. & Bascom, L. D. (1990). *Full Circle: The Near-Death Experience and Beyond.* New York: Pocket Books.

CHAPTER 6

Alighieri, D (2011). *The Divine Comedy* (Complete and Illustrated by Gustove Dore). ICU Publishing.

Burpo, T. (2010). *Heaven is for Real*. Nashville, TN: Thomas Nelson.

Bush, N. E. (2012). *Dancing Past the Dark: Distressing Near-Death Experiences.* Oak Island, NC: Nancy Evans Bush.

Clark, K. (1984). Visual perception during the naturalistic near-death out-of-body experience. *Journal of Near-Death Studies*, 7, 107-120.

De Morgan, S. E.(1863) *Matter to Spirit*, https://openlibrary.org/books/OL13499069M/From_matter_to_spirit. Retrieved April 14, 2014.

Fenwick, P. & Fenwick, E. (2001). *The Truth in the Light*. Guilford, UK: White Crow Books.

Gallup, G. (1982). *Adventures in Immortality: A Look Beyond the Threshold of Death*. New York: McGraw Hill.

Greyson, B. (1983). The near-death experience scale: Construction, reliability, and validity. *Journal of Nervous and Mental Disease*. 171(6), 369-375.

Greyson, B. & Bush, N.E. (1992). Distressing near-death experiences. *Psychiatry*. 55(1), 95-110.

IANDS, Blocked by a Golden Being. http://www.iands.org/experiences/nde-accounts/860-blocked-by-a-golden-being.html. Retrieved April 14, 2013.

IANDS (2002 -2004). Confirmation of Eternity. http://iands.org/experiences/nde-accounts/733-confirmation-of-eternity.html. Retrieved April 14, 2013.

Lawrence, M. (2012). *Dancing Past the Dark: Distressing Near-Death Experiences by N. E. Bush*. (book review) *Journal of Near-Death Studies*, 30(3) 178-186.

Lawrence, M. (1997). *In a World of Their Own, Experiencing Unconsciousness*. Westport: Praeger.

Moody, R. (1975). *Life after Life*. New York: Bantam.

Ring, K. (1982). *Life at Death: A Scientific Investigation of the Near-Death Experience*. New York: William Morrow & Co.

Ring, K (1984). *Heading Toward Omega: In Search of the Meaning of the Near-Death Experience*. New York, NY: Morrow.

Ring, K., Lawrence, M. (1993). Veridical Perceptions During Near-Death Experiences, *Journal of Near-Death Studies*, 7, 107-120.

Ring, K. & Cooper, S. (1997).Near-Death and Out-of-Body Experiences in the Blind: A Study of Apparent Eyeless Vision. *Journal of Near-Death Studies*, 16(12), 101-147.

Rommer, B. (2000). *Blessing in Disguise: Another Side of the Near-Death Experience*. St. Paul, MN: Llewellyn.

Sabom, M.B. (1982). Recollections of Death: Medical Investigation. New York, NY: Harper and Row.

Sutherland, C. (1989). Psychic phenomena following near-death experiences: An Australian study. Journal of Near-Death Studies, 8(2) 93-102.

Williams, K. Jayne Smith's Near-Death Experience. http://www.near-death.com/smith.html Retrieved June 14, 2014.

Whitfield, B. H. & Bascom, L. D. (1990). *Full Circle: The Near-Death Experience and Beyond.* New York: Pocket Books.

CHAPTER 7

Barrett, W. (2011). *Deathbed Visions.* Guildford, UK: White Crow Books.

Bonenfant, R. (2001). A Child's Encounter with the Devil: An Unusual Near-Death Experience with Both Blissful and Frightening Elements. *Journal of Near-Death Studies*, 20(2), 87-100.

Bush, N. E. (2002). Afterward: Making meaning after a frightening near-death experience. *Journal of Near-Death Studies*, 21(2), pp. 99-133.

Bush, N. E. (2012). *Dancing Past the Dark: Distressing Near-Death Experiences.* Cleveland, TN: Parson's Porch Books.

Byrne, L. (2013). My Near Death Experience. http://www.opencenter.org/my-near-death- experience-by-lorna-byrne/ retrieved April 9, 2014.

Byrne, L. (2009). *Angels in My Hair.* New York: Three Rivers Press.

Chorvinsky, M. (1997). Encounters with the Grim Reaper. *Strange Magazine*, 18, 6-14.

Chorvinsky, M. (1992). Our Strange World. *Fate*, 45(7), 31-35.

Dickens, C. (1991). *A Christmas Carol.* New York: Dover Publications.

Do Angels Exist? (2008). http://www.freerepublic.com/focus/religion/2152137/ posts retrieved April 17, 2014.

Heathcote-James, E. (2002). *Seeing Angels.* London: John Blake Publishing.

Lawrence, M. (1995). The unconscious experience. *American Journal of Critical Care*, 4 (3), 227-32

Lawrence, M. (1997). *In a World of Their Own, Experiencing Unconsciousness.* Westport: Praeger.

Lester, K. (2013). Senator Kirk speaks for the first time about his stroke. Daily Herald. http://www.dailyherald.com/article/20130102/news/701029938/. Retrieved April 17, 2014.

Lundahl, C. (1992). Angels in near-death experiences. *Journal of Near-Death Studies,* 11(1), 49-56.

Malarkey, K. & Malarkey, A. (2010). *The Boy Who Came Back from Heaven: A Remarkable Account of Miracles, Angels, and Life beyond this World.* Cambridge, England: Tyndale Momentum.

Moody, R. & Perry, P. (1988). *The Light Beyond.* New York: Bantam Press.

Morse, M., Perry, P. & Moody, R. (1991). *Closer to the Light.* Ivy books

Offutt, J. (2009). Shadow people stalk dying man. From the shadows. Retrieved April 16, 2014 http://from-the-shadows.blogspot.com/2009/01/shadow-people-stalk-dying-man.html

Offutt, J. (2009). *Darkness Walks: The Shadow People Among Us.* San Antonio, Texas: Anomalist book.

Osis, K. (1961). *Deathbed Observations by Physicians and Nurses.* New York: Parapsychology Foundation, Inc.

Stark, R. (2008). *What Americans Really Believe.* Texas: Baylor University Press.

Wagner, S. (2005). Hooded Beings. *Fate,* 58, p. 11.

Woerlee, G.M. (2005). *Mortal Minds: The Biology of Near-Death Experiences.* New York: Prometheus Press.

CHAPTER 8

Barrett, W. (2011). *Deathbed Visions.* UK: White Crow Books.

Brajtman S. (2005). Terminal restlessness: perspectives of an interdisciplinary palliative care team. *Int J Palliat Nurs.* 11(4), 170-178.

Cobbe, F.P. (1882). *The Peak in Darien, An Octave of Essays.* Boston: George H. Ellis

Callahan, M. & Kelley, P. (1992). *Final Gifts.* New York: Simon and Schuster Paperbacks.

Head, B. & Faul, A. (2005). Terminal restlessness as perceived by hospice professionals. *Am J Hosp Palliat Care.* 22(4), 277-282.

Houran, J. & Lange R (1997). Hallucinations that comfort: contextual mediation of deathbed visions. *Percept Mot Skills.* 84(30, 1491-504.

Jones, W. & Anderson, J. R. (1987). Short and long-term memory retrieval: A comparison of the effects of information load and relatedness. *Journal of Experimental Psychology.* 116, 137-153.

Lawrence, M. & Repede, E. (2013). The incidence of deathbed communications and their impact on the dying process. *American Journal of Hospice and Palliative Medicine,* 30 (7), 632-639.

Matsumoto, D., Frank, M. & Hwang, H. (2012). Nonverbal Communication: Science and Applications. Thousand Oaks, CA: Sage Publications.

Osis, K. (1961). *Deathbed Observations by Physicians and Nurses,* New York: Parapsychology Foundation, Inc.

Osis, K. & Haraldsson, E. (2012). *At the Hour of Death: A New Look at Evidence for Life after Death.* UK: White Crow Books.

Simpson, M. (2011). A sister's eulogy for Steve Jobs. *The New York Times.* http://www.nytimes.com/2011/10/30/opinion/mona-simpsons-eulogy-for-steve-jobs.html?pagewanted=3&_r=0

CHAPTER 9

Adhiyaman, V., Adhiyaman, S. & Sundaram, R. (2007). The Lazarus Phenomenon. *Journal of Royal Society of Medicine,* 100 (12), 552-557.

Alexander, E. (2012). *Proof of Heaven: A Neurosurgeon's Journey into the Afterlife.* New York: Simon & Schuster.

All Nurses (2013) *Patients who die right after the family leaves the room.* http://allnurses.com/hospice-nursing/patients-who-die-845879.html retrieved April 20, 2014.

Arriero, E. (2013). After nearly 65 years together, couple die hours apart. *Charlotte Observer.* http://www.charlotteobserver.com/2013/12/02/4512192/after-nearly-65-years-together.html#.U1Pz2W2OGuY#storylink=cpy retrieved April 20, 2014.

Carroll, (2013). Died of a broken heart? The science behind close couple deaths. *Today.* http://www.today.com/health/died-broken-heart-science-behind-close-couple-deaths-8C11018276. Retrieved April, 24, 2014.

FoxNews (2008). Woman wakes after heart stopped: Rigor mortis set in. http://www.foxnews.com/story/2008/05/23/woman-wakes-after-heart-stopped-rigor-mortis-set-in. Retrieved June 8, 2014.

Inbar, M. (2014). Moms hugs revives baby who was pronounced dead. *Today Show.* http://www.today.com/id/38988444/ns/today-parenting_and_family/t/moms-hug-revives-baby-was-pronounced-dead/#.U1KXHm2OGuY retrieved April 20, 2014.

Kindela, K. (2013). Harold and Ruth Knapke married 65 years die 11 hours apart. ABC News. http://abcnews.go.com/blogs/lifestyle/2013/08/harold-and-ruth-knapke-married-65-years-die-11-hours-apart/ retrieved April 20, 2013.

Lawrence, M. (1997). *In A World of Their Own: Experiencing Unconsciousness.* Westport: Praeger.

Lawrence, M. (2014). Personal recollections. April 20, 2014.

Lupkin, S. (2013). Ohio Man Declared Dead Comes Back to Life. ABC News. http://abcnews.go.com/Health/ohio-man-declared-dead-back-life/story?id=20027401 retrieved April 23, 2014.

Maleck. W.H., Piper, S.N., Triem, J, Boldt, J. & Zittel, F.U. (1998). Unexpected return of spontaneous circulation after cessation of resuscitation (Lazarus phenomenon). *Resuscitation,* 39,125–8.

Moisse, K. (2014). Mississippi man declared dead wakes up in body bag. ABC News. http://abcnews.go.com/blogs/health/2014/02/28/miss-man-declared-dead-wakes-up-in-body-bag/ Retrieved April 22, 2014.

Moody, R. (2001). *Life after Life.* San Francisco: Harper.

Nykamp D. Titak JA. Takotsubo cardiomyopathy, or broken-heart syndrome. *Annals of Pharmacotherapy.* 44(3):590-3, 2010 Mar.

Ruiz, R. (2013). Lifetime of love: Couple married 75 years die a day apart. *Today Show.* http://www.today.com/news/lifetime-love-couple-married-75-years-die-day-apart-6C10786498. Retrieved April 20, 2014.

Salkeld, L. (2011). Inseparable in life and death: Couple who were devoted to each other for over half a century died MINUTES apart. *Daily Mail, UK.* http://www.dailymail.co.uk/news/article-1352788/

Donald-Rosemary-Dix-Devoted-couple-die-minutes-apart.html#ixzz2z-R9gXa9G retrieved April 20, 2014.

Sims, P. (2009). Devoted couple die within minutes of one another after suffering heart attacks.

Daily Mail. http://www.dailymail.co.uk/news/article-1221492/Double-tragedy-husband-wife-die-minutes-heart-attacks.html retrieved April 24, 2014.

Uniform Law Commission (2014). Determination of Death Act. http://www.uniformlaws.org/ActSummary.aspx?title=Determination%20of%20Death%20Act. Retrieved April 20, 2014.

Walsh, M. (2014). Canadian "miracle" baby starts breathing again after being pronounced legally dead. New York Daily News. http://www.nydailynews.com/news/world/miracle-baby-breaths-declared-dead-article-1.1718030#ixzz2z0EhXoMC retrieved April 24, 2014.

CHAPTER 10

Barrett, W. (2011). *Deathbed Visions.* Guilford, UK: White Crow Books.

Chawla, L.S., Akst, S., Junker, C., Jacobs,B. & Seneff, M. G. (2009). Surges of electroencephalogram activity at the time of death: a case series. *Journal of Palliative Medicine.* 12(12), 1095-1100.

Cobbe, F. P. (2013). *The Peak in Darien: An Octave of Essays.* Lexington, Kentucky: Ulan Press.

Donnelly, S.M. & Donnelly CN. (2009). The experience of the moment of death in a specialist palliative care unit (SPCU). *Irish Medical Journal,* 102(5),143-6.

Donnelly, S. & Battley, J. (2010). Relatives' experience of the moment of death in a tertiary referral hospital. *Mortality,* 15(1).

Fenwick, P. & Fenwick, E. (2008). *The Art of Dying.* New York: Bloomsbury Academic.

Koike, A., Shimizu, H., Suzuki, I., Ishijima, B. &, Sugishita, M. (1996). Preserved musical abilities following right temporal lobectomy. J Neurosurg. 85(6),1000-4.

Korotkov,K. (2002). *Human Energy Field: Study with GDV Bioelectrography.* New York: Blackbone Publishing Co.

Lawrence, M. (2010). *New directions for near-death experience research.* IANDS chapter conference, Durham, NC.

Lawrence, M. & Repede, E. (2013) Incidence of deathbed communications and their impact on the dying experience. *American Journal of Hospice and Palliative Medicine.* 30, 632-639.

MacDougall, D. (1907). Hypothesis concerning soul substance, together with experimental evidence of the existence of such substance. *Journal of the American Society for Psychical Research,* 1(5), 237-244.

Milner, B. (1962). Laterality effects in audition, in Mountcastle VB (ed): *Interhemispheric Relations and Cerebral Dominance.* Baltimore: The John Hopkins Press, pp 177-195.

Oldfield, H. & Coghill, R. (1991). *The Dark Side of the Brain: Major Discoveries in the Use of Kirlian Photography and Electrocrystal Therapy.* Rockport, Mass: Element Books Ltd.

Schneider, G., Gelb, A. W. Schmeller, B., Taschaker, & Kochs, E. (2203). Detection of awareness in surgical patients with EEG-based Indices bispectral index and patient state index. *British Journal of Anaesthesia,* 91 (3), 329-35

Virtue, D. (2012). *The Angel Therapy Handbook.* Carlsbad, CA: Hay House.

Willin, M. (1999). *Paramusicology: An investigation of music and paranormal phenomena.* Sheffield, UK: University of Sheffield.

Willin, M. (1996). A Ganzfeld experiment using musical targets with previous high scorers from the general population. *Journal of the Society for Psychical Research,* 61 (843), 103-108.

Willin, M. (1997). Music and Spiritualism. *Journal of the Society for Psychical Research,* 62 (848), 46-57.

CHAPTER 11

Arcangel, D. & Schwartz, G. (2005). *Afterlife Encounters: Ordinary People, Extraordinary Experiences.* Newburyport, Massachusetts: Hampton Road Publishing Company.

Bazett, L. M. (1920). *After-Death Communications. Ann Arbor,* Michigan: University of Michigan library. Botkin, A.L. and Hogan, R.C. (2005). *Induced*

After-Death Communication: A New Therapy for Healing Grief and Trau-matic Loss. Hampton Roads Publishing Company.

Botkin, A.L. (2000). The induction of after-death communications utilizing eye-movement desensitization and reprocessing: A new discovery. *The Journal of Near-Death Studies.* Vol.18, No.3, spring 2000.

Diane S's ADC (2002). Communication with father at the time of death. http://www.adcrf.org/archived_2002.htm. retrieved May 9, 2014.

Daggett, L. (2005). Continued encounters: The experience of after-death com-munication. Journal of Holistic Nursing, 23(2) 191-207).

Fenwick, P. & Fenwick, E. (2011) The Truth in the Light. Guildford, UK: White Crow Books.

Grimby, A. (1993). Bereavement among elderly people: Grief reactions, post-bereavement hallucinations and quality of life. *Acta Psychiatrica Scandi-navica,* 87(1), 72-80.

Grimby, A. (1998). Hallucinations following the loss of a spouse: Common and nor-mal events among the elderly. *Journal of Clinical Geropsychology,* 4(1), 65-74.

Guggenheim, B. & Guggenheim, J. (1995). *Hello from Heaven.* New York: Ban-tam Books.

Haraldsson, E. (1988). Survey of claimed encounters with the dead. *Omega,* 19 (2) 103-113.

Jeff M's ADC (2002. Teenager's recent ADC with his grandmother. http://www.adcrf.org/adcrf_research.htm\ retrieved May 9, 2014.

Kelly, R. E. (2002). Post mortem contact by fatal injury victims with emergency service workers at the scenes of their death. *Journal of Near-Death Stud-ies,* 21(1), 25-33.

Larry J ADC (2012). ADC with Grandmother. http://www.adcrf.org/adcrf_re-search.htm\ Retrieved May 9, 2014.

Lawrence, M. (2010). New directions for near-death experience research. IANDS chapter conference, Durham, NC.

McMahon, J. & Lascurain, A. (1997). *Shopping for Miracles.* Los Angeles, CA: Roxbury Park.

Moody, R. & Perry, P. (1993). Reunions: Visionary Encounters With Departed *Loved Ones.* New York: Villard.

Randi, James; Clarke, Arthur C. (1997). An Encyclopedia of Claims, Frauds, and Hoaxes of the Occult and Supernatural. St. Martin's Press.

Sidgwick, H., Johnson, A., Myers, A.T., Podmore, F. and Sidgwick, E. (1894) Report on the Census of Hallucinations. Proceedings of the Society for Psychical Research. 26 (10) 25-422.

Streit-Horn, Jenny. *A Systematic Review of Research on After-Death Communication (ADC).* Denton, Texas. UNT Digital Library. http://digital.library.unt.edu/ark:/67531/metadc84284/. Accessed June 25, 2014.

Tymn, M. (2011). *The Afterlife Explorers.* Guildford, UK: White Crow Books.

CHAPTER 12

Alexander, E. (2012). *Proof of Heaven: A Neurosurgeon's Journey into the Afterlife.* New York: Simon and Schuster.

Alvarado, C. S. (1997). Mapping the characteristics of out-of-body experiences. *J Am Soc Psychical Res.* 91,15-32

Blackmore,S. J. (1984). A postal survey of OBEs and other experiences. *J Soc Psychical Res 52, 225-244.*

Bonenfant, R. J. (2004). A comparative study of near-death experience and non-near-death experience outcomes in 56 survivors of clinical death. *Journal of Near-Death Studies,* 22(3), 155-178.

Callanan, M. & Kelley, P. (2012). *Final Gifts: Understanding the Special Awareness, Needs, and Communications of the Dying.* New York: Simon and Schuster.

Clark, K. (1984). Visual perception during the naturalistic near-death out-of-body experience. *Journal of Near-Death Studies,* 7, 107-120.

Fenwick, P. & Fenwick, E. (2011). *The Truth in the Light: An Investigation of Over 300 Near-Death Experiences.* Guildford, UK: White Crow Books.

Long, J. & Perry, P. (2011). *Evidence of the Afterlife: The Science of Near-Death Experiences.* Paperback. New York: HarperOne.

Flynn, C. (1982). Meanings and Implications of NDEr Transformations: Some Preliminary Findings and Implications. *Anabiosis: Journal of Near-Death Studies* 2: 7

Gallup, G. & Proctor,W. (1982). *Adventures in Immortality: A Look Beyond the Threshold of Death*. New York, NY: McGraw-Hill.

Grey, M. (1985). *Return from Death: An Exploration of the Near-Death Experience*. London, England: Arkana.

Greyson, B. (1981). Near-Death Experiences and Attempted Suicide. *Suicide and Life-Threatening Behavior*. 11, 10-16.

Greyson, B. (1983). The near-death experience scale: Construction, reliability, and validity. *Journal of Nervous and Mental Disease*. 171(6), 369-375.

Greyson, B. (1991). Near-Death Experiences Precipitated by Suicide Attempt: Lack of Influence of Psychopathology, Religion, and Expectations. *Journal of Near-Death Studies*. 9:3,

Greyson, B. (2003). Incidence and Correlates of Near-Death Experiences in a Cardiac Care Unit. *General Hospital Psychiatry*. 25:269-276.

Greyson, B. & Bush, N.E. (1992). Distressing near-death experiences. *Psychiatry*. 55(1), 95-110.

Greyson, B., & Liester, M. B. (2011). *Electromagnetic phenomena questionnaire*. Unpublished manuscript.

Knoblauch, H., et al. (2001). Different Kinds of Near-Death Experience: A Report on a Survey of Near-Death Experiences in Germany. *Journal of Near-Death Studies*, 20, 15-29.

Lawrence, M. (1997). *In a World of Their Own, Experiencing Unconsciousness*. Westport: Praeger.

Lawrence, M. (2010). New directions for near-death experience research. IANDS chapter conference, Durham, NC.

Lai, C.F., Kao, T.W., Wu, M.S., Chiang, S.S., Chang, C.H., et al. (2007). Impact of near-death experiences on dialysis patients: A multicenter collaborative study. *Am J Kidney Dis*. 50(101), 123-32.

Milne, C. (1995). Cardiac electrophysiology studies and the near-death experience. Official Journal of the Canadian Association of Critical Care Nurses. 6(1), 16-9.

Monroe, R. (1977). *Journeys Out of the Body*. Anchor Press.

Moody, R. (1975). *Life after Life*. Mockingbird Books.

Nouri, F. M. (2008). Electromagnetic aftereffects of near-death experiences. *Dissertation International Abstracts*, UMI No. 3352121. Retrieved June 2, 2014 from Proquest Dissertations and Thesis Database.

Olson, M. (1988). Incidence of out-of-body experiences in hospitalized patients. *Journal of Near-Death Studies*, 6(3).

Palmer, J. C. (2001). On becoming a parapsychologist, in Palmer, J. Rhine, J.B., Dalton, K. & Feather, S. R. *Parapsychology and the Rhine Research Center.* Durham, NC: Parapsychology Press.

Parnia, S., Waller, D. G., Yeates, R., & Fenwick, P. (2001). A qualitative and quantitative study of the incidence, features and aetiology of near-death experiences in cardiac arrest survivors. *Resuscitation*, 48, 149-156.

Peat, J. (2002). *Health Science Research: A Handbook of Quantitative Methods.* Sage Publications Ltd.

Perera, M., et al. (2005). Prevalence of Near-Death Experiences in Australia. *Journal of Near-Death Studies*, 24, 109.

Persinger, M. A., Roll, W. G., Tiller, S. G., Koren, S. A., & Cook, C. M. (2002). Remote viewing with the artist Ingo Swann. *Perceptual and Motor Skills*, 94, 927-949.

Ring, K. (1980). *Life at Death.* Coward, McCann & Geoghegan.

Ring, K., Lawrence, M. (1993). Veridical Perceptions During Near-Death Experiences, *Journal of Near-Death Studies*, 7, 107-120.

Ring, K. & Cooper, S. (1997). Near-Death and Out-of-Body Experiences in the Blind: A Study of Apparent Eyeless Vision. *Journal of Near-Death Studies*, 16(12), 101-147.

Sabom, M. (1982). Recollections of Death: A Medical Investigation. New York: Simon & Schuster.

Satori, P. (2006). Prospectively Studied Near-Death Experience with Corroborated Out-of-Body Perceptions and Unexplained Healing. *The Journal of Near-Death Studies*, 25(2), 69–84.

Schwaninger, J., Eisenberg, P. R., Schechtman, K. B., & Weiss, A. N. (2002). A prospective analysis of near-death experiences in cardiac arrest patients. *Journal of Near-Death Studies.* 20(4), 215-232.

Sharp, K. C. (1995). *After the Light: What I Discovered on the Other Side of Life that can Change Your World.* New York: Morrow.

Sutherland, C. (1990). Changes in Religious Beliefs, Attitudes, and Practices Following Near-Death Experiences: An Australian Study. *Journal of Near-Death Studies.* 9: 24.

Turning Point – "Life after death: Personal experiences." ABC television, aired 1995.https://www.youtube.com/watch?v=PZywS7ZKbS8 retrieved, June 6, 2014.

van Lommel, P., van Wees, R., Meyers, V., & Elfferich, I. (2001). Near-death experience in survivors of cardiac arrest. *The Lancet* 358, 2039-2045.

CHAPTER 13

Barrett, W. (2011). *Deathbed Visions.* UK: White Crow Books.

Bauer, M. (1985). Near-Death Experiences and Attitudinal Change. *Anabiosis: Journal of Near-Death Studies.* 5. 39-46.

Christian, S. R. (2006). Marital satisfaction and stability following a near-death experience of one of the marital partners. *Dissertation Abstracts International, Section A: Humanities and Social Sciences*, 66(11-A), 3925.

Cobbe, F. P. (1882). *The Peak in Darien: An Octave of Essays.* Boston: George H. Ellis

Callahan, M. & Kelley, P. (1992). *Final Gifts.* New York: Simon and Schuster Paperbacks.

Christian, S. R. (2005). Marital satisfaction and stability following a near-death experience of one of the marital partners. University of North Texas Dissertation. Available at http://www.unt.edu/etd/all/ August2005/Open/christian_sandra_rozan/index.htm retrieved, June 20, 2014.

David A. Cook, D. A. & Beckman, T. J. (2006). Current Concepts in Validity and Reliability for Psychometric Instruments: Theory and Application. *The American Journal of Medicine* 119.

Drewry, M. D. (2003). Purported after-death communication and its role in the recovery of bereaved individuals: A phenomenological study. *Proceedings of the Academy of Religion and Psychical Research*, 74-87.

Flynn, Charles. (1982). Meanings and Implications of NDEr Transformations: Some Preliminary Findings and Implications. *Anabiosis: Journal of Near-Death Studies*, 2, 3-14.

Fracasso, C. & Friedman, H. (2012). Electromagnetic Aftereffects of Near-Death Experiences: A Preliminary Report on a Series of Studies Currently Under Way. *Journal of Transpersonal Research*, 4 (2), 34-55.

Fracasso, C. L. (2012). Near-death experiences and electromagnetic aftereffects: An exploratory study. Ph.D. dissertation, Saybrook University, United States — California. *Dissertation International Abstracts. Electromagnetic Aftereffects of Near-Death Experiences: A Preliminary Report* UMI No. 3509447. Retrieved June 19, 2014, from ProQuest Dissertations & Theses Database: Full Text. (Publication No. AAT 3509447).

Gottman, J. (1999). *The Marriage Clinic: A Scientifically Based Marital Therapy*. New York: W.W. Norton & Company.

Grey, M. (1985). *Return from Death: An Exploration of the Near-Death Experience*. London, England, Arkana.

Greyson, B. (1992). Reduced Death Threat in Near-Death Experiencers. *Death Studies*. 16, 533-46.

Greyson, B. (1983). Increase in Psychic Phenomena Following Near-Death Experiences. *Theta*, 11, 26-29.

Greyson, B & Liester, M. B. (2004). Auditory hallucinations following near-death experiences. *J Humanistic Psychol*, 44, 320-336.

Greyson, B. & Ring, K. (2004). The life changes inventory-revised. *Journal of Near-Death Studies*, 23(1), 41-54.

Grimby, A. (1993). Bereavement among elderly people: Grief reactions, post-bereavement hallucinations and quality of life. *Acta Psychiatrica Scandinavica*, 87(1), 72-80.

Grimby, A. (1998). Hallucinations following the loss of a spouse: Common and normal events among the elderly. *Journal of Clinical Geropsychology*, 4(1), 65-74.

Groth-Marnat, G & Summers, R. (1998). Altered Beliefs, Attitudes, and Behaviors Following Near-Death Experiences. *Journal of Humanistic Psychology*, 8(2),110-125.

Guggenheim, B. & Guggenheim, J. (1995). *Hello from Heaven*. New York: Bantam Books.

Haraldsson, E. (1988). Survey of claimed encounters with the dead. *Omega*, 19 (2) 103-113.

Houran, J. & Lange R (1997). Hallucinations that comfort: contextual mediation of deathbed visions. *Percept Mot Skills.* 84(30), 1491-504.

Insinger, M. (1991).The impact of a near-death experience on family relationships. *Journal of Near-Death Studies,* 9(3),141-181.

Irwin, H., & Rodriguez, P. (1999). Parapsychological phenomena near the time of death. *Journal of Palliative Care,* 15(2), 30-37.

Knittweis, J. (1997). Electrical sensitivity of near-death experiencers. *Journal of Near-Death Studies,* 15(3), 223-225.

Kohr. R. L. (1982). Near-death experience and its relationship to psi and various altered states. *Theta,* 1982, 10, 50-53.

Lawrence, M. (1997). *In a World of Their Own: Experiencing Unconsciousness.* Westport, CT.: Greenwood Publishing Group.

Lawrence, M. & Repede, E. (2013). The incidence of deathbed communications and their impact on the dying process. *American Journal of Hospice and Palliative Medicine,* 30(7), 632-9.

Locke, H.J. & Wallace, K.M. (1959) Short marital adjustment and prediction tests: Their reliability and validity. *Marriage and Family Living,* 21, 251-255.

Morse, M. & Perry, P. (1992). *Transformed by the Light: The Powerful Effect of Near-Death Experiences on People's Lives.* New York:Villard.

Nouri, F. M. (2008). Electromagnetic aftereffects of near-death experiences. *Dissertation International Abstracts,* UMI No. 3352121. Retrieved December 1, 2014, from Proquest Dissertations and Thesis Database.

Noyes, Russell. (1980). Attitude Changes Following Near-Death Experiences. *Psychiatry,* 43,234-242.

Palmer, J. (1979). A community mail survey of psychic experiences. *Journal of the American Society for Psychical Research,* 73,221-251.

Robert, R. A. (1993). *Death Anxiety Handbook: Research, Instrumentation, and Application.* UK: Taylor & Francis.

Osis, K (1961). *Deathbed Observations by Physicians and Nurses.* New York: Parapsychology Foundation, Inc.

Osis, K & Haraldsson, E. (2012). *At the Hour of Death: A New Look at Evidence for Life after Death.* UK: White Crow Books.

Parkes, C. M. (1965). Bereavement and mental illness. *British Journal of Medical Psychology*, 38(1), 1-26.

Parkes, C. M. (1970). The first year of bereavement: A longitudinal study of the reaction of London widows to the death of their husbands. *Psychiatry*, 33, 444-467.

Podmore, F. and Sidgwick, E. (1894). Report on the Census of Hallucinations. *Proceedings of the Society for Psychical Research*. 26 (10) 25-422.

Rees, D. (1971). The Hallucinations of Widowhood. *British Medical Journal*, 37-41

Ring, K. (1980). *Life at Death*. New York, NY: Quill.

Ring, K. (1984). *Heading Toward Omega: In Search of the Meaning of the Near-Death Experience*. New York: William Marrow and Company, Inc.

Ring, K. (1992). *The Omega Project: Near-Death Experiences, UFO Encounters, and Mind at Large*. New York, NY: William Morrow and Company, Inc.

Sidgwick, H.,Sidgwick, E., & Johnson, A. (1894). Report on the census of hallucinations. *Proceedings of the Society for Psychical Research*, 10, 25-422.

Silverman, P. R., & Nickman, S. L. (1998). Children's construction of their dead parents. Am J Orthopsychiatry, 68(1), 126-34.

D. Klass, P. R. Silverman, & S. L. Nickman (Eds.), *Continuing Bonds: New Understandings of Grief* (pp. 73-86). London: Taylor & Francis

Streit-Horn, Jenny. *A Systematic Review of Research on After-Death Communication* (ADC). Denton, Texas. UNT Digital Library. http://digital.library.unt.edu/ark:/67531/metadc84284/. Accessed June 25, 2014.

Sutherland, C. (1989). Psychic phenomena following near-death experiences: An Australian study. *Journal of Near-Death Studies*, 8(2), 93-102.

Sutherland, C. (1990). Changes in Religious Beliefs, Attitudes, and Practices Following Near-Death Experiences: An Australian Study. *Journal of Near-Death Studies*, 9 (1), 21-31.

van Lommel, P., van Wees, R., Meyers, V., & Elfferich, I. (2001). Near-death experience in survivors of cardiac arrest: A prospective study in the Netherlands. *The Lancet*, 358, 2039-2045.

Yamamoto, J., Okonogi, K., Iwasaki, T., & Yoshimura, S. (1969). Mourning in Japan. *American Journal of Psychiatry*, 125 (12), 1660-1665.

CHAPTER 14

Baker, J. (1954). *The Exteriorization of the Mental Body:A Scientific Interpretation of the Out-of-the-Body Experience known as Pneumakinesis.* William-Frederick Press.

Barrett, W. (2011). *Deathbed Visions.* UK: White Crow Books.

Buckley, T., Sunari, D., Marshall, A., Bartrop, R., McKinley, S & Tofler, G. (2010). Physiological correlates of bereavement and the impact of bereavement interventions. *Dialogues Clin Neurosci.,* 14(2), 129–139.

Gabbard, G. O., and Twemlow, S. W. (1984). *With the Eyes of the Mind: An Empirical Analysis of Out-of-Body States.* New York,NY: Praeger Publishing Company.

Gibson, A. (1999). *Fingerprints of God: Evidences from Near-Death Studies, Scientific Research on Creation & Mormon Theology.* Traverse City, MI:Horizon Pub & Dist Inc

Greyson, B., and Bush, N. E. (1996). Distressing near-death experiences. In Bailey, L. W., and Yates, J. (Eds.), *The Near-Death Experience: A Reader* (pp. 207-230). New York, NY: Routledge.

Guggenheim, B. & Guggenheim, J. (1995). *Hello from Heaven.* New York: Bantam Books.

Heller, K. J. (2006). The cognitive psychology of circumstantial evidence. *The Michigan Law Review,* 105(2), 241-306.

Lawrence, M. (1997). *In a World of Their Own: Experiencing Unconsciousness.* Westport, CT: Praeger Books.

Lawrence, M. (2014). Vision of Mary at Medjugorje. Unpublished interview.

Lawrence, M. & Repede, E. (2013). The incidence of deathbed communications and their impact on the dying process. *American Journal of Hospice and Palliative Medicine,* 30(7), 632-9.

McVea. C. (2013). *Waking up in Heaven.* New York: Howard Books.

Olson, M. (1988). Incidence of out-of-body experiences in hospitalized patients. *Journal of Near-Death Studies,* 6(3).

Satori, P. (2006). Prospectively Studied Near-Death Experience with Corroborated Out-of-Body Perceptions and Unexplained Healing. *The Journal of Near-Death Studies,* 25(2), 69–84.

Streit-Horn, Jenny. *A Systematic Review of Research on After-Death Communication (ADC)*. Denton, Texas. UNT Digital Library. http://digital.library. unt.edu/ark:/67531/metadc84284/. Accessed June 25, 2014.

INDEX

Paperbacks also available from
White Crow Books

Jesus of Nazareth with Simon Parke—
Conversations with Jesus of Nazareth
ISBN 978-1-907661-41-9

Thomas à Kempis with Simon
Parke—*The Imitation of Christ*
ISBN 978-1-907661-58-7

Julian of Norwich with Simon
Parke—*Revelations of Divine Love*
ISBN 978-1-907661-88-4

Allan Kardec—*The Spirits Book*
ISBN 978-1-907355-98-1

Allan Kardec—*The Book on Mediums*
ISBN 978-1-907661-75-4

Emanuel Swedenborg—*Heaven and Hell*
ISBN 978-1-907661-55-6

P.D. Ouspensky—*Tertium Organum:
The Third Canon of Thought*
ISBN 978-1-907661-47-1

Dwight Goddard—*A Buddhist Bible*
ISBN 978-1-907661-44-0

Michael Tymn—*The Afterlife Revealed*
ISBN 978-1-970661-90-7

Michael Tymn—*Transcending the
Titanic: Beyond Death's Door*
ISBN 978-1-908733-02-3

Guy L. Playfair—*If This Be Magic*
ISBN 978-1-907661-84-6

Guy L. Playfair—*The Flying Cow*
ISBN 978-1-907661-94-5

Guy L. Playfair —*This House is Haunted*
ISBN 978-1-907661-78-5

Carl Wickland, M.D.—
Thirty Years Among the Dead
ISBN 978-1-907661-72-3

John E. Mack—*Passport to the Cosmos*
ISBN 978-1-907661-81-5

Peter & Elizabeth Fenwick—
The Truth in the Light
ISBN 978-1-908733-08-5

Erlendur Haraldsson—
Modern Miracles
ISBN 978-1-908733-25-2

Erlendur Haraldsson—
At the Hour of Death
ISBN 978-1-908733-27-6

Erlendur Haraldsson—
The Departed Among the Living
ISBN 978-1-908733-29-0

Brian Inglis—*Science and Parascience*
ISBN 978-1-908733-18-4

Brian Inglis—*Natural and Supernatural:
A History of the Paranormal*
ISBN 978-1-908733-20-7

Ernest Holmes—*The Science of Mind*
ISBN 978-1-908733-10-8

Victor & Wendy Zammit —*A Lawyer
Presents the Evidence For the Afterlife*
ISBN 978-1-908733-22-1

Casper S. Yost—*Patience
Worth: A Psychic Mystery*
ISBN 978-1-908733-06-1

William Usborne Moore—
Glimpses of the Next State
ISBN 978-1-907661-01-3

William Usborne Moore—
The Voices
ISBN 978-1-908733-04-7

John W. White—
The Highest State of Consciousness
ISBN 978-1-908733-31-3

Stafford Betty—
The Imprisoned Splendor
ISBN 978-1-907661-98-3

Paul Pearsall, Ph.D. —
Super Joy
ISBN 978-1-908733-16-0

All titles available as eBooks, and selected titles available in Hardback and Audiobook formats from www.whitecrowbooks.com

CPSIA information can be obtained
at www.ICGtesting.com
Printed in the USA
FFOW04n0355280115
10659FF